Christopher Marlowe (1564–1593) was born in Canterbury the year of Shakespeare's birth. Like Shakespeare, he was of a prosperous middle-class family, but unlike Shakespeare, he went to a university, Corpus Christi College, Cambridge, where he received the bachelor's degree in 1584 and the master's degree in 1587. The terms of his scholarship implied that he was preparing for the clergy but he did not become a clergyman. Shortly before he received his M.A., the University seems to have wished to withhold it, apparently suspecting him of conversion to Roman Catholicism, but the Queen's Privy Council intervened on his behalf, stating that he "had done her majesty good service" and had been employed "in matters touching the benefit of the country." His precise service is unknown. After Cambridge, Marlowe went to London, where he apparently lived a turbulent life (he had two brushes with the law and was said to be disreputable) while pursuing a career as a dramatist. He wrote seven plays—the dates of which are uncertain—before he was yet again in legal difficulties. In 1593 Marlowe was arrested, accused of atheism. He was not imprisoned, and before his case could be decided, he was dead, having been stabbed in a tavern while quarreling over the bill.

Sylvan Barnet received a B.A. from New York University and an M.A. and a Ph.D. from Harvard University. At Tufts University, where he served as chair of the Department of English, he taught courses ranging from Chaucer to twentieth-century literature, though he specialized in courses on Renaissance drama. He is the general editor of the Signet Classics Shakespeare, the author of numerous essays on Shakespeare as well as of *A Short Guide to Shakespeare*, and the author and coauthor of several dramatic texts, including editions of selected plays by Oscar Wilde and George Bernard Shaw.

The Tragicall History of the Life and Death

of *Doctor Faustus*.

With new Additions.

VVritten by *Ch. Mar.*

LONDON,
Printed for *Iohn Wright*, and are to be sold at his shop without
Newgate, at the signe of the Bible. 1619.

Title page (1619) of *Doctor Faustus*. Notice the announcement of "new Additions." In fact, this version of the play (the so-called B-text) had already been published in 1616, but without this announcement. A shorter version of the play (conventionally called the A-text) was first published in 1604. Although the woodcut certainly does not seek to give a sense of what a production on an Elizabethan stage looked like, it nevertheless may tell us something about the costumes (Faustus wears a doctor's gown), the props (Faustus holds a magic wand and a conjuring book), and even some details of the staging (Faustus conjures within a magic circle inscribed on the floor of the study, which is furnished with books and a cross; a devil enters through a trapdoor at the lower right).

DOCTOR FAUSTUS

Christopher Marlowe

Edited and with an Introduction
by Sylvan Barnet

SIGNET CLASSICS

SIGNET CLASSICS
Published by New American Library, a division of
Penguin Group (USA) Inc., 375 Hudson Street,
New York, New York 10014, USA
Penguin Group (Canada), 90 Eglinton Avenue East, Suite 700, Toronto,
Ontario, Canada M4P 2Y3 (a division of Pearson Penguin Canada Inc.)
Penguin Books Ltd., 80 Strand, London WC2R 0RL, England
Penguin Ireland, 25 St. Stephen's Green, Dublin 2,
Ireland (a division of Penguin Books Ltd.)
Penguin Group (Australia), 250 Camberwell Road, Camberwell, Victoria 3124,
Australia (a division of Pearson Australia Group Pty. Ltd.)
Penguin Books India Pvt. Ltd., 11 Community Centre, Panchsheel Park,
New Delhi - 110 017, India
Penguin Group (NZ), 67 Apollo Drive, Rosedale, North Shore 0632,
New Zealand (a division of Pearson New Zealand Ltd.)
Penguin Books (South Africa) (Pty.) Ltd., 24 Sturdee Avenue,
Rosebank, Johannesburg 2196, South Africa

Penguin Books Ltd., Registered Offices:
80 Strand, London WC2R 0RL, England

Published by Signet Classics, an imprint of New American Library,
a division of Penguin Group (USA) Inc.

First Signet Classic Printing, May 1969
First Signet Classics Printing (Revised Edition), April 2010
10   9   8   7   6   5   4   3   2   1

CONTENTS

INTRODUCTION

Dr. Johann Faust, or Faustus, a magician and an astrologer who was born in Württemberg at an unknown date and who died about 1538, has entered the English language via the term "Faustian bargain." These two words are commonly taken to refer to the belief—one might say to the myth at the heart of Western culture—that we can remake reality to suit our desires. Thus, to quote an Earth Day special edition of *Time* magazine (Spring 2000), "Water development, like nuclear energy, is a Faustian bargain between civilization and the natural world." Or one reads that Al Gore made a "Faustian bargain," serving as Clinton's vice president so that he might become president himself. Putting aside the merits of the individual instances, the idea of the Faustian bargain, as it is commonly understood, is that some people are so eager to gain immediate power that they engage in actions that they know are evil.

Are such actions "tragic"? The word "tragedy" has been discussed for two and a half millennia—this Introduction later will add a few words—but we can at the start say that the term "Faustian bargain" in popular usage seems to mean not much more than selling one's soul to the devil for some temporary advantage. This is supposedly what the historical Johann Faust did, but the term can also have a richer, more tragic meaning if we think of the works of Marlowe and of Goethe, the poets who in fact have made the wretched German trickster immortal. (When one thinks about it, most of the most famous figures of history are immortal because poets have recreated them. What do we know about the historical Helen of Troy, except what Homer tells us of her in *The Iliad,* and what Marlowe and Goethe tell us? The historical Helen is dust, but she is immortal for most readers because Marlowe's Faustus says of her, "Was this the face that launched a thousand ships / And burnt the topless towers of Ilium?") In Marlowe and Goethe, at least intermittently Faustus is motivated not merely by self-interest but by lofty ideals, and the tragedy resides not merely in his choice of evil in an effort to advance himself, but in the corruption of those lofty ideals and in the waste of greatness. Interestingly, two recent books have used the term "Faustian bargain" in the title: William J. Robinson's *A Faustian Bargain: U.S. Intervention in the Nicaraguan Elections and American Foreign Policy in the Post-Colonial War Era* (1992) and Jonathan Petropoulos's *The Faustian Bargain: The Art World in Nazi Germany* (2000). Both of these books suggest that the people who made the Faustian bargains were not little guys who were seeking merely to advance their own careers. Rather, in many instances they were persons of considerable talent, and they were motivated by lofty ideals. To take the clearer case: The Nazi art museum directors who knowingly received stolen art treasures were highly talented, highly educated men who genuinely believed they were helping establish Germany's preeminence as the world's greatest contemporary culture. Without in any way minimizing the almost unspeakable tragedy of their victims, we can say that such individuals—persons who engaged in monstrous acts in the name of a higher good—are the most memorable examples, the most moving examples, of persons who make Faustian bargains.

PROBLEMS OF AUTHORSHIP

But for a moment let us put aside what indeed is the most interesting aspect of Marlowe's play and briefly turn our attention to a basic question: What *is* Marlowe's play? When we pick up a printed play—let's say *Doctor Faustus*—we assume that it is by the playwright whose name is on the cover, in this case Christopher Marlowe. We realize, of course, that the playwright did not create the work out of nothing: The author may draw on history, as Shakespeare does in many plays, for instance in *Antony and Cleopatra,* which is indebted not only to history but (in some passages) to the specific words of Sir Thomas North, whose translation of the Roman biographer Plutarch provided Shakespeare not only with episodes but even occasionally with speeches. Beyond such source material, a playwright may well be indebted to a director and to actors who persuade the writer to revise this scene, to drop that scene, and to make this speech a bit more speakable. A famous example is Oscar Wilde's comedy *The Importance of Being Earnest* (1894): Wilde originally wrote it in four acts, but when it was first staged (1895) the producer persuaded him to revise it into three acts. The three-act version, with some later small improvements in the dialogue, is what Wilde then published, and it is this version that is most widely known. (The omitted material, however, can be read in a few editions, including the Signet Classics edition of *The Importance of Being Earnest and Other Plays.*) Wilde of course is rightly regarded as the author of the three-act version but, again, this version was in some sense done with the collaboration of the producer, and the additional dialogue, too, may well owe something to changes that were worked out with actors during rehearsals.

With Elizabethan plays, the problem of "Whose play is it?" is greatly magnified since the playwright normally had nothing to do with publication. A playwright sold a script to the theatrical company and had no further claim on it. What finally got published (and many plays never did get published) might be a scribe's copy of the playwright's script, or it might be an acting version prepared by the theatrical company from the script, amplified not only with stage directions but perhaps with some additions by the players—and also reduced by substantial cuts to bring it within the allotted playing time. In any case, *Doctor Faustus* was first published in 1604, eleven years after Marlowe's death, and at least twelve years after the first performance of the play. In 1616 a very different version was published. The 1616 text omits a few short passages, totaling 36 lines, but it gives some 676 lines of new material, making the text about one-third longer than the 1604 text. Even in passages that are largely the same in the two texts, there are numerous small verbal differences. How are we to account for the differences in the two texts? We know that in 1602 an Elizabethan theater manager, Philip Henslowe, paid William Birde and Samuel Rowley £4 "for ther adicyones in doctor fostes," but we have no idea of which passages are these additions. The additions conceivably are among the passages found only in the longer version, but, equally conceivably, they are present in the shorter version. And Marlowe himself may have made additions at some point after the original staging. Some passages, too, especially in the abundant low comedy, may be amplifications by actors who may have added stock bits of business, such as a servant aping his master. We have Shakespeare's authority that comic actors sometimes made additions in performance. In *Hamlet,* the prince warns the traveling players:

> And let those that play your clowns speak no more than is set down for them, for there be of them that will themselves laugh, to set on some quantity of barren spectators to laugh, too, though in the meantime some necessary question of the play be then to be considered. That's villainous and shows a most pitiful ambition in the fool that uses it.
>
> (3.2.40–47)

In the past, many scholars tended to assume that the loftier parts of *Doctor Faustus* are by Marlowe and the low comic scenes perhaps by a collaborator or in some instances by actors, but such a view perhaps proceeds from a fastidious literary taste and from a lack of theatrical sense. Indeed, there is now a tendency to argue that much of the comedy is integral, exposing Faustus's sins by parodying them. Possibly Marlowe wrote comic scenes for this very purpose, but the performers dropped or shortened some of this material for an acting version, and this acting version survives in the shorter (1604) text. But the issue may not be *either/or.* It may be *both/and*; some comic material may be Marlowe's, some may be a collaborator's, and some may be additions by actors. The 1604 text may be close to the play as it was performed in an abbreviated version, and the 1616 text may be close to Marlowe's fuller manuscript and to a full-scale production. This issue of the two texts is gone into in a little further detail on pages 93–97; here it must suffice to say that although the relationship between the two texts and their relative closeness to Marlowe's original script remain uncertain, we will of course continue to speak of *Doctor Faustus* as Marlowe's play.

THE RENAISSANCE FAUSTUS

The historical Doctor Faustus apparently was a man of shreds and patches, a disreputable astrologer and necromancer known chiefly in German inns. Possibly he was the Johannes Faust who was granted a B.A. in divinity at Heidelberg in 1509, but even this is uncertain; his only well-attested accomplishment is a cruel practical joke: While imprisoned, he offered, in exchange for wine, to show a chaplain how to remove hair from his face without a razor; the chaplain provided the wine and Faustus provided the chaplain with a salve of arsenic, which removed not only the hair but the flesh. Around this charlatan there accumulated a host of legends, including some that earlier had been associated with Simon Magus, who had sought to buy the gift of the Holy Spirit, and who was said to have flown through the air until Peter caused him to fall to his death. The uninspired material and the uninspiring hero that Marlowe inherited can be seen in his source, the so-called English Faustbook, printed in large part at the rear of this volume; but Doctor Faustus owes his eternal life to Marlowe and to Goethe rather than to his own accomplishments.

In the Faust-book the legends concerning Faustus were gathered together and unified by the idea that pride will have a fall. The arrogant and powerful Faustus of the legends is at last carried off by the devils. In the words of the Faust-book,

> give none blame but thine own self-will, thy proud and aspiring mind, which both brought thee into the wrath of God and utter damnation.

In Marlowe's play, the Chorus tells us early on that Faustus flourished

> Till swoll'n with cunning, of a self-conceit,
> His waxen wings did mount above his reach
> And melting, heavens conspired his overthrow!

And at the end of the play the Chorus returns to summarize:

> Faustus is gone: regard his hellish fall,
> Whose fiendful fortune may exhort the wise
> Only to wonder at unlawful things,
> Whose deepness doth entice such forward wits
> To practice more than heavenly power permits.

His fortune, in short, teaches us to adhere to traditional Christian behavior rather than to practice the unlawful things that exceptional minds give themselves to. This is a simple enough moral, and perhaps some such reading of the play inspired the late Professor R. M. Dawkins to his epigram: the play tells "the story of a Renaissance man who had to pay the medieval price for being one." And because Faustus has so often been seen as the symbol of the Renaissance, it seems reasonable here to try to sketch some of the qualities of the Renaissance, now often called the Early Modern Period.

In 1860 Jacob Burckhardt published his *Civilization of the Renaissance in Italy*; it is scarcely an exaggeration to say that all subsequent discussions of the Renaissance are footnotes to Burckhardt. Burckhardt argued—as Renaissance men themselves had argued—that the Renaissance marked "the discovery of the world and of man." Put a little differently, the Renaissance saw the emergence of the individual: Private man made his way through a world in which the traditional sanctions—

especially medieval *humilitas*—no longer operated powerfully. (It is no accident that Marlowe's towering Faustus is born of "parents base of stock.") In England, the dissolution of the monasteries meant that one-fifth of England's land was put up for sale, and much of it was acquired by merchants and lawyers. Capitalism, with its attendant colonialism, double-entry bookkeeping, and technological advances—notably printing—made for a relatively open society in which a young man of humble origins could rise to wealth and power. The Renaissance, indeed, is the age that saw the birth of literature as a profession. Chaucer had been an amateur author, writing his books after hours, but Spenser, Shakespeare, Jonson, Milton, and, of course, Marlowe were professionals who carved out their careers with their pens. Moreover, none of these men came from an aristocratic family: Spenser's father was a tailor, Shakespeare's a dealer in farm commodities, Jonson's stepfather a bricklayer, Milton's father a scrivener, and Marlowe's a prosperous shoemaker. This is not to say that the old aristocratic families and the old authorities ceased to exist, or that the Renaissance is simply antiauthoritarian. One can find innumerable statements, in the best and the worst Renaissance writers, that support authority (Marlowe's Chorus in *Doctor Faustus* is a case in point), but the fact remains that, during the Renaissance, man's horizons became bigger and there was a widespread sense that the traditional authorities were no longer adequate.

Burckhardt's remark about "the discovery of the world and of man" can most obviously be supported by reference first to the geographical explorations, which extended man's outer world, and second to the revival of pagan classical learning, which extended man's inner world. Portrait painting offers additional evidence of man's heightened discovery of himself and his attempt to record his personality and his achievements on earth. In the Middle Ages there are pictures of faces, but there is scarcely anything that can be called portraiture; it is not until the Renaissance that we find painters sufficiently materialistic to be concerned with the physical looks (rather than only the spiritual or regal qualities) of their sitters. Yet another index, and one especially relevant to *Doctor Faustus,* is the concept of wisdom. For the Middle Ages, the highest wisdom was knowledge of divine things, which was achieved through God's grace, bestowed in revelation. In the Renaissance, however, one finds abundant deprecation of the contemplative life rooted in faith and abundant praise of the active life, of the study of political and social man. The monasteries that the Middle Ages built harbor (it was held in the Renaissance) idlers, caterpillars of the commonwealth, men who must be fools because they lack the experience of the world. Milton's disparagement of "cloistered virtue" is only the best known of many Renaissance statements to the same effect, insisting that the *vita contemplativa* is inferior to the *vita activa.* The family man, the soldier, and especially the statesman, who serves a prince and his community rather than God, acquire esteem; the paradigm of virtue is no longer the doctor of theology.

A few words about Marlowe's own life may be appropriate here, although much of his life remains mysterious. He was born in Canterbury, the son of a shoemaker, in 1564—the same year that Shakespeare was born—and in 1578 he became a student at King's School, Canterbury. In 1580 he was awarded a scholarship to Corpus Christi College in Cambridge. In 1584 he passed his bachelor's examinations, and he remained in Cambridge on a scholarship for two additional years, probably on the assumption that he would enter holy orders. In 1587, however, Cambridge University refused to award Marlowe his master's degree, perhaps because he had failed to continue his clerical career, or perhaps because he was suspected of harboring Roman Catholic sympathies and of visiting the English Catholic seminary at Rheims. The Queen's Privy Council intervened, ordering the university to give Marlowe his degree, and saying that he had been "engaged ... in matters touching the benefit of his country." Probably this means that he had been employed as a spy in Queen Elizabeth's secret service, perhaps spying on Catholics abroad.

Probably while he was a student at Cambridge he wrote his first popular play, *Tamburlaine the Great,* which apparently was staged in 1587, and soon after its success he wrote a sequel, *The Second Part of Tamburlaine.* His next play was presumably *The Jew of Malta,* usually dated 1589. In any case, certainly in 1589 his friend Thomas Watson was accused of killing a man, and Marlowe was accused of being an accomplice, but both were acquitted on grounds of self-defense. In 1591 he shared lodgings with the playwright Thomas Kyd, author of *The Spanish Tragedy* (c. 1588–90); later Kyd would describe Marlowe as "intemperate and of a cruel heart." Around 1591, we assume, Marlowe wrote *Edward II,* and he may have written *Doctor Faustus* soon thereafter—proposed dates for *Faustus* differ, but 1592 is a good guess. In 1593 Thomas Kyd was arrested, and he said that heretical books found in his lodgings belonged to Marlowe. Marlowe was arrested but was in effect put on probation. On 30 May he was feasting with three friends at Deptford when a quarrel broke out about the bill. Apparently Marlowe struck Ingram Frizer (or Friser) with the handle of Frizer's dagger. They grappled, and Frizer then stabbed Marlowe in the skull, through the eye, "in such sort that his brains coming out at the dagger point, he shortly after died." Marlowe was posthumously accused of atheism, of treason, and of holding the opinion "that they that love not tobacco and boys were fools." Whether he in fact held any or all of these views is not known. In recent years the theory has developed that Marlowe was murdered on the orders of the government, i.e., he was a spy who now was being terminated, and the whole affair of a brawl in a tavern was a contrivance. No evidence supports this view, but of course it may conceivably be true. What surely is not true is the theory that in fact he was not murdered; the whole business with Frizer has been said (on no evidence whatsoever) to have been a plot to seem to get rid of Marlowe, but to allow him in fact to go on living in seclusion, during which period he went on to write the plays attributed to Shakespeare.

Putting aside the flights of unbridled fantasy that invented a Marlowe who wrote Shakespeare's plays, and even adopting a skeptical view toward the accusations that were made against Marlowe in his lifetime and shortly thereafter, e.g., that he said "the first beginning of religion was only to keep men in awe," we can say this: The point is not the truth or falsity of the accusation; the point is that in the Renaissance a way of life that is not centered in God becomes a believable possibility. Modern readers who feel that the charges against Marlowe must have had at least some truth behind them tend to hear in *Doctor Faustus* the heretical Marlowe, glorifying unfettered aspiration, attacking traditional sanctities, and only adding an unconvincing pious ending as a sop to conventional belief. Faustus the magician is not a worshiper of God, but an operator who manages to impose his will on the material world. He is, in short, an applied scientist, rejoicing in power rather than in contemplation, and in this view, he is a symbol of the Renaissance, that second great attempt (after Periclean Athens) to free the mind from dogma and, by means of reason and experiment, to understand phenomena in terms of cause and effect.

But there is another way of looking at Faustus, Marlowe, and the Renaissance. One can see the Renaissance as the period when thinking took a bad turn and entered upon the course it still pursues. In this view, unappeasable curiosity catastrophically banished intuition and faith. Etienne Gilson in *Les idées et les lettres* puts it thus: "The difference between the Renaissance and the Middle Ages was not a difference by addition but by subtraction. The Renaissance, as it has been described to us, was not the Middle Ages plus man, but the Middle Ages minus God, and the tragedy is that in losing God the Renaissance was losing man himself." Some Renaissance texts themselves can be summoned to support Gilson's charge that secularism diminished man's possibilities. For example, John Lyly's Euphues in 1579 asked himself, "Is Aristotle more dear to thee with his books, than Christ with his blood?" Faustus, of course, centers his life on the quest for knowledge, and for the power that knowledge confers, rather than on God. Marlowe is careful to show us that in his egoism Faustus deludes himself into thinking that magic, which means control over nature, is "heavenly," and that, for example, Helen's kiss—or rather, worse yet, the kiss of a demon impersonating Helen—confers immortality. Faustus's unwillingness, or inability, to see things as they evidently are, to see evil as evil, is nicely indicated early in the play, when Mephostophilis first appears. Faustus says,

> I charge thee to return and change thy shape,
> Thou art too ugly to attend on me.
> Go, and return an old Franciscan friar:
> That holy shape becomes a devil best.

There is a crude anti-Catholic joke here, of course, but there is more: The speech reveals Faustus's perverse simplification of reality by fiddling with surface matters. Several of his other speeches make this point unambiguously. In 1.3, for example, Faustus jauntily asserts that

> This word "damnation" terrifies not me
> For I confound hell in Elysium:
> My ghost be with the old philosophers!

This superficiality is too much even for Mephostophilis, who, agitated by the memory of the vision of the God that he lost through pride and insolence, is moved to pity the man whom he has come to capture:

> Think'st thou that I who saw the face of God
> And tasted the eternal joys of heaven
> Am not tormented with ten thousand hells
> In being deprived of everlasting bliss?
> O Faustus, leave these frivolous demands
> Which strikes a terror to my fainting soul!

Faustus replies:

> What, is great Mephostophilis so passionate
> For being deprivèd of the joys of heaven?
> Learn thou of Faustus manly fortitude
> And scorn those joys thou never shalt possess.

We do not have to wait until later in the play, when we see Faustus's jauntiness give way to cringing, to hear in these words not only scorn and arrogance but also a foolish rejection of traditional wisdom. Similarly, the trivial ends to which on the whole Faustus puts his magic—the "belly-cheer" that includes satisfying his palate and his lust—reveal Faustus's reduction of spiritual realities to physical states. The spectacle of the Seven Deadly Sins, for instance, moves him to exclaim, "O, how this sight doth delight my soul," whereas a wiser man (i.e., one not merely learned but imbued with faith and drawing upon instinct as well as intellect) would reject this activity as diminishing rather than nourishing. At his lowest, Doctor Faustus sounds almost like the absurd old Doctor in Italian popular comedy— pedantic, gluttonous, amorous, and thoroughly foolish.

But of course there is another side, too. Faustus's aspirations are curiously mixed: He studies medicine so that he may "heap up gold," but he also would "make men to live eternally." In him we occasionally hear the voice of the Renaissance humanist, the man refreshed by the greatness of the pagan past and anxious to live an ampler life than his father had lived. Faustus, for example, has "made blind Homer sing" to him, an accomplishment especially resonant when we recall that Petrarch (1304–74), one of the first humanists, failed to master Greek and had to be content with Homer's epics in Latin versions. Most notable, of course, is the famous apostrophe to Helen: We can say that the speech is mistaken (Helen cannot confer immortality) and that images of destruction undermine the opulence, but the fact remains that Marlowe's ability as a poet infuses in Faustus an unmistakable grandeur that is not wholly eradicated by commonsense reflections:

> Was this the face that launched a thousand ships
> And burnt the topless towers of Ilium?
> Sweet Helen, make me immortal with a kiss.
> Her lips suck forth my soul. See where it flies!
> Come Helen, come, give me my soul again.
> Here will I dwell, for heaven is in these lips
> And all is dross that is not Helena.

We can go through the text and find abundant evidence that Faustus is foolish and corrupt, but we ought not to deny that at times his imaginings capture our imagination and evoke awe, or at least rapt attention rather than censure. His ideals are corrupted, but they reveal an abundance of energy that makes Faustus indisputably greater (not better, of course) than any of the other mortals in the play. The danger in reading the play is that we will see only either the heroic humanist or the fool; we may have difficulty in understanding that Faustus can be both.

We can say that Faustus makes a choice, and that he is responsible for his choice, but there is in the play a suggestion—sometimes explicit, sometimes only very dimly implicit—that Faustus comes to destruction not merely through his own actions but through the actions of a hostile cosmos that entraps him. In this sense, too, there is something of Everyman in Faustus. The story of Adam, for instance, insists on Adam's culpability; Adam, like Faustus, made himself, rather than God, the center of his existence. And yet, despite the traditional expositions, one cannot entirely suppress the common-sense response that if the Creator knew Adam would fall, the Creator rather than Adam is responsible for the fall; Adam ought to have been created of better stuff.

To what degree is Faustus, or any tragic hero, victimized? Lear sees himself "more sinned against than sinning," Othello sees himself as one "ensnared" by a "demi-devil," and there are similar statements in almost all of the major tragedies, from Aeschylus's *Prometheus Bound* onward. It can be argued, of course, that the devils cannot control Faustus; they can come to him only when he has laid himself open to them. Mephostophilis says something to this effect when he explains that he has come to Faustus not because Faustus's invocation is compelling, but because Faustus has made himself vulnerable to attack:

> . . . when we hear one rack the name of God,
> Abjure the Scriptures and his savior Christ,
> We fly in hope to get his glorious soul.
> Nor will we come unless he use such means
> Whereby he is in danger to be damned.
> Therefore the shortest cut for conjuring
> Is stoutly to abjure the Trinity
> And pray devoutly to the prince of hell.

This suggests that the devils are not so much independent external creatures as they are aspects of Faustus
himself, symbols perhaps of his pride. On the other
hand, one can argue that given Faustus's character—his
extraordinary abilities that can find no satisfaction in
the trivial pursuits of ordinary men—he is not entirely
responsible for his actions. He clearly is of a nature different from that of his fellow scholars, whose attain-
ments are far beneath his, and it is not at all evident that
such a nature could find satisfaction and fulfill itself in
the allowed activities. Faustus's initial speech, in which
he masters and tires of four branches of learning, each
of which would normally require a lifetime—the liberal
arts, medicine, law, and divinity—suggests that he is the
victim of the intellectual abilities that were given to him
by his Creator.

There are, moreover, some passages that explicitly
say that Faustus is trapped—although they do not entirely obliterate our sense that we are watching a man
who freely acts and who then reaps the consequences of
his actions. For example, while Faustus signs the bond,
giving his soul to Lucifer, Mephostophilis in an aside
says, "What will not I do to obtain his soul!" Even more
explicit is Mephostophilis's confession, late in the play,
that he has ensnared Faustus's soul. To Faustus's charge,
" 'Twas thy temptation/Hath robbed me of eternal happiness," Mephostophilis replies,

I do confess it Faustus, and rejoice.
'Twas I, that when thou wert i' the way to heaven
Dammed up thy passage. When thou took'st the book
To view the scriptures, then I turned the leaves
And led thine eye.

One can trace this voice of motiveless malignity (Coleridge's description of Iago) through such figures as Iago, and Aaron in *Titus Andronicus,* back to the Vice of medieval drama, but to call attention to the literary tradition does not diminish the voice itself. Again, one can say that to some degree the diabolic voices are aspects of Faustus himself, like the Good and Bad Angels, and the Old Man, but one cannot entirely dismiss the personages as shadowy allegoric representations of Faustus; these personages have their independent reality too.

Moreover, the idea that Faustus is in some measure trapped is implicitly strengthened by the stage business at the beginning of 5.2 and perhaps at the beginning of 1.3. To take the more certain episode first: The stage direction at 5.2 reads thus: "Enter Lucifer, Belzebub, and Mephostophilis." The ensuing dialogue suggests that they rise through a trapdoor and then climb to a playing area above the main stage, so that like cosmic powers they gaze down upon their plaything beneath them:

Thus from infernal Dis do we ascend
To view the subjects of our monarchy,
Those souls which sin seals the black sons of hell.
'Mong which as chief, Faustus, we come to thee,
Bringing with us lasting damnation
To wait upon thy soul. The time is come
Which makes it forfeit.

Possibly in 1.3 also, where Lucifer and four devils enter and remain unseen while Faustus seeks to conjure them up, the devils are above; but even if they merely hover on one side of the main stage, their presence and Faustus's ignorance of them suggests that they dominate him, or at least that they lie in wait for him.

But perhaps we need not worry too much about whether Faustus trapped himself or was trapped by diabolic creatures (though it seems reasonable to say that the play suggests not an *either/or* situation, but *both/and*); it is a tragic play, and tragic plays are not philosophic treatises on the freedom of the will. Still, a reader or a spectator—at least if he has been corrupted by too much education—inevitably tries to make sense out of his experiences and is reluctant merely to have the experience itself. What sense, then, can we make out of *Doctor Faustus*? The "meaning" of the play, of course, is the play itself; any paraphrase, and certainly any reduction to a moral tag, inevitably simplifies the work. The play "means" what it says, beginning with the Chorus's first entry and concluding with its final exit.

Still, if we stand back from the play, perhaps we can see in it something rather like what Sir Philip Sidney, writing at about the time that Marlowe was beginning his theatrical career, suggested could be found in all tragedies: a depiction of "the uncertainty of this world, and upon how weak foundation gilden roofs are builded." This depiction, Sidney says, evokes wonder (his word is "admiration," used with a suggestion of its Latin meaning) and pity. Perhaps we can say that the protagonist's vitality and the cosmic order's power both evoke wonder. That the protagonist is destroyed by the vitality that brings him into conflict with the order is pitiful. Perhaps, then, we can amplify Professor Dawkins's epigram (Faustus is "a Renaissance man who had to pay the medieval price for being one") into something along these lines: Doubtful of traditional authority, anxious to exert himself to the fullest, Faustus drove himself—and was driven—into experiences that were exhilarating but that brought him into conflict with a basic law of life. His displays of pride and will evoke both wonder and pity; there is something magnificent about Faustus, but his magnificence is corrupt because it is founded on egoism rather than on love and service, and so the magnificence is destroyed by the moral order with which it conflicts. Faustus partly willingly and partly blindly rejects the inherent limitations of life, thereby becoming both hero and villain.

Let the last words be Marlowe's: Faustus dies with "fearful shrieks," yet his limbs are given due burial because "he was a scholar once admired/For wondrous knowledge." His gifts were indisputable, and, as indisputably, they destroyed him:

> Cut is the branch that might have grown full straight
> And burnèd is Apollo's laurel bough
> That sometime grew within this learnèd man.

—SYLVAN BARNET
Tufts University

DOCTOR
FAUSTUS

[Speaking Characters

Chorus
Doctor Faustus
Wagner, his student and servant
Good Angel
Bad Angel
Valdes ⎫
Cornelius ⎬ *magicians*
Three Scholars
Lucifer, prince of devils
Mephostophilis, a devil
Robin, a Clown
Belzebub, a devil
Pride ⎫
Covetousness │
Envy │
Wrath ⎬ *the Seven Deadly Sins*
Gluttony │
Sloth │
Lechery ⎭
Dick, a clown
Pope Adrian
Raymond, King of Hungary
Bruno, rival Pope appointed by the Emperor
Two Cardinals
Archbishop of Rheims
Friars
Vintner
Martino ⎫
Frederick ⎬ *gentlemen at the Emperor's court*
Benvolio ⎭
The German Emperor, Charles the Fifth
Duke of Saxony
Two Soldiers   *Duke of Vanholt*
Horse-courser, a clown *Duchess of Vanholt*
Carter, a clown   *Servant*
Hostess of a Tavern   *Old Man*

Mute Characters

Darius of Persia, Alexander the Great, Alexander's Paramour, Helen of Troy, Devils, Piper, Cardinals, Monks, Friars, Attendants, Soldiers, Servants, Two Cupids]

[Prologue] *Enter Chorus.*°

Not marching in the fields of Trasimene°
Where Mars did mate° the warlike Carthagens,
Nor sporting in the dalliance of love
In courts of kings where state° is overturned,
Nor in the pomp of proud audacious deeds   5
Intends our muse° to vaunt° his heavenly verse.
Only this, gentles—We must now perform
The form of Faustus' fortunes, good or bad:
And now to patient judgments we appeal
And speak for Faustus in his infancy.   10
Now is he born of parents base of stock
In Germany within a town called Rhode;°
At riper years to Wittenberg he went
Whereas° his kinsmen chiefly brought him up.
So much he profits in divinity   15
That shortly he was graced° with doctor's name,
Excelling all, and sweetly can dispute
In th' heavenly matters of theology;
Till swoll'n with cunning, of a self-conceit,°
His waxen wings° did mount above his reach   20
And melting, heavens conspired his overthrow!

Prologue s.d. **Chorus** a single actor (here, perhaps, Wagner, Faustus' servant-student) 1 **Trasimene** Lake Trasimene, site of one of Hannibal's victories over the Romans, 217 B.C. (Marlowe is not known to have written on this subject, though lines 3–4 may refer to his *Edward II,* and line 5 to his *Tamburlaine*) 2 **Mars did mate** i.e., the Roman army encountered 4 **state** government 6 **muse** poet 6 **vaunt** proudly display 12 **Rhode** Roda 14 **Whereas** where 16 **graced** (alluding to the official "grace" permitting the student to take his degree) 19 **cunning, of a self-conceit** ingenuity, born of arrogance 20 **waxen wings** (alluding to Icarus, who flew by means of wings made of feathers waxed to a framework; despite the warning of his father, Icarus soared too near the sun, the wax melted, and he plunged to his death)

3

For falling to a devilish exercise
And glutted now with learning's golden gifts
He surfeits upon cursèd necromancy:°
25   Nothing so sweet as magic is to him
Which he prefers before his chiefest bliss°—
And this the man that in his study sits.

>   *Exit.*

[1.1] *Faustus in his study.*°

Faustus. Settle thy studies Faustus, and begin
To sound the depth of that thou wilt profess.°
Having commenced,° be a divine in show—
Yet level° at the end of every art
5   And live and die in Aristotle's works.
Sweet *Analytics,*° 'tis thou hast ravished me.
Bene disserere est finis logices.°
Is to dispute well logic's chiefest end?
Affords this art no greater miracle?
10   Then read no more, thou has attained that end.
A greater subject fitteth Faustus' wit:°
Bid *on kai me on*° farewell, and Galen° come:
Be a physician Faustus, heap up gold,
And be eternized for some wondrous cure.
15   *Summum bonum medicinae sanitas,*°
The end of physic° is our body's health.
Why Faustus hast thou not attained that end?

24 **necromancy** (literally divination by means of the spirits of the dead, but here probably equivalent to black magic)   26 **prefers before his chiefest bliss** sets above his hope of salvation   1.1 s.d. **Faustus in his study** (probably at his last line the Chorus drew back a curtain at the rear of the stage, disclosing Faustus)   2 **profess** study and teach   3 **commenced** taken a degree   4 **level** aim   6 **Analytics** title of two treatises on logic by Aristotle   7 **Bene . . . logices** the end (i.e., purpose) of logic is to argue well (Latin)   11 **wit** intelligence   12 **on kai me on** being and not being (Greek)   12 **Galen** Greek authority on medicine, 2nd century A.D.   15 **Summum . . . sanitas** health is the greatest good of medicine (Latin, translated from Aristotle's *Nichomachean Ethics*)   16 **physic** medicine

Are not thy bills° hung up as monuments
Whereby whole cities have escaped the plague
And thousand desperate maladies been cured?   20
Yet art thou still but Faustus and a man.
Could'st thou make men to live eternally
Or being dead raise them to life again,
Then this profession were to be esteemed.
Physic farewell! Where is Justinian?°   25
Si una eademque res legatur duobus, alter rem, alter
Valorem rei, et cetera.°
A petty case of paltry legacies.
Exhereditare filium non potest pater, nisi°—
Such is the subject of the *Institute*   30
And universal body of the law!
This study fits a mercenary drudge
Who aims at nothing but external trash,
Too servile and illiberal for me.
When all is done, divinity is best.   35
Jerome's Bible,° Faustus, view it well.
Stipendium peccati mors est.° Ha! *Stipendium et*
cetera. The reward of sin is death? That's hard: *Si*
peccasse negamus, fallimur, et nulla est in nobis
veritas.° If we say that we have no sin, we deceive   40
ourselves, and there is no truth in us. Why, then
belike, we must sin, and so consequently die.
Ay, we must die an everlasting death.

18 **bills** prescriptions   25 **Justinian** Roman emperor and authority on
law (483–565) who ordered the compilation of the *Institutes* (see line
30)   26–27 **Si … et cetera** if one thing is willed to two persons, one of them
shall have the thing itself, the other the value of the thing, and so forth
(Latin)   29 **Exhereditare … nisi** a father cannot disinherit his son unless (Latin)   36 **Jerome's Bible** the Latin translation made by St. Jerome
(c.340–420)   37 **Stipendium … est** the wages of sin is death (Romans 6:23;
if Faustus had gone on to read the rest of the verse, he would have found
that "the gift of God is eternal life through Jesus Christ our Lord")   38–
40 **Si … veritas** from 1 John 1:8, translated in the next two lines; Faustus
neglects the following verse: "If we confess our sins, He is faithful and just
to forgive us our sins, and to cleanse us from all unrighteousness"

45   What doctrine call you this? *Che serà, serà:*°
      What will be, shall be! Divinity, adieu!
      These metaphysics° of magicians
      And negromantic° books are heavenly;
      Lines, circles, letters, characters—
50   Ay, these are those that Faustus most desires.
      O, what a world of profit and delight,
      Of power, of honor, and omnipotence
      Is promised to the studious artisan!°
      All things that move between the quiet° poles
55   Shall be at my command: emperors and kings
      Are but obeyed in their several provinces
      But his dominion that exceeds in this°
      Stretcheth as far as doth the mind of man:
      A sound magician is a demi-god!
60   Here tire my brains to get° a deity!

                    Enter Wagner.

      Wagner, commend me to my dearest friends,
      The German Valdes and Cornelius.
      Request them earnestly to visit me.

Wagner. I will, sir.   *Exit.*

65   *Faustus.* Their conference° will be a greater help to me
      Than all my labors, plod I ne'er so fast.

          Enter the [*Good*] *Angel and* [*the Evil*] *Spirit.*°

      Good Angel. O Faustus, lay that damnèd book aside
      And gaze not on it lest it tempt thy soul

---

45 **Che serà, serà** (Italian, translated in the first half of the next line)   47
metaphysics subjects lying beyond (or studied after) physics 48 **negromantic** black magical (though probably here also associated with "necromantic," i.e., concerned with raising the spirits of the dead) 53 **artisan**
i.e., expert   54 **quiet** motionless   57 **this** i.e., magic   60 **get** beget   65
conference conversation   67 s.d. **Spirit** Bad Angel, devil (the two angels
probably enter the stage from separate doors)

And heap God's heavy wrath upon thy head!
Read, read the Scriptures— that° is blasphemy!   70

Bad Angel. Go forward Faustus, in that famous art
Wherein all nature's treasure is contained.
Be thou on earth as Jove is in the sky,
Lord and commander of these elements!
                              Exeunt Angels.

Faustus. How am I glutted with conceit of this!°   75
Shall I make spirits fetch me what I please?
Resolve me of° all ambiguities?
Perform what desperate enterprise I will?
I'll have them fly to India° for gold,
Ransack the ocean for orient° pearl,   80
And search all corners of the new-found world
For pleasant fruits and princely delicates;
I'll have them read me strange philosophy
And tell the secrets of all foreign kings;
I'll have them wall all Germany with brass   85
And make swift Rhine circle fair Wittenberg;
I'll have them fill the public schools° with silk
Wherewith the students shall be bravely° clad.
I'll levy soldiers with the coin they bring
And chase the Prince of Parma° from our land   90
And reign sole king of all the provinces!
Yea, stranger engines for the brunt° of war
Than was the fiery keel° at Antwerp bridge
I'll make my servile spirits to invent.

---

70 **that** i.e., the book of magic   75 **conceit of this** i.e., the conception of being a magician   77 **Resolve me of** explain to me   79 **India** either the West
Indies (America) or the East Indies   80 **orient** lustrous and precious   87
public schools universities   88 **bravely** splendidly   90 **Prince of Parma**
Spanish governor-general of the Low Countries during 1579–92   92 **brunt**
assault   93 **fiery keel** burning ship sent by the Netherlanders in 1585
against a bridge erected by Parma to blockade Antwerp (Antwerp here is
an adjective, not genetive)

Enter Valdes and Cornelius.

95 Come German Valdes and Cornelius
    And make me blest with your sage conference.
    Valdes, sweet Valdes, and Cornelius,
    Know that your words have won me at the last
    To practice magic and concealèd arts.
100 Philosophy is odious and obscure,
    Both law and physic are for petty wits,
    Divinity is basest of the three—
    Unpleasant, harsh, contemptible, and vile.
    'Tis magic, magic, that hath ravished me!
105 Then, gentle friends, aid me in this attempt
    And I, that have with subtle syllogisms
    Graveled° the pastors of the German church
    And made the flow'ring pride of Wittenberg
    Swarm to my problems° as th' infernal spirits
110 On sweet Musaeus° when he came to hell,
    Will be as cunning as Agrippa° was,
    Whose shadows made all Europe honor him.

Valdes. Faustus, these books, thy wit, and our experi-
        ence
    Shall make all nations to canonize us.
115 As Indian Moors° obey their Spanish lords,
    So shall the spirits of every element
    Be always serviceable to us three:
    Like lions shall they guard us when we please,
    Like Almain rutters° with their horsemen's staves
120 Or Lapland giants trotting by our sides;

---

107 **Graveled** confounded 109 **problems** questions proposed for disputation 110 **Musaeus** legendary Greek poet 111 **Agrippa** Cornelius Agrippa of Nettesheim (1486–1535), German author of *De occulta philosophia,* a survey of Renaissance magic; Agrippa was believed to have raised spirits ("shadows") from the dead 115 **Indian Moors** American Indians 119 **Almain rutters** German cavalrymen

Sometimes like women or unwedded maids
Shadowing° more beauty in their airy brows
Than has the white breasts of the queen of love;
From Venice shall they drag huge argosies
And from America the golden fleece   125
That yearly stuffs old Philip's° treasury,
If learnèd Faustus will be resolute.

Faustus. Valdes, as resolute am I in this
As thou to live; therefore object it not.

Cornelius. The miracles that magic will perform   130
Will make thee vow to study nothing else.
He that is grounded in astrology,
Enriched with tongues, well seen° in minerals,
Hath all the principles magic doth require.
Then doubt not Faustus but to be renowned   135
And more frequented for this mystery°
Than heretofore the Delphian oracle.°
The spirits tell me they can dry the sea
And fetch the treasure of all foreign wracks,
Yea, all the wealth that our forefathers hid   140
Within the massy° entrails of the earth.
Then tell me Faustus, what shall we three want?°

Faustus. Nothing, Cornelius. O, this cheers my soul!
Come, show me some demonstrations magical
That I may conjure° in some bushy grove   145
And have these joys in full possession.

Valdes. Then haste thee to some solitary grove,
And bear wise Bacon's° and Albanus'° works,

122 **Shadowing** sheltering   126 **Philip** King Philip II of Spain (1527–
98)   133 **well seen** skilled   136 **frequented for this mystery** resorted to
for this art   137 **Delphian oracle** oracle of Apollo at Delphi   141 **massy**
massive   142 **want** lack   145 **conjure** raise spirits   148 **Bacon** Roger Bacon, medieval friar and scientist   148 **Albanus** perhaps Pietro d'Abano,
medieval writer on medicine and philosophy

The Hebrew Psalter, and New Testament;
150 And whatsoever else is requisite
We will inform thee ere our conference cease.

Cornelius. Valdes, first let him know the words of art,
And then, all other ceremonies learned,
Faustus may try his cunning by himself.

155 *Valdes.* First I'll instruct thee in the rudiments,
And then wilt thou be perfecter than I.

Faustus. Then come and dine with me, and after meat
We'll canvass every quiddity° thereof,
For ere I sleep I'll try what I can do:
160 This night I'll conjure though I die therefor!
Exeunt omnes.°

[1.2] *Enter two Scholars.*

1 Scholar. I wonder what's become of Faustus that was
wont to make our schools ring with *sic probo.*°

Enter Wagner.

2 Scholar. That shall we presently° know. Here
comes his boy.°

5 *1 Scholar.* How now sirrah,° where's thy master?

Wagner. God in heaven knows.

1 Scholar. Why, dost not thou know then?

Wagner. Yes, I know, but that follows not.

158 **canvass every quiddity** discuss every essential detail 160 s.d. **omnes** all
(Latin) 1.2.2 **sic probo** thus I prove it (Latin) 3 **presently** at once 4 **boy**
servant (an impoverished student) 5 **sirrah** (term of address used to an
inferior)

1 Scholar. Go to° sirrah, leave your jesting and tell
    us where he is.   10

Wagner. That follows not by force of argument,
    which you, being licentiates,° should stand
    upon;° therefore acknowledge your error and
    be attentive.

2 Scholar. Then you will not tell us?   15

Wagner. You are deceived, for I will tell you. Yet if
    you were not dunces,° you would never ask me
    such a question. For is he not *corpus naturale*?
    And is not that *mobile?*° Then wherefore should
    you ask me such a question? But that I am by   20
    nature phlegmatic,° slow to wrath, and prone
    to lechery—to love, I would say—it were not
    for you to come within forty foot of the place of
    execution°—although I do not doubt but to see
    you both hanged the next sessions.° Thus, hav-   25
    ing triumphed over you, I will set my counte-
    nance like a precisian° and begin to speak thus:
    Truly, my dear brethren, my master is within at
    dinner, with Valdes and Cornelius, as this wine,
    if it could speak, would inform your worships;   30
    and so, the Lord bless you, preserve you, and
    keep you, my dear brethren.   *Exit.*

1 Scholar. O Faustus, then I fear that which I have
    long suspected,
    That thou art fall'n into that damnèd art

9 **Go to** (exclamation of impatience)   12 **licentiates** possessors of a degree
preceding the master's degree   12–13 **stand upon** make much of   17 **dunces**
(1) fools (2) hairsplitters   18–19 **corpus naturale ... mobile** natural matter ...
movable (Latin, scholastic definition of the subject matter of physics)   21
phlegmatic sluggish   23–24 **the place of execution** the place of action, i.e., the
dining room (with quibble on gallows)   25 **sessions** sittings of a court   27
precisian Puritan (Wagner goes on to parody the style of the Puritans)

For which they two are infamous through the
35   world.

2 Scholar. Were he a stranger, not allied to me,
     The danger of his soul would make me mourn.
     But come, let us go and inform the rector.°
     It may be his grave counsel may reclaim him.

40   *1 Scholar.* I fear me nothing will reclaim him now.

     2 Scholar. Yet let us see what we can do.   *Exeunt.*

     [1.3] *Thunder. Enter Lucifer and four Devils.°*
          Faustus to them with this speech.

Faustus. Now that the gloomy shadow of the night,
     Longing to view Orion's° drizzling look,
     Leaps from th' antarctic world unto the sky
     And dims the welkin° with her pitchy breath,
5   Faustus, begin thine incantations
     And try if devils will obey thy hest,
     Seeing thou hast prayed and sacrificed to them.
     Within this circle° is Jehovah's name
     Forward and backward anagrammatized,
10   Th' abbreviated names of holy saints,
     Figures of every adjunct to° the heavens,
     And characters of signs and erring stars,°
     By which the spirits are enforced to rise:
     Then fear not, Faustus, to be resolute
15   And try the utmost magic can perform. [*Thunder.*]

38 **rector** head of the university   1.3 s.d. **Enter ... Devils** (they are invisible to Faustus; perhaps they enter through a trapdoor and climb to the
upper playing area, as implied in 5.2 s.d.)   2 **Orion** constellation appearing at the beginning of winter, associated with rain   4 **welkin** sky   8 **circle**
circle the conjuror draws around him on the ground, to call the spirits
and to protect himself from them   11 **adjunct to** heavenly body fixed to
12 **signs and erring stars** signs of the Zodiac and planets

Sint mihi dei Acherontis propitii! Valeat numen
triplex Iehovae! Ignei, aerii, aquatici, spiritus, sal-
vete! Orientis princeps, Belzebub inferni ardentis
monarcha, et Demogorgon, propitiamus vos ut ap-
pareat et surgat Mephostophilis! Quid tu moraris?   20
Per Iehovam, Gehennam, et consecratam aquam
quam nunc spargo, signumque crusis quod nunc
facio, et per vota nostra, ipse nunc surgat nobis di-
catus Mephostophilis!°

Enter a Devil.°

I charge thee to return and change thy shape,   25
Thou art too ugly to attend on me.
Go, and return an old Franciscan friar:
That holy shape becomes a devil best. *Exit Devil.*
I see there's virtue in my heavenly words.
Who would not be proficient in this art?   30
How pliant is this Mephostophilis,
Full of obedience and humility,
Such is the force of magic and my spells.

Enter Mephostophilis.

Mephostophilis. Now Faustus, what wouldst thou
      have me do?

16–24 **Sint ... Mephostophilis** may the gods of the lower region be favor-
able to me. Away with the trinity of Jehovah. Hail, spirits of fire, air, water.
Prince of the east, Belzebub monarch of burning hell, and Demogorgon,
we pray to you that Mephostophilis may appear and rise. Why do you
delay? By Jehovah, Gehenna, and the holy water which now I sprinkle,
and the sign of the cross which now I make, and by our vows, may Mephostophilis himself now rise to serve us (Latin)   24 s.d. **Devil** (the word
"dragon" oddly appears, after "surgat Mephostophilis," in the preceding conjuration. It makes no sense in the sentence, and it has therefore
been omitted from the present text, but perhaps it indicates that a dragon
briefly appears at that point, or perhaps the devil referred to in the present
stage direction is disguised as a dragon)

35 *Faustus.* I charge thee wait upon me whilst I live
         To do whatever Faustus shall command,
         Be it to make the moon drop from her sphere
         Or the ocean to overwhelm the world.

     Mephostophilis. I am a servant to great Lucifer
40   And may not follow thee without his leave.
         No more than he commands must we perform.

     Faustus. Did not he charge thee to appear to me?

     Mephostophilis. No, I came now hither of mine own
         accord.

     Faustus. Did not my conjuring raise thee? Speak.

     Mephostophilis. That was the cause, but yet *per*
45   *accidens*:°
         For when we hear one rack° the name of God,
         Abjure the Scriptures and his savior Christ,
         We fly in hope to get his glorious° soul.
         Nor will we come unless he use such means
50   Whereby he is in danger to be damned.
         Therefore the shortest cut for conjuring
         Is stoutly to abjure the Trinity
         And pray devoutly to the prince of hell.

     Faustus. So Faustus hath already done, and holds this
         principle,
55   There is no chief but only Belzebub:
         To whom Faustus doth dedicate himself.
         This word "damnation" terrifies not me
         For I confound hell in Elysium:°
         My ghost° be with the old° philosophers!

---

45 **per accidens** the immediate (but not ultimate) cause (Latin)   46 **rack**
torture   48 **glorious** (1) splendid (2) presumptuous   58 **confound hell in
Elysium** do not distinguish between hell and Elysium 59 **ghost** spirit   59
old i.e., pre-Christian

But leaving these vain trifles of men's souls,   60
Tell me, what is that Lucifer thy lord?

Mephostophilis. Arch-regent and commander of all
    spirits.°

Faustus. Was not that Lucifer an angel once?

Mephostophilis. Yes Faustus, and most dearly loved
    of God.

Faustus. How comes it then that he is prince of   65
    devils?

Mephostophilis. O, by aspiring pride and insolence,
For which God threw him from the face of
    heaven.

Faustus. And what are you that live with Lucifer?

Mephostophilis. Unhappy spirits that fell with Lucifer,
Conspired against our God with Lucifer,   70
And are forever damned with Lucifer.

Faustus. Where are you damned?

Mephostophilis. In hell.

Faustus. How comes it then that thou art out of
    hell?

Mephostophilis. Why this is hell, nor am I out of it.   75
Think'st thou that I who saw the face of God
And tasted the eternal joys of heaven
Am not tormented with ten thousand hells
In being deprived of everlasting bliss?
O Faustus, leave these frivolous demands   80
Which strikes° a terror to my fainting soul!

---

62 **spirits** devils   81 **strikes** (it is not unusual to have a plural subject—
especially when it has a collective force—take a verb ending in -s)

Faustus. What, is great Mephostophilis so passion-
    ate°
    For being deprivèd of the joys of heaven?
    Learn thou of Faustus manly fortitude
85   And scorn those joys thou never shalt possess.
    Go bear these tidings to great Lucifer:
    Seeing Faustus hath incurred eternal death
    By desperate thoughts against Jove's deity,
    Say he surrenders up to him his soul
90   So he will spare him four and twenty years,
    Letting him live in all voluptuousness,
    Having thee ever to attend on me,
    To give me whatsoever I shall ask,
    To tell me whatsoever I demand,
95   To slay mine enemies and to aid my friends
    And always be obedient to my will.
    Go and return to mighty Lucifer
    And meet me in my study at midnight,
    And then resolve° me of thy master's mind.

100 *Mephostophilis.* I will, Faustus.

Faustus. Had I as many souls as there be stars
    I'd give them all for Mephostophilis.
    By him I'll be great emperor of the world,
    And make a bridge through° the moving air
105   To pass the ocean with a band of men;
    I'll join the hills that bind the Afric shore
    And make that country continent to° Spain,
    And both contributary to my crown;
    The Emperor shall not live but by my leave,
110   Nor any potentate of Germany.
    Now that I have obtained what I desired

---

82 **passionate** emotional 99 **resolve** inform 104 **through** (pronounced
"thorough") 107 **continent to** continuous with

I'll live in speculation° of this art
Till Mephostophilis return again.   *Exit.*
                      [Exeunt Lucifer and Devils.]

    [1.4] *Enter Wagner and [Robin] the Clown.*°

Wagner. Come hither, sirrah boy.

Robin. Boy! O, disgrace to my person! Zounds,° boy
    in your face! You have seen many boys with
    such pickadevants,° I am sure.

Wagner. Sirrah, hast thou no comings in?°   5

Robin. Yes, and goings out too, you may see sir.

Wagner. Alas, poor slave! See how poverty jests in
    his nakedness. I know the villain's out of ser-
    vice, and so hungry that I know he would give
    his soul to the devil for a shoulder of mutton,   10
    though it were blood-raw.

Robin. Not so, neither! I had need to have it well
    roasted, and good sauce to it, if I pay so dear, I
    can tell you.

Wagner. Sirrah, wilt thou be my man and wait on me?   15
    And I will make thee go like *Qui mihi discipulus.*°

Robin. What, in verse?

Wagner. No, slave, in beaten° silk and stavesacre.°

112 **speculation** contemplation   1.4 s.d. **Clown** buffoon   2 **Zounds** by
God's wounds   4 **pickadevants** pointed beards   5 **comings in** income (the
Clown then quibbles on "goings out," i.e., expenses and also holes in his
clothes through which his body pokes)   16 **Qui mihi discipulus** one who is
my disciple, i.e., like the servant of a learned man (the Latin is the beginning
of a poem, familiar to Renaissance schoolboys, on proper behavior)   18
beaten embroidered (leading to the quibble on the sense "hit")   18 **stavesacre** preparation from seeds of delphinium, used to kill vermin

Robin. Stavesacre? That's good to kill vermin! Then,
20   belike, if I serve you I shall be lousy.

Wagner. Why, so thou shalt be, whether thou dost it
or no; for sirrah, if thou dost not presently bind
thyself to me for seven years, I'll turn all the lice
about thee into familiars° and make them tear
25   thee in pieces.

Robin. Nay sir, you may save yourself a labor, for
they are as familiar with me as if they paid for
their meat and drink, I can tell you.

Wagner. Well sirrah, leave your jesting and take
30   these guilders.°

Robin. Yes marry° sir, and I thank you too.

Wagner. So, now thou art to be at an hour's warning whensoever and wheresoever the devil shall
fetch thee.

35 *Robin.* Here, take your guilders, I'll none of 'em!

Wagner. Not I, thou art pressed.° Prepare thyself, for
I will presently raise up two devils to carry thee
away. Banio! Belcher!

Robin. Belcher! And° Belcher come here I'll belch
40   him. I am not afraid of a devil!

Enter two Devils.

Wagner. How now sir, will you serve me now?

Robin. Ay, good Wagner, take away the devil then.

24 **familiars** attendant demons   30 **guilders** Dutch coins   31 **marry** indeed (a mild oath, from "by the Virgin Mary")   36 **pressed** enlisted into
service   39 **And** if

Wagner. Spirits, away! [*Exeunt Devils.*] Now sirrah,
    follow me.

Robin. I will sir! But hark you master, will you teach   *45*
    me this conjuring occupation?

Wagner. Ay sirrah, I'll teach thee to turn thyself to a
    dog or a cat or a mouse or a rat or anything.

Robin. A dog or a cat or a mouse or a rat? O brave°
    Wagner!   *50*

Wagner. Villain, call me Master Wagner. And see
    that you walk attentively, and let your right eye
    be always diametrally° fixed upon my left heel,
    that thou mayst *quasi vestigiis nostris insistere.*°

Robin. Well sir, I warrant you.   *Exeunt.*   *55*

[2.1] *Enter Faustus in his study.*

Faustus. Now, Faustus, must thou needs be damned;
    Canst thou not be saved!
    What boots° it then to think on God or heaven?
    Away with such vain fancies, and despair—
    Despair in God and trust in Belzebub!   *5*
    Now go not backward. Faustus, be resolute!
    Why waver'st thou? O something soundeth in
       mine ear,
    "Abjure this magic, turn to God again."
    Ay, and Faustus will turn to God again.
    To God? He loves thee not;   *10*
    The god thou serv'st is thine own appetite
    Wherein is fixed the love of Belzebub!

---

49 **brave** splendid   53 **diametrally** directly   54 **quasi vestigiis nostris in-
sistere** as if to step in our footsteps   2.1.3 **boots** avails

To him I'll build an altar and a church
And offer lukewarm blood of newborn babes!

Enter the two Angels.

15 *Bad Angel.* Go forward, Faustus, in that famous art.

Good Angel. Sweet Faustus, leave that execrable art.

Faustus. Contrition, prayer, repentance, what of these?

Good Angel. O, they are means to bring thee unto
heaven.

Bad Angel. Rather illusions, fruits of lunacy,
20 That make men foolish that do use them most.

Good Angel. Sweet Faustus, think of heaven and
heavenly things.

Bad Angel. No Faustus, think of honor and of wealth.
Exeunt Angels.

Faustus. Wealth!
Why, the signory of Emden° shall be mine!
25 When Mephostophilis shall stand by me
What power can hurt me? Faustus, thou art safe.
Cast no more doubts! Mephostophilis, come,
And bring glad tidings from great Lucifer.
Is't not midnight? Come Mephostophilis,
30 *Veni, veni, Mephostophile!°*

Enter Mephostophilis.

Now tell me, what saith Lucifer thy lord?

---

24 **signory of Emden** lordship of the rich German port at the mouth of the
Ems   30 **Veni, veni, Mephostophile** come, come, Mephostophilis (Latin)

Mephostophilis. That I shall wait on Faustus whilst
    he lives,
  So he will buy my service with his soul.

Faustus. Already Faustus hath hazarded that for thee.

Mephostophilis. But now thou must bequeath it
    solemnly   *35*
  And write a deed of gift with thine own blood,
  For that security craves Lucifer.
  If thou deny it I must back to hell.

Faustus. Stay Mephostophilis and tell me
  What good will my soul do thy lord?   *40*

Mephostophilis. Enlarge his kingdom.

Faustus. Is that the reason why he tempts us thus?

*Mephostophilis. Solamen miseris socios habuisse
  doloris.*°

Faustus. Why, have you any pain that torture other?°

Mephostophilis. As great as have the human souls
    of men.   *45*
  But tell me, Faustus, shall I have thy soul—
  And I will be thy slave and wait on thee
  And give thee more than thou hast wit to ask?

Faustus. Ay Mephostophilis, I'll give it him.°

Mephostophilis. Then, Faustus, stab thy arm coura-
    geously   *50*
  And bind thy soul that at some certain day
  Great Lucifer may claim it as his own.
  And then be thou as great as Lucifer!

43 **Solamen . . . doloris** misery loves company (Latin) 44 **other** others 49 **him** i.e., to Lucifer

Faustus. Lo, Mephostophilis, for love of thee
    Faustus hath cut his arm and with his proper°
55   blood
    Assures° his soul to be great Lucifer's,
    Chief lord and regent of perpetual night.
    View here this blood that trickles from mine arm
    And let it be propitious for my wish.

60 *Mephostophilis.* But Faustus,
    Write it in manner of a deed of gift.

Faustus. Ay so I do—But Mephostophilis,
    My blood congeals and I can write no more.

Mephostophilis. I'll fetch thee fire to dissolve it
    straight.   *Exit.*

65 *Faustus.* What might the staying of my blood portend?
    Is it unwilling I should write this bill?°
    Why streams it not that I may write afresh:
    "Faustus gives to thee his soul"? O there it
    stayed.
    Why shouldst thou not? Is not thy soul thine
    own?
70   Then write again: "Faustus gives to thee his soul."

    Enter Mephostophilis with the chafer° of fire.

Mephostophilis. See Faustus, here is fire. Set it° on.

Faustus. So, now the blood begins to clear again.
    Now will I make an end immediately.

Mephostophilis. [*aside*] What will not I do to obtain
    his soul!

---

55 **proper** own   56 **Assures** conveys by contract   66 **bill** contract   70 s.d.
chafer portable grate   71 **it** i.e., the receptacle containing the congealed
blood

Faustus. Consummatum est!° This bill is ended: 75
    And Faustus hath bequeathed his soul to Lucifer.
    —But what is this inscription on mine arm?
    Homo fuge!° Whither should I fly?
    If unto God, He'll throw me down to hell.
    My senses are deceived, here's nothing writ.   80
    O yes, I see it plain! Even here is writ
    Homo fuge! Yet shall not Faustus fly!

Mephostophilis. [*aside*] I'll fetch him somewhat to
    delight his mind.   *Exit.*

*Enter Devils giving crowns and rich apparel to
    Faustus. They dance and then depart.*

Enter Mephostophilis.

Faustus. What means this show? Speak, Mepho-
    stophilis.

Mephostophilis. Nothing Faustus, but to delight thy
    mind   85
    And let thee see what magic can perform.

Faustus. But may I raise such spirits when I please?

Mephostophilis. Ay Faustus, and do greater things
    than these.

Faustus. Then, Mephostophilis, receive this scroll,
    A deed of gift of body and of soul: 90
    But yet conditionally that thou perform
    All covenants and articles between us both.

Mephostophilis. Faustus, I swear by hell and Lucifer
    To effect all promises between us both.

75 **Consummatum est** it is finished (Latin; a blasphemous repetition of Christ's
words on the Cross; see John 19:30)   78 **Homo fuge** fly, man (Latin)

95   *Faustus.* Then hear me read it, Mephostophilis:
            "On these conditions following:
            First, that Faustus may be a spirit° in form and
               substance.
            Secondly, that Mephostophilis shall be his servant
100   and be by him commanded.
            Thirdly, that Mephostophilis shall do for him and
               bring him whatsoever.
            Fourthly, that he shall be in his chamber or house
               invisible.
105   Lastly, that he shall appear to the said John Faus-
               tus at all times in what form or shape soever
               he please:
            I, John Faustus of Wittenberg, Doctor, by these
               presents, do give both body and soul to Lucifer,
110   prince of the east, and his minister Mephosto-
               philis, and furthermore grant unto them that,
               four and twenty years being expired, and these
               articles above written being inviolate,° full
               power to fetch or carry the said John Faustus,
115   body and soul, flesh, blood, or goods, into their
               habitation wheresoever.
                                     By me John Faustus.

      Mephostophilis. Speak Faustus, do you deliver this
            as your deed?

      Faustus. Ay, take it, and the devil give thee good of it!

      Mephostophilis. So now Faustus, ask me what thou
120   wilt.

      Faustus. First will I question with thee about hell.
            Tell me, where is the place that men call hell?

97 **spirit** evil spirit, devil (but to see Faustus as transformed now into a
devil deprived of freedom to repent is to deprive the remainder of the play
of much of its meaning)   113 **inviolate** unviolated

Mephostophilis. Under the heavens.

Faustus. Ay, so are all things else, but whereabouts?

Mephostophilis. Within the bowels of these elements   125
    Where we are tortured and remain forever.
    Hell hath no limits nor is circumscribed
    In one self place, but where we are is hell,
    And where hell is there must we ever be.
    And to be short, when all the world dissolves   130
    And every creature shall be purified
    All places shall be hell that is not heaven!

Faustus. I think hell's a fable.

Mephostophilis. Ay, think so still—till experience
    change thy mind!

Faustus. Why, dost thou think that Faustus shall be
    damned?   135

Mephostophilis. Ay, of necessity, for here's the scroll
    In which thou hast given thy soul to Lucifer.

Faustus. Ay, and body too; but what of that?
    Think'st thou that Faustus is so fond° to imagine
    That after this life there is any pain?   140
    No, these are trifles and mere old wives' tales.

Mephostophilis. But I am an instance to prove the
    contrary,
    For I tell thee I am damned and now in hell!

Faustus. Nay, and this be hell, I'll willingly be
    damned—
    What, sleeping, eating, walking, and disputing?   145
    But leaving this, let me have a wife, the fairest

139 **fond** foolish

maid in Germany, for I am wanton and lascivi-
ous and cannot live without a wife.

Mephostophilis. Well Faustus, thou shalt have a wife.
　　　He fetches in a woman Devil [*with fireworks*].

150　*Faustus.* What sight is this?

Mephostophilis. Now Faustus, wilt thou have a wife?

Faustus. Here's a hot whore indeed! No, I'll no wife.

Mephostophilis. Marriage is but a ceremonial toy,°
　　　　　　　　　　　　　　　　[*Exit She-devil.*]
　　And if thou lovest me, think no more of it.
155　I'll cull thee out° the fairest courtesans
　　And bring them every morning to thy bed.
　　She whom thine eye shall like thy heart shall
　　　　have,
　　Were she as chaste as was Penelope,°
　　As wise as Saba,° or as beautiful
160　As was bright Lucifer before his fall.
　　Here, take this book and peruse it well.
　　The iterating° of these lines brings gold;
　　The framing° of this circle on the ground
　　Brings thunder, whirlwinds, storm, and lightning;
165　Pronounce this thrice devoutly to thyself,
　　And men in harness° shall appear to thee,
　　Ready to execute what thou command'st.

Faustus. Thanks Mephostophilis for this sweet book.
　　This will I keep as chary as my life.　　　*Exeunt.*°

---

153 **toy** trifle　　155 **cull thee out** select for you　　158 **Penelope** wife of Ulysses, famed for her fidelity　159 **Saba** the Queen of Sheba　162 **iterating**
repetition　163 **framing** drawing　166 **harness** armor　169 s.d. **Exeunt** (a
scene following this stage direction has probably been lost. Earlier Wagner
hired the Clown; later the Clown is an ostler possessed of one of Faustus'
conjuring books. Possibly, then, the lost scene was a comic one, showing
the Clown stealing a book and departing)

[2.2] *Enter Faustus in his study and Mephostophilis.*

Faustus. When I behold the heavens, then I repent
    And curse thee, wicked Mephostophilis,
    Because thou has deprived me of those joys.

Mephostophilis. 'Twas thine own seeking Faustus,
    thank thyself.
    But think'st thou heaven is such a glorious thing?   5
    I tell thee, Faustus, it is not half so fair
    As thou or any man that breathe on earth.

Faustus. How prov'st thou that?

Mephostophilis. 'Twas made for man; then he's more
    excellent.

Faustus. If heaven was made for man, 'twas made
    for me!   10
    I will renounce this magic and repent.

            Enter the two Angels.

Good Angel. Faustus, repent: yet° God will pity thee!

Bad Angel. Thou art a spirit: God cannot pity thee!

Faustus. Who buzzeth in mine ears I am a spirit?
    Be I a devil, yet God may pity me—   15
    Yea, God will pity me if I repent.

Bad Angel. Ay, but Faustus never shall repent.
                   Exit Angels.

Faustus. My heart is hardened, I cannot repent.
    Scarce can I name salvation, faith, or heaven,
    Swords, poison, halters, and envenomed steel   20
    Are laid before me to dispatch myself.

2.2.12 **yet** still, even now

And long ere this I should have done the deed
Had not sweet pleasure conquered deep despair.
Have not I made blind Homer sing to me
25   Of Alexander's love and Oenone's° death?
And hath not he° that built the walls of Thebes
With ravishing sound of his melodious harp
Made music with my Mephostophilis?
Why should I die then or basely despair?
30   I am resolved, Faustus shall not repent!
Come Mephostophilis, let us dispute again
And reason of divine astrology.
Speak, are there many spheres above the moon?
Are all celestial bodies but one globe
35   As is the substance of this centric° earth?

Mephostophilis. As are the elements, such° are the
    heavens,
Even from the moon unto the empyreal orb
Mutually folded in each others' spheres,
And jointly move upon one axle-tree,
40   Whose terminè° is termed the world's wide pole.
Nor are the names of Saturn, Mars, or Jupiter
Feigned but are erring stars.°

Faustus. But have they all one motion,
Both *situ et tempore*?°

45   *Mephostophilis.* All move from east to west in four and
    twenty hours upon the poles of the world but dif-
    fer in their motions upon the poles of the zodiac.

---

25 **Alexander ... Oenone** Paris, also called Alexander, was Oenone's lover,
but he later deserted her for Helen of Troy, causing the Trojan War, the subject of Homer's *Iliad*   26 **he** Amphion, whose music charmed stones to form
the walls of Thebes   35 **centric** central   36 **such** i.e., separate but combined;
the idea is that the heavenly bodies are separate but their spheres are con-
centric ("folded"), and all—from the nearest (the moon) to the farthest ("the
empyreal orb" or empyrean)—move on one axle-tree   40 **terminè** end, extremity   42 **erring stars** planets   44 **situ et tempore** in place and in time

Faustus. These slender questions Wagner can decide.
   Hath Mephostophilis no greater skill?
   Who knows not the double motion of the planets?   *50*
   That the first is finished in a natural day.°
   The second thus: Saturn in thirty years;
   Jupiter in twelve; Mars in four; the sun, Venus,
   and Mercury in a year; the moon in twenty-eight
   days. These are freshmen's suppositions.° But   *55*
   tell me, hath every sphere a dominion or *intel-*
   ligentia?°

Mephostophilis. Ay.

Faustus. How many heavens or spheres are there?

Mephostophilis. Nine: the seven planets, the firma-   *60*
   ment, and the empyreal heaven.

Faustus. But is there not *coelum igneum et crystal-*
   linum?°

Mephostophilis. No Faustus, they be but fables.

Faustus. Resolve me then in this one question. Why   *65*
   are not conjunctions, oppositions, aspects,
   eclipses all at one time,° but in some years we
   have more, in some less?

Mephostophilis. Per inaqualem motum respectu
   totius.°   *70*

Faustus. Well, I am answered. Now tell me, who
   made the world?

Mephostophilis. I will not.

---

51 **natural day** twenty-four hours   55 **suppositions** premises   56–57 **dominion or intelligentia** governing angel or intelligence (believed to impart motion
to the sphere)   62–63 **coelum igneum et crystallinum** a heaven of fire and
a crystalline sphere (Latin)   67 **at one time** i.e., at regular intervals   69–70
Per ... totius because of unequal speed within the system (Latin)

Faustus. Sweet Mephostophilis, tell me.

75 *Mephostophilis.* Move° me not, Faustus!

Faustus. Villain, have not I bound thee to tell me
        anything?

Mephostophilis. Ay, that is not against our kingdom.
        This is. Thou art damned. Think thou of hell!

Faustus. Think, Faustus, upon God, that made the
80   world.

Mephostophilis. Remember this!   *Exit.*

Faustus. Ay, go accursèd spirit to ugly hell!
        'Tis thou hast damned distressèd Faustus' soul.—
        Is't not too late?

            Enter the two Angels.

85 *Bad Angel.* Too late.

Good Angel. Never too late, if Faustus will repent.

Bad Angel. If thou repent, devils will tear thee in
        pieces.

Good Angel. Repent, and they shall never raze° thy
        skin.   *Exeunt Angels.*

Faustus. O Christ, my savior, my savior!
90   Help to save distressèd Faustus' soul.

        Enter Lucifer, Belzebub, and Mephostophilis.

Lucifer. Christ cannot save thy soul, for He is just.
        There's none but I have interest in° the same.

75 **Move** anger   88 **raze** scratch   92 **interest in** legal claim on

Faustus. O, what art thou that look'st so terribly?

Lucifer. I am Lucifer
   And this is my companion prince in hell.   95

Faustus. O Faustus, they are come to fetch thy soul!

Belzebub. We are come to tell thee thou dost injure us.

Lucifer. Thou call'st on Christ contrary to thy promise.

Belzebub. Thou should'st not think on God.

Lucifer.   Think on the Devil.

Belzebub. And his dam° too.   100

Faustus. Nor will Faustus henceforth. Pardon him
   for this,
   And Faustus vows never to look to heaven!
   Never to name God or to pray to Him,
   To burn His Scriptures, slay His ministers,
   And make my spirits pull His churches down.   105

Lucifer. So shalt thou show thyself an obedient
   servant,
   And we will highly gratify thee for it.

Belzebub. Faustus, we are come from hell in person
   to show thee some pastime. Sit down and thou
   shalt behold the Seven Deadly Sins° appear to   110
   thee in their own proper shapes and likeness.

Faustus. That sight will be as pleasant to me as Paradise was to Adam the first day of his creation.

Lucifer. Talk not of Paradise or creation but mark
   the show. Go Mephostophilis, fetch them in.   115

100 **dam** mother   110 **Seven Deadly Sins** (so called because they cause
spiritual death; they are Pride, Covetousness, Envy, Wrath, Gluttony, Sloth,
Lechery)

Enter the Seven Deadly Sins [led by a Piper].

Belzebub. Now Faustus, question them of their
names and dispositions.

Faustus. That shall I soon. What art thou, the first?

Pride. I am Pride. I disdain to have any parents. I am
120   like to Ovid's flea,° I can creep into every corner
of a wench: sometimes, like a periwig I sit upon
her brow; next, like a necklace I hang about her
neck; then, like a fan of feathers I kiss her; and
then, turning myself to a wrought smock,° do what
125   I list—But fie, what a smell is here! I'll not speak a
word more for a king's ransom unless the ground
be perfumed and covered with cloth of arras.°

Faustus. Thou art a proud knave indeed. What art
thou, the second?

130 *Covetousness.* I am Covetousness, begotten of an old
churl in a leather bag;° and might I now obtain
my wish, this house, you and all, should turn to
gold that I might lock you safe into my chest. O
my sweet gold!

135 *Faustus.* And what art thou, the third?

Envy. I am Envy, begotten of a chimney-sweeper
and an oyster-wife.° I cannot read and therefore wish all books burned. I am lean with
seeing others eat. O, that there would come a
140   famine over all the world that all might die and
I live alone! Then thou shouldst see how fat I'd

---

120 **Ovid's flea** flea in *Carmen de pulce,* a lewd poem mistakenly attributed to Ovid   124 **wrought smock** decorated petticoat   127 **cloth of
arras** Flemish cloth used for tapestries   131 **leather bag** moneybag (?)
136–137 **chimney-sweeper … oyster-wife** i.e., dirty and smelly

be. But must thou sit and I stand? Come down,
with a vengeance!

Faustus. Out, envious wretch! But what art thou, the
fourth?

Wrath. I am Wrath. I had neither father nor mother. I   *145*
leapt out of a lion's mouth when I was scarce an
hour old and ever since have run up and down
the world with these case° of rapiers, wounding
myself when I could get none to fight withal. I
was born in hell! And look to it, for some of you   *150*
shall be my father.

Faustus. And what art thou, the fifth?

Gluttony. I am Gluttony. My parents are all dead, and
the devil a penny they have left me, but a small
pension: and that buys me thirty meals a day and   *155*
ten bevers,° a small trifle to suffice nature. I come
of a royal pedigree. My father was a gammon° of
bacon, and my mother was a hogshead of claret
wine. My godfathers were these: Peter Pickled-
herring and Martin Martlemas-beef.° But my   *160*
godmother, O, she was an ancient gentlewoman:
her name was Margery March-beer.° Now Faustus, thou hast heard all my progeny,° wilt thou
bid me to supper?

Faustus. Not I.   *165*

Gluttony. Then the devil choke thee!

Faustus. Choke thyself, glutton! What art thou, the
sixth?

148 **these case** this pair   156 **bevers** snacks (literally drinks)   157 **gam-
mon** haunch   160 **Martlemas-beef** cattle slaughtered at Martinmas (11
November) and salted for winter consumption   162 **March-beer** strong
beer brewed in March   163 **progeny** ancestry

Sloth. Heigh-ho!° I am Sloth. I was begotten on a
170   sunny bank. Heigh-ho, I'll not speak a word
          more for a king's ransom.

Faustus. And what are you, Mistress Minx, the sev-
          enth and last?

Lechery. Who, I, I sir? I am one that loves an inch of raw
175   mutton° better than an ell of fried stockfish,° and
          the first letter of my name begins with Lechery.

Lucifer. Away to hell, away! On, piper!
                              Exeunt the Seven Sins.

Faustus. O, how this sight doth delight my soul!

Lucifer. But Faustus, in hell is all manner of delight.

180 *Faustus.* O, might I see hell and return again safe,
          how happy were I then!

Lucifer. Faustus, thou shalt. At midnight I will send
          for thee.
          Meanwhile peruse this book and view it thoroughly,
          And thou shalt turn thyself into what shape thou
          wilt.

185 *Faustus.* Thanks mighty Lucifer.
          This will I keep as chary° as my life.

Lucifer. Now Faustus, farewell.

Faustus. Farewell great Lucifer. Come Mephostoph-
          ilis.   *Exeunt omnes several° ways.*

---

169 **Heigh-ho** (a yawn or tired greeting)   174–175 **inch of raw mutton** i.e.,
penis ("mutton" in a bawdy sense commonly alludes to a prostitute, but
since here the speaker is a woman, the allusion must be to a male)   175 **an
ell of . . . stockfish** forty-five inches of dried cod 186 **chary** carefully   188
s.d. **several** various

[2.3] *Enter [Robin] the Clown.*

Robin. What, Dick, look to the horses there till I
come again! I have gotten one of Doctor Faustus' conjuring books, and now we'll have such
knavery as't passes.

Enter Dick.

Dick. What, Robin, you must come away and walk   *5*
the horses.

Robin. I walk the horses? I scorn't, 'faith. I have
other matters in hand. Let the horses walk
themselves an° they will. [*Reading*] A *per se*°—
a; t, h, e—the; o *per se*—o; deny orgon—gorgon.°   *10*
Keep further from me, O thou illiterate and un-
learned hostler!

Dick. 'Snails,° what hast thou got there, a book?
Why, thou canst not tell ne'er a word on't.

Robin. That thou shalt see presently. Keep out of the
circle, I say, lest I send you into the hostry° with   *15*
a vengeance.

Dick. That's like, 'faith! You had best leave your
foolery, for an my master come, he'll conjure
you, 'faith.

Robin. My master conjure me? I'll tell thee what. An   *20*
my master come here, I'll clap as fair a pair of
horns° on's head as e'er thou sawest in thy life.

2.3.9 **an** if   9 **per se** by itself (Latin; the idea is, "A by itself spells A")   10
deny orgon—gorgon (Robin is trying to read the name "Demogor-
gon")   12 **'Snails** by God's nails   15 **hostry** hostelry, inn   22 **horns** (as
the next speech indicates, horns were said to adorn the head of a man
whose wife was unfaithful)

Dick. Thou need'st not do that, for my mistress hath
    done it.

25 *Robin.* Ay, there be of us here that have waded as
    deep into matters as other men—if they were
    disposed to talk.

Dick. A plague take you! I thought you did not
    sneak up and down after her for nothing. But I
30   prithee tell me in good sadness° Robin, is that a
    conjuring book?

Robin. Do but speak what thou't have me to do,
    and I'll do't. If thou't dance naked, put off thy
    clothes, and I'll conjure thee about presently. Or
35   if thou't go but to the tavern with me, I'll give
    thee white wine, red wine, claret wine, sack,°
    muscadine, malmsey, and whippincrust°—hold-
    belly-hold. And we'll not pay one penny for it.

Dick. O brave! Prithee let's to it presently, for I am
40   as dry as a dog.

Robin. Come then, let's away.   *Exeunt.*

[3] *Enter the Chorus.*

Learnèd Faustus,
To find the secrets of astronomy
Graven in the book of Jove's high firmament,
Did mount him up to scale Olympus' top:
5 Where, sitting in a chariot burning bright
Drawn by the strength of yokèd dragons' necks,
He views the clouds, the planets, and the stars,

---

30 **in good sadness** seriously   36 **sack** sherry   37 **whippincrust** illiterate
pronunciation of "hippocras," a spiced wine

The tropics, zones,° and quarters of the sky,
From the bright circle° of the hornèd moon
Even to the height of *primum mobile*:°   10
And whirling round with this circumference
Within the concave compass of the pole,
From east to west his dragons swiftly glide
And in eight days did bring him home again.
Not long he stayed within his quiet house   15
To rest his bones after his weary toil
But new exploits do hale him out again.
And mounted then upon a dragon's back,
That with his wings did part the subtle air,
He now is gone to prove cosmography,°   20
That measures coasts and kingdoms of the earth,
And as I guess will first arrive at Rome
To see the Pope and manner of his court
And take some part of holy Peter's feast,
The which this day is highly solemnized.   *Exit.*   25

[3.1] *Enter Faustus and Mephostophilis.*

Faustus. Having now, my good Mephostophilis,
Passed with delight the stately town of Trier,°
Environed round with airy mountain tops,
With walls of flint, and deep-entrenchèd lakes,°
Not to be won by any conquering prince: 5
From Paris next, coasting the realm of France,
We saw the river Main fall into Rhine,
Whose banks are set with groves of fruitful vines:
Then up to Naples, rich Campania,

3 Chorus   8 **zones** segments of the sky   9 **circle** orbit   10 **primum mobile** the outermost sphere, the empyrean   20 **prove cosmography** test maps, i.e., explore the universe   3.1.2 **Trier** German city on the Moselle, also known as Trèves   4 **deep-entrenchèd lakes** moats

10   Whose buildings fair and gorgeous to the eye,
       The streets straight forth and paved with finest
          brick,
       Quarters the town in four equivalents.
       There saw we learnèd Maro's° golden tomb,
       The way he cut an English mile in length
15   Through° a rock of stone in one night's space.
       From thence to Venice, Padua, and the rest,
       In one of which a sumptuous temple stands
       That threats the stars with her aspiring top,
       Whose frame is paved with sundry colored stones
20   And roofed aloft with curious work in gold.
       Thus hitherto hath Faustus spent his time.
       But tell me now, what resting-place is this?
       Hast thou, as erst I did command,
       Conducted me within the walls of Rome?

Mephostophilis. I have, my Faustus, and for proof
25   thereof
       This is the goodly palace of the Pope,
       And 'cause we are no common guests
       I choose his privy chamber for our use.

Faustus. I hope his Holiness will bid us welcome.

Mephostophilis. All's one, for we'll be bold with his
30   venison.
       But now my Faustus, that thou may'st perceive
       What Rome contains for to delight thine eyes,
       Know that this city stands upon seven hills
       That underprop the groundwork of the same:
35   Just through the midst runs flowing Tiber's stream
       With winding banks that cut it in two parts,

13 **Maro** Vergil (Publius Vergilius Maro, 70–19 B.C.)   15 **Through** (pronounced "thorough")

Over the which four stately bridges lean°
That make safe passage to each part of Rome.
Upon the bridge called Ponte Angelo
Erected is a castle passing strong   40
Where thou shalt see such store of ordinance
As that the double cannons forged of brass
Do match the number of the days contained
Within the compass of one complete year,
Beside the gates and high pyramides°   45
That Julius Caesar brought from Africa.

Faustus. Now, by the kingdoms of infernal rule,
Of Styx, of Acheron, and the fiery lake
Of ever-burning Phlegethon,° I swear
That I do long to see the monuments   50
And situation of bright-splendent Rome.
Come therefore, let's away.

Mephostophilis. Nay stay my Faustus. I know you'd
    see the Pope
And take some part of holy Peter's feast,
The which this day with high solemnity,   55
This day, is held through Rome and Italy
In honor of the Pope's triumphant victory.

Faustus. Sweet Mephostophilis, thou pleasest me.
Whilst I am here on earth let me be cloyed
With all things that delight the heart of man.   60
My four and twenty years of liberty
I'll spend in pleasure and in dalliance,
That Faustus' name, whilst this bright frame doth
    stand,
May be admirèd through the furthest land.

37 **lean** bend   45 **pyramides** obelisk (pronounced py-ràm-i-des) 48–49 **Styx, Acheron, Phlegethon** rivers of the underworld

Mephostophilis. 'Tis well said, Faustus, come then,
65   stand by me
       And thou shalt see them come immediately.

Faustus. Nay stay, my gentle Mephostophilis,
       And grant me my request, and then I go.
       Thou know'st, within the compass of eight days
70   We viewed the face of heaven, of earth, and hell.
       So high our dragons soared into the air
       That looking down the earth appeared to me
       No bigger than my hand in quantity—
       There did we view the kingdoms of the world,
75   And what might please mine eye I there beheld.
       Then in this show let me an actor be
       That this proud Pope may Faustus' cunning see!

Mephostophilis. Let it be so, my Faustus, but first stay
       And view their triumphs° as they pass this way.
80   And then devise what best contents thy mind
       By cunning in thine art to cross the Pope
       Or dash the pride of this solemnity—
       To make his monks and abbots stand like apes
       And point like antics° at his triple crown,
85   To beat the beads about the friars' pates,
       Or clap huge horns upon the cardinals' heads,
       Or any villainy thou canst devise—
       And I'll perform it, Faustus. Hark, they come!
       This day shall make thee be admired° in Rome!

*Enter the Cardinals and Bishops, some bearing
crosiers, some the pillars; Monks and Friars singing
their procession; then the Pope and Raymond King
of Hungary, with Bruno° led in chains.*

79 **triumphs** spectacular displays   84 **antics** grotesque figures, buffoons
89 **admired** wondered at   89 s.d. **Raymond King of Hungary ... Bruno** (un-
historical figures; Bruno is the emperor's nominee for the papal throne)

Pope. Cast down our footstool.

Raymond.   Saxon Bruno, stoop,   *90*
   Whilst on thy back his Holiness ascends
   Saint Peter's chair and state° pontifical.

Bruno. Proud Lucifer, that state belongs to me—
   But thus I fall to Peter, not to thee.

Pope. To me and Peter shalt thou grov'lling lie   *95*
   And crouch before the papal dignity!
   Sound trumpets then, for thus Saint Peter's heir
   From Bruno's back ascends Saint Peter's chair!

A flourish° while he ascends.

   Thus as the gods creep on with feet of wool
   Long ere with iron hands they punish men,   *100*
   So shall our sleeping vengeance now arise
   And smite with death thy hated enterprise.
   Lord Cardinals of France and Padua,
   Go forthwith to our holy consistory°
   And read amongst the statutes decretal°   *105*
   What by the holy council held at Trent°
   The sacred synod° hath decreed for him
   That doth assume the papal government
   Without election and a true consent.
   Away, and bring us word with speed!   *110*

1 Cardinal. We go my Lord. *Exeunt [two] Cardinals.*

Pope. Lord Raymond—   [*Talks to him apart.*]

Faustus. Go haste thee, gentle Mephostophilis,

---

92 **state** throne   98 s.d. **flourish** trumpet fanfare   104 **consistory** i.e.,
meeting-place of the papal consistory or senate   105 **statutes decretal** i.e.,
ecclesiastical laws   106 **council held at Trent** (intermittently from 1545 to
1563)   107 **synod** council

Follow the cardinals to the consistory
115   And as they turn their superstitious books
Strike them with sloth and drowsy idleness
And make them sleep so sound that in their
      shapes
Thyself and I may parley with this Pope,
This proud confronter of the Emperor!
120   —And in despite of all his holiness
Restore this Bruno to his liberty
And bear him to the states of Germany!

Mephostophilis. Faustus, I go.

Faustus. Dispatch it soon.
125   The Pope shall curse that Faustus came to Rome.
                         Exit Faustus and Mephostophilis.

Bruno. Pope Adrian, let me have some right of law:
I was elected by the Emperor.

Pope. We will depose the Emperor for that deed
And curse the people that submit to him.
130   Both he and thou shalt stand excommunicate
And interdict from church's privilege
And all society of holy men.
He grows too proud in his authority,
Lifting his lofty head above the clouds,
135   And like a steeple overpeers the church.
But we'll pull down his haughty insolence.
And as Pope Alexander,° our progenitor,°
Trod on the neck of German Frederick,
Adding this golden sentence to our praise:
140   "That Peter's heirs should tread on emperors
And walk upon the dreadful adder's back,
Treading the lion and the dragon down,

137 **Pope Alexander** Pope Alexander III (d. 1181) compelled the Emperor
Frederick Barbarossa to kneel before him   137 **progenitor** predecessor

And fearless spurn the killing basilisk"°—
So will we quell that haughty schismatic
And by authority apostolical   145
Depose him from his regal government.

Bruno. Pope Julius swore to princely Sigismond,
  For him and the succeeding Popes of Rome,
  To hold the emperors their lawful lords.

Pope. Pope Julius did abuse the church's rites   150
  And therefore none of his decrees can stand.
  Is not all power on earth bestowed on us?
  And therefore though we would, we cannot err.
  Behold this silver belt whereto is fixed
  Seven golden keys fast sealed with seven seals   155
  In token of our sevenfold power from heaven
  To bind or loose, lock fast, condemn, or judge,
  Resign° or seal, or whatso pleaseth us.
  Then he and thou and all the world shall stoop—
  Or be assurèd of our dreadful curse   160
  To light as heavy as the pains of hell.

Enter Faustus and Mephostophilis like the cardinals.

Mephostophilis. [*aside*] Now tell me Faustus, are we
    not fitted well?

Faustus. [*aside*] Yes Mephostophilis, and two such
    cardinals
  Ne'er served a holy Pope as we shall do.
  But whilst they sleep within the consistory   165
  Let us salute his reverend Fatherhood.

Raymond. Behold my lord, the cardinals are returned.

143 **basilisk** fabulous monster said to kill with a glance   158 **Resign**
unseal

Pope. Welcome grave fathers, answer presently,°
What have our holy council there decreed
170   Concerning Bruno and the Emperor
In quittance of° their late conspiracy
Against our state and papal dignity?

Faustus. Most sacred patron of the church of Rome,
By full consent of all the synod
175   Of priests and prelates it is thus decreed:
That Bruno and the German Emperor
Be held as lollards° and bold schismatics
And proud disturbers of the church's peace.
And if that Bruno by his own assent,
180   Without enforcement of the German peers,
Did seek to wear the triple diadem
And by your death to climb Saint Peter's chair,
The statutes decretal have thus decreed:
He shall be straight condemned of heresy
185   And on a pile of fagots burnt to death.

Pope. It is enough. Here, take him to your charge
And bear him straight to Ponte Angelo
And in the strongest tower enclose him fast.
Tomorrow, sitting in our consistory
190   With all our college of grave cardinals
We will determine of his life or death.
Here, take his triple crown along with you
And leave it in the church's treasury.
Make haste again,° my good lord cardinals,
195   And take our blessing apostolical.

Mephostophilis. [*aside*] So, so! Was never devil thus
blessed before.

---

168 **presently** immediately   171 **quittance of** requital for   177 **lollards**
heretics   194 **again** i.e., to return

Faustus. [*aside*] Away sweet Mephostophilis, be gone!
   The cardinals will be plagued for this anon.
   Exeunt Faustus and Mephostophilis [*with Bruno*].

Pope. Go presently and bring a banquet forth,
   That we may solemnize Saint Peter's feast   *200*
   And with Lord Raymond, King of Hungary,
   Drink to our late and happy victory.   *Exeunt.*

   [3.2] *A sennet° while the banquet is brought in,*
      and then enter Faustus and Mephostophilis
            in their own shapes.

Mephostophilis. Now Faustus, come prepare thyself
      for mirth.
   The sleepy cardinals are hard at hand
   To censure Bruno, that is posted hence,
   And on a proud-paced steed as swift as thought
   Flies o'er the Alps to fruitful Germany,   *5*
   There to salute the woeful Emperor.

Faustus. The Pope will curse them for their sloth today
   That slept both Bruno and his crown away.
   But now, that Faustus may delight his mind
   And by their folly make some merriment,   *10*
   Sweet Mephostophilis, so charm me here
   That I may walk invisible to all
   And do whate'er I please unseen of any.

Mephostophilis. Faustus, thou shalt. Then kneel down
      presently,
         Whilst on thy head I lay my hand   *15*

3.2 s.d. **sennet** set of notes played on a trumpet signaling an approach or
a departure

And charm thee with this magic wand.
First wear this girdle, then appear
Invisible to all are here:
The planets seven, the gloomy air,
20   Hell, and the Furies' forkèd hair,°
Pluto's blue fire, and Hecat's° tree
With magic spells so compass thee
That no eye may thy body see.
So Faustus, now for all their holiness,
25   Do what thou wilt, thou shalt not be discerned.

Faustus. Thanks Mephostophilis. Now friars, take heed
Lest Faustus make your shaven crowns to bleed.

Mephostophilis. Faustus, no more. See where the cardinals come.

Enter Pope [and Friars] and all the Lords [with King Raymond and the Archbishop of Rheims]. Enter the [two] Cardinals with a book.

Pope. Welcome lord cardinals. Come, sit down.
30   Lord Raymond, take your seat. Friars, attend,
And see that all things be in readiness
As best beseems this solemn festival.

1 Cardinal. First may it please your sacred Holiness
To view the sentence of the reverend synod
35   Concerning Bruno and the Emperor.

Pope. What needs this question? Did I not tell you
Tomorrow we would sit i' th' consistory

---

20 **Furies' forkèd hair** (the hair of the Furies consisted of snakes, whose forked tongues may be implied here)   21 **Hecat** Hecate, goddess of magic (possibly her "tree" is the gallows-tree, but possibly "tree" is a slip for "three," Hecate being the triple goddess of heaven, earth, and hell)

And there determine of his punishment?
You brought us word, even now, it was decreed
That Bruno and the cursèd Emperor   40
Were by the holy council both condemned
For loathèd lollards and base schismatics.
Then wherefore would you have me view that
    book?

1 Cardinal. Your Grace mistakes. You gave us no
    such charge.

Raymond. Deny it not; we all are witnesses   45
That Bruno here was late delivered you
With his rich triple crown to be reserved
And put into the church's treasury.

Both Cardinals. By holy Paul we saw them not.

Pope. By Peter you shall die   50
Unless you bring them forth immediately.
Hale them to prison, lade their limbs with gyves.°
False prelates, for this hateful treachery
Cursed be your souls to hellish misery.
    [*Exeunt Attendants with two Cardinals.*]

Faustus. So, they are safe. Now Faustus, to the feast. 55
The Pope had never such a frolic guest.

Pope. Lord Archbishop of Rheims, sit down with us.

Archbishop. I thank your Holiness.

Faustus. Fall to,° the devil choke you an you spare!

Pope. Who's that spoke? Friars, look about.   60
Lord Raymond, pray fall to. I am beholding
To the Bishop of Milan for this so rare a present.

---

52 **gyves** fetters   59 **Fall to** set to work (here, as commonly, "start eating")

Faustus. [*aside*] I thank you, sir! [*Snatches the dish.*]

Pope. How now! Who snatched the meat from me?
65   Villains, why speak you not?
       My good Lord Archbishop, here's a most dainty
          dish
       Was sent me from a cardinal in France.

Faustus. [*aside*] I'll have that too! [*Snatches the dish.*]

Pope. What lollards do attend our Holiness
70   That we receive such great indignity!
       Fetch me some wine.

Faustus. [*aside*] Ay, pray do, for Faustus is adry.

Pope. Lord Raymond, I drink unto your Grace.

Faustus. [*aside*] I pledge your Grace.
                              [*Snatches the goblet.*]

75 *Pope.* My wine gone too? Ye lubbers, look about
       And find the man that doth this villainy,
       Or by our sanctitude you all shall die.
       I pray, my lords, have patience at this trouble-
          some banquet.

Archbishop. Please it your Holiness, I think it be
80   some ghost crept out of purgatory, and now is
       come unto your Holiness for his pardon.

Pope. It may be so:
       Go then, command our priests to sing a dirge
       To lay the fury of this same troublesome ghost.
                              [*Exit Attendant.*]

[*The Pope crosses himself before eating.*]

Faustus. How now! Must every bit be spicèd with a   85
  cross?
  Nay then, take that!   [*Strikes the Pope.*]

Pope. O, I am slain! Help me my lords!
  O come and help to bear my body hence.
  Damned be this soul forever for this deed.
                    Exeunt the Pope and his train.

Mephostophilis. Now Faustus, what will you do now?   90
  For I can tell you, you'll be cursed with bell, book,
  and candle.°

Faustus. Bell, book, and candle. Candle, book, and
  bell.
  Forward and backward, to curse Faustus to hell!

          *Enter the Friars, with bell, book,
            and candle for the dirge.*

1 Friar. Come brethren, let's about our business with   95
  good devotion.
  Cursèd be he that stole his Holiness' meat from
  the table.
      Maledicat Dominus!°
  Cursèd be he that struck his Holiness a blow on
  the face.
      Maledicat Dominus!   100
                    [*Faustus strikes a Friar.*]
  Cursèd be he that took Friar Sandelo a blow on
  the pate.
      Maledicat Dominus!

91–92 **bell, book, and candle** implements used in excommunicating (the
bell was tolled, the book closed, the candle extinguished)   98 **Maledicat
Dominus** may the Lord curse him (Latin)

Cursèd be he that disturbeth our holy dirge.
        Maledicat Dominus!
105 Cursèd be he that took away his Holiness' wine.
        Maledicat Dominus!

[*Faustus and Mephostophilis*] *beat the Friars, fling*
        fireworks among them and exeunt.

[3.3] *Enter* [*Robin the*] *Clown and Dick with a cup.*

Dick. Sirrah Robin, we were best look that your devil
        can answer the stealing of this same cup, for the
        vintner's boy follows us at the hard heels.°

Robin. 'Tis no matter, let him come! An he follow us
5   I'll so conjure him as he was never conjured in
        his life, I warrant him. Let me see the cup.

            Enter Vintner.

Dick. Here 'tis. Yonder he comes. Now Robin, now
        or never show thy cunning.

Vintner. O, are you here? I am glad I have found you.
10   You are a couple of fine companions!° Pray,
        where's the cup you stole from the tavern?

Robin. How, how! We steal a cup? Take heed what
        you say. We look not like cup-stealers, I can tell
        you.

15 *Vintner.* Never deny't, for I know you have it, and
        I'll search you.

3.3.3 **at the hard heels** hard at heel, closely   10 **companions** fellows
(contemptuous)

Robin. Search me? Ay, and spare not! [*Aside*] Hold
    the cup, Dick.—Come, come. Search me, search
    me.   [*Vintner searches him.*]

Vintner. Come on sirrah, let me search you now.   20

Dick. Ay ay, do do. [*Aside*] Hold the cup, Robin.— I
    fear not your searching. We scorn to steal your
    cups, I can tell you.   [*Vintner searches him.*]

Vintner. Never outface me for the matter, for sure
    the cup is between you two.   25

Robin. Nay, there you lie! 'Tis beyond us both.°

Vintner. A plague take you. I thought 'twas your knav-
    ery to take it away. Come, give it me again.

Robin. Ay, much! When, can you tell?° [*Aside*] Dick,
    make me a circle and stand close at my back and   30
    stir not for thy life. Vintner, you shall have your
    cup anon. [*Aside*] Say nothing, Dick! O *per se,* o;
    Demogorgon, Belcher, and Mephostophilis!

        Enter Mephostophilis. [*Exit Vintner.*]

Mephostophilis. You princely legions of infernal rule,
    How am I vexèd by these villains' charms!   35
    From Constantinople have they brought me now
    Only for pleasure of these damnèd slaves.

Robin. By lady sir, you have had a shrewd° journey
    of it. Will it please you to take a shoulder of
    mutton to supper and a tester° in your purse   40
    and go back again?

---

26 **beyond us both** (apparently Robin has managed to place the cup at
some distance from where he now stands)   29 **When, can you tell** (a
scornful reply)   38 **shrewd** bad   40 **tester** sixpence

Dick. Ay, I pray you heartily, sir. For we called you
    but in jest, I promise you.

Mephostophilis. To purge the rashness of this cursèd
    deed,
45   First be thou turnèd to this ugly shape,
    For apish° deeds transformèd to an ape.

Robin. O brave! An ape! I pray sir, let me have the
    carrying of him about to show some tricks.

Mephostophilis. And so thou shalt. Be thou trans-
50   formed to a dog and carry him upon thy back.
    Away, be gone!

Robin. A dog! That's excellent. Let the maids look
    well to their porridge-pots, for I'll into the
    kitchen presently. Come Dick, come.
                         Exeunt the two Clowns.

Mephostophilis. Now with the flames of ever-burn-
55   ing fire
    I'll wing myself and forthwith fly amain
    Unto my Faustus, to the Great Turk's court. *Exit.*

[4] *Enter Chorus.*

When Faustus had with pleasure ta'en the view
Of rarest things and royal courts of kings,
He stayed his course and so returnèd home,
Where such as bare his absence but with grief,
5   I mean his friends and nearest companions,
Did gratulate° his safety with kind words.
And in their conference° of what befell

----

46 **apish** (1) foolish (2) imitative 4 Chorus 6 **gratulate** express joy in
7 **conference** discussion

Touching his journey through the world and air
They put forth questions of astrology
Which Faustus answered with such learnèd skill   10
As they admired and wondered at his wit.
Now is his fame spread forth in every land.
Amongst the rest the Emperor is one,
Carolus the Fifth,° at whose palace now
Faustus is feasted 'mongst his noblemen.   15
What there he did in trial of his art
I leave untold, your eyes shall see performed. *Exit.*

[4.1] *Enter Martino and Frederick at several° doors.*

Martino. What ho, officers, gentlemen!
　　Hie to the presence° to attend the Emperor.
　　Good Frederick, see the rooms be voided straight,°
　　His Majesty is coming to the hall.
　　Go back and see the state° in readiness.   5

Frederick. But where is Bruno, our elected Pope,
　　That on a fury's back came post from Rome?
　　Will not his Grace consort° the Emperor?

Martino. O yes, and with him comes the German
　　　　conjurer,
　　The learnèd Faustus, fame of Wittenberg,   10
　　The wonder of the world for magic art:
　　And he intends to show great Carolus
　　The race of all his stout progenitors
　　And bring in presence of his Majesty
　　The royal shapes and warlike semblances   15
　　Of Alexander and his beauteous paramour.°

14 **Carolus the Fifth** Charles V (1500–58), Holy Roman Emperor   4.1 s.d. **several** separate   2 **presence** presence-chamber   3 **voided straight** emptied immediately   5 **state** chair of state, throne   8 **consort** attend   16 **Alexander and his beauteous paramour** Alexander the Great and his mistress Thaïs

Frederick. Where is Benvolio?

Martino.   Fast asleep, I warrant you.
He took his rouse with stoups° of Rhenish wine
So kindly yesternight to Bruno's health
20   That all this day the sluggard keeps his bed.

Frederick. See, see, his window's ope. We'll call to
him.

Martino. What ho, Benvolio!

Enter Benvolio above at a window, in his nightcap,
buttoning.

Benvolio. What a devil ail you two?

Martino. Speak softly sir, lest the devil hear you,
25   For Faustus at the court is late arrived
And at his heels a thousand furies wait
To accomplish whatsoever the doctor please.

Benvolio. What of this?

Martino. Come, leave thy chamber first, and thou
shalt see   .
30   This conjurer perform such rare exploits
Before the Pope° and royal Emperor
As never yet was seen in Germany.

Benvolio. Has not the Pope enough of conjuring
yet?
He was upon the devil's back late enough!
35   And if he be so far in love with him
I would he would post with him to Rome again.

Frederick. Speak, wilt thou come and see this sport?

18 **took his rouse with stoups** had drinking bouts with full goblets   31 **the**
Pope i.e., Bruno

Benvolio.   Not I.

Martino. Wilt thou stand in thy window and see it
    then?

Benvolio. Ay, and I fall not asleep i' th' meantime.

Martino. The Emperor is at hand, who comes to see   40
    What wonders by black spells may compassed be.

Benvolio. Well, go you attend the Emperor. I am con-
    tent for this once to thrust my head out at a win-
    dow, for they say if a man be drunk overnight
    the devil cannot hurt him in the morning. If that   45
    be true, I have a charm in my head shall control
    him as well as the conjurer, I warrant you.
                    Exit [Martino with Frederick. Benvolio
                            remains at window]. °

[4.2] *A sennet.* ° *Charles the German Emperor,*
Bruno, [Duke of] Saxony, Faustus, Mephostophilis,
Frederick, Martino, and Attendants.

Emperor. Wonder of men, renownèd magician,
    Thrice-learnèd Faustus, welcome to our court.
    This deed of thine in setting Bruno free
    From his and our professèd enemy,
    Shall add more excellence unto thine art   5
    Than if by powerful necromantic spells
    Thou could'st command the world's obedience.

---

47 s.d. **Benvolio remains at window** (because Benvolio does not leave the
stage, this scene cannot properly be said to be ended. But the present edition, following its predecessors for convenience of reference, begins a new
scene)   4.2 s.d. **sennet** trumpet fanfare (the absence of a verb in the rest
of the stage direction perhaps indicates that the Emperor and his party do
not enter but rather are "discovered" as Faustus may have been discovered at the beginning of 1.1, if the Chorus drew back a curtain)

For ever be beloved of Carolus!
And if this Bruno thou hast late redeemed°
10   In peace possess the triple diadem
And sit in Peter's chair despite of chance,
Thou shalt be famous through all Italy
And honored of the German Emperor.

Faustus. These gracious words, most royal Carolus,
15   Shall make poor Faustus to his utmost power
Both love and serve the German Emperor
And lay his life at holy Bruno's feet.
For proof whereof, if so your Grace be pleased,
The doctor stands prepared by power of art
20   To cast his magic charms that shall pierce through
The ebon gates of ever-burning hell,
And hale the stubborn furies from their caves
To compass whatsoe'er your Grace commands.

Benvolio. Blood! He speaks terribly. But for all that
25   I do not greatly believe him. He looks as like a
conjurer as the Pope to a costermonger.°

Emperor. Then Faustus, as thou late didst promise
us,
We would behold that famous conqueror
Great Alexander and his paramour
30   In their true shapes and state majestical,
That we may wonder at their excellence.

Faustus. Your Majesty shall see them presently.—
Mephostophilis away,
And with a solemn noise of trumpets' sound
35   Present before this royal Emperor
Great Alexander and his beauteous paramour.

Mephostophilis. Faustus, I will.   [*Exit.*]

9 **redeemed** freed   26 **costermonger** fruit-seller

Benvolio. Well master doctor, an your devils come
    not away quickly, you shall have me asleep
    presently. Zounds,° I could eat myself for anger   *40*
    to think I have been such an ass all this while to
    stand gaping after the devils' governor and can
    see nothing.

Faustus. I'll make you feel something anon if my art
    fail me not!   *45*
  My lord, I must forewarn your Majesty
  That when my spirits present the royal shapes
  Of Alexander and his paramour,
  Your Grace demand no questions of the King
  But in dumb silence let them come and go.   *50*

Emperor. Be it as Faustus please; we are content.

Benvolio. Ay ay, and I am content too. And thou bring
    Alexander and his paramour before the Em-
    peror, I'll be Actaeon° and turn myself to a stag.

Faustus. [*aside*] And I'll play Diana and send you the   *55*
    horns presently.

*Sennet. Enter at one [door] the Emperor Alexander,
at the other Darius.° They meet. Darius is thrown
down. Alexander kills him, takes off his crown, and
offering to go out, his Paramour meets him. He
embraceth her and sets Darius' crown upon her
head, and coming back both salute the Emperor;
who leaving his state offers to embrace them, which
Faustus seeing suddenly stays him. Then trumpets
cease and music sounds.*

---

40 **Zounds** by God's wounds   54 **Actaeon** legendary hunter who saw the
naked goddess Diana bathing. She transformed him into a stag, and he was
torn to pieces by his own hounds   56 s.d. **Darius** King of Persia, defeated
by Alexander in 334 B.C.

My gracious lord, you do forget yourself.
These are but shadows, not substantial.

Emperor. O pardon me, my thoughts are so ravished
60   With sight of this renownèd Emperor,
That in mine arms I would have compassed° him.
But Faustus, since I may not speak to them,
To satisfy my longing thoughts at full,
Let me this tell thee: I have heard it said
65   That this fair lady whilst she lived on earth,
Had on her neck a little wart or mole.
How may I prove that saying to be true?

Faustus. Your Majesty may boldly go and see.

Emperor. Faustus, I see it plain!
70   And in this sight thou better pleasest me
Than if I gained another monarchy.

Faustus. Away, be gone!   *Exit show.*
See, see, my gracious lord, what strange beast is
yon that thrusts his head out at the window!

75   *Emperor.* O wondrous sight! See, Duke of Saxony,
Two spreading horns most strangely fastened
Upon the head of young Benvolio.

Saxony. What, is he asleep or dead?

Faustus. He sleeps my lord, but dreams not of his
horns.

Emperor. This sport is excellent. We'll call and wake
80   him.
What ho, Benvolio!

Benvolio. A plague upon you! Let me sleep awhile.

61 **compassed** encompassed, embraced

Emperor. I blame thee not to sleep much, having
    such a head of thine own.

Saxony. Look up Benvolio! 'Tis the Emperor calls.   85

Benvolio. The Emperor! Where? O zounds, my head!

Emperor. Nay, and thy horns hold, 'tis no matter for
    thy head, for that's armed sufficiently.

Faustus. Why, how now Sir Knight? What, hanged by
    the horns?° This is most horrible! Fie fie, pull   90
    in your head for shame! Let not all the world
    wonder at you.

Benvolio. Zounds doctor, is this your villainy?

Faustus. Oh, say not so sir: The doctor has no skill,
  No art, no cunning to present these lords   95
  Or bring before this royal Emperor
  The mighty monarch, warlike Alexander.
  If Faustus do it, you are straight resolved
  In bold Actaeon's shape to turn a stag.
  And therefore my lord, so please your Majesty,   100
  I'll raise a kennel of hounds shall hunt him so
  As all his footmanship shall scarce prevail
  To keep his carcass from their bloody fangs.
  Ho, Belimote, Argiron, Asterote!

Benvolio. Hold, hold! Zounds, he'll raise up a kennel   105
    of devils I think, anon. Good my lord, entreat for
    me. 'Sblood,° I am never able to endure these
    torments.

Emperor. Then good master doctor,
  Let me entreat you to remove his horns.   110
  He has done penance now sufficiently.

89–90 **hanged by the horns** (the spreading horns prevent Benvolio from
pulling his head inside of the window)   107 **'Sblood** by God's blood

Faustus. My gracious lord, not so much for injury done
      to me, as to delight your Majesty with some mirth,
      hath Faustus justly requited this injurious° knight;
115   which being all I desire, I am content to remove
      his horns. Mephostophilis, transform him. And
      hereafter sir, look you speak well of scholars.

Benvolio. [*aside*] Speak well of ye! 'Sblood, and schol-
      ars be such cuckold-makers to clap horns of
120   honest men's heads o' this order, I'll ne'er trust
      smooth faces and small ruffs° more. But an I be
      not revenged for this, would I might be turned to
      a gaping oyster and drink nothing but salt water.
                               [*Exit.*]

Emperor. Come Faustus, while the Emperor lives,
125   In recompense of this thy high desert,
      Thou shalt command the state of Germany
      And live beloved of mighty Carolus.
                            Exeunt omnes.

[4.3] *Enter Benvolio, Martino, Frederick,*
and Soldiers.

Martino. Nay, sweet Benvolio, let us sway thy
      thoughts
      From this attempt against the conjurer.

Benvolio. Away! You love me not to urge me thus.
      Shall I let slip° so great an injury
5   When every servile groom jests at my wrongs
      And in their rustic gambols proudly say,
      "Benvolio's head was graced with horns today"?

114 **injurious** insulting   121 **small ruffs** (worn by scholars, in contrast to
the large ruffs worn by courtiers)   4.3.4 **let slip** ignore

O, may these eyelids never close again
Till with my sword I have that conjurer slain!
If you will aid me in this enterprise,   10
Then draw your weapons and be resolute;
If not, depart. Here will Benvolio die
But° Faustus' death shall quit° my infamy.

Frederick. Nay, we will stay with thee, betide what
    may,
And kill that doctor if he come this way.   15

Benvolio. Then, gentle Frederick, hie thee to the
    grove
And place our servants and our followers
Close in an ambush there behind the trees.
By this, I know, the conjurer is near.
I saw him kneel and kiss the Emperor's hand   20
And take his leave laden with rich rewards.
Then soldiers, boldly fight. If Faustus die,
Take you the wealth, leave us the victory.

Frederick. Come soldiers, follow me unto the grove.
Who kills him shall have gold and endless love.   25
                  Exit Frederick with the Soldiers.

Benvolio. My head is lighter than it was by th' horns—
But yet my heart more ponderous than my head,
And pants until I see that conjurer dead.

Martino. Where shall we place ourselves, Benvolio?

Benvolio. Here will we stay to bide the first assault.   30
O, were that damnèd hell-hound but in place
Thou soon should'st see me quit my foul disgrace.

             Enter Frederick.

13 **But** unless 13 **quit** avenge

Frederick. Close, close! The conjurer is at hand
  And all alone comes walking in his gown.
35 Be ready then and strike the peasant° down!

Benvolio. Mine be that honor then! Now sword,
  strike home!
  For horns he gave I'll have his head anon.

   Enter Faustus with the false head.

Martino. See see, he comes.

Benvolio.   No words. This blow ends all!
          [Strikes Faustus.]
  Hell take his soul, his body thus must fall.

40 *Faustus.* O!

Frederick. Groan you, master doctor?

Benvolio. Break may his heart with groans! Dear
  Frederick, see,
  Thus will I end his griefs immediately.

   [Cuts off Faustus' false head.]

Martino. Strike with a willing hand! His head is off.

45 *Benvolio.* The devil's dead, the furies now may laugh.

Frederick. Was this that stern aspect, that awful frown,
  Made the grim monarch of infernal spirits
  Tremble and quake at his commanding charms?

Martino. Was this that damnèd head whose heart
  conspired
50 Benvolio's shame before the Emperor?

35 **peasant** low fellow

Benvolio. Ay, that's the head, and here the body lies
   Justly rewarded for his villainies.

Frederick. Come let's devise how we may add more
      shame
   To the black scandal of his hated name.

Benvolio. First, on his head in quittance of my wrongs   55
   I'll nail huge forkèd horns and let them hang
   Within the window where he yoked me first
   That all the world may see my just revenge.

Martino. What use shall we put his beard to?

Benvolio. We'll sell it to a chimney-sweeper. It will   60
   wear out ten birchen brooms, I warrant you.

Frederick. What shall eyes do?

Benvolio. We'll put out his eyes, and they shall serve
      for buttons to his lips to keep his tongue from
      catching cold.   65

Martino. An excellent policy! And now sirs, having
      divided him, what shall the body do?
                              [*Faustus rises.*]

Benvolio. Zounds, the devil's alive again!

Frederick. Give him his head for God's sake!

Faustus. Nay keep it. Faustus will have heads and
      hands,   70
   Ay, all your hearts, to recompense this deed.
   Knew you not, traitors, I was limited
   For four and twenty years to breathe on earth?
   And had you cut my body with your swords
   Or hewed this flesh and bones as small as sand,   75
   Yet in a minute had my spirit returned
   And I had breathed a man made free from harm.

But wherefore do I dally my revenge?
Asteroth, Belimoth, Mephostophilis!

Enter Mephostophilis and other Devils.

80 Go horse these traitors on your fiery backs
And mount aloft with them as high as heaven,
Thence pitch them headlong to the lowest hell.
Yet stay, the world shall see their misery,
And hell shall after plague their treachery.
85 Go Belimoth, and take this caitiff° hence
And hurl him in some lake of mud and dirt:
Take thou this other, drag him through the woods
Amongst the pricking thorns and sharpest briars:
Whilst with my gentle Mephostophilis
90 This traitor flies unto some steepy rock
That rolling down may break the villain's bones
As he intended to dismember me.
Fly hence, dispatch my charge immediately!

Frederick. Pity us, gentle Faustus, save our lives!

Faustus. Away!

95 *Frederick.*   He must needs go that the devil drives.
                    Exeunt Spirits with the Knights.

Enter the ambushed Soldiers.

1 Soldier. Come sirs, prepare yourselves in readiness.
Make haste to help these noble gentlemen.
I heard them parley with the conjurer.

2 Soldier. See where he comes, dispatch, and kill the
slave!

85 **caitiff** wretch

Faustus. What's here, an ambush to betray my life?   *100*
    Then Faustus, try thy skill. Base peasants, stand!
    For lo, these trees remove° at my command
    And stand as bulwarks 'twixt yourselves and me
    To shield me from your hated treachery!
    Yet to encounter this your weak attempt   *105*
    Behold an army comes incontinent.°

*Faustus strikes the door, and enter a Devil playing
on a drum, after him another bearing an ensign, and
divers with weapons: Mephostophilis with fireworks:
they set upon the Soldiers and drive them out.
[Exeunt all.]*

[4.4] *Enter at several doors Benvolio, Frederick, and
Martino, their heads and faces bloody and besmeared
with mud and dirt, all having horns on their heads.*

Martino. What ho, Benvolio!

Benvolio.   Here! What, Frederick, ho!

Frederick. O, help me gentle friend. Where is Mar-
    tino?

Martino. Dear Frederick, here,
    Half smothered in a lake of mud and dirt,
    Through which the furies dragged me by the heels.   *5*

Frederick. Martino, see, Benvolio's horns again.

Martino. O misery! How now Benvolio?

Benvolio. Defend me, heaven! Shall I be haunted°
    still?

102 **remove** move   106 **incontinent** immediately   4.4.8 **haunted** (the following line suggests that there is a quibble on "hunted," Benvolio now
resembling a stag)

Martino. Nay fear not man, we have no power to kill.

Benvolio. My friends transformèd thus! O hellish
10   spite,
    Your heads are all set with horns.

Frederick.   You hit it right:
    It is your own you mean. Feel on your head.

Benvolio. Zounds, horns again!

Martino.   Nay chafe° not man, we all are sped.°

Benvolio. What devil attends this damned magician,
15   That spite of spite our wrongs are doubled?

Frederick. What may we do that we may hide our
        shames?

Benvolio. If we should follow him to work revenge
    He'd join long asses' ears to these huge horns
    And make us laughing-stocks to all the world.

20 *Martino.* What shall we then do, dear Benvolio?

Benvolio. I have a castle joining near these woods,
    And thither we'll repair and live obscure
    Till time shall alter this our brutish shapes.
    Sith° black disgrace hath thus eclipsed our fame,
25 We'll rather die with grief than live with shame.
                              Exeunt omnes.

[4.5] *Enter Faustus and the Horse-courser.*°

Horse-courser. I beseech your worship, accept of
        these forty dollars.°

---

13 **chafe** fret   13 **sped** done for, ruined (because of the horns)   24 **Sith**
since   4.5 s.d. **Horse-courser** horse trader   2 **dollars** German coins

Faustus. Friend, thou canst not buy so good a horse
for so small a price. I have no great need to sell
him, but if thou likest him for ten dollars more,   *5*
take him, because I see thou hast a good mind
to him.

Horse-courser. I beseech you sir, accept of this. I am
a very poor man and have lost very much of
late by horse-flesh,° and this bargain will set me   *10*
up again.

Faustus. Well, I will not stand° with thee. Give me
the money. Now sirrah, I must tell you that you
may ride him o'er hedge and ditch and spare
him not. But, do you hear, in any case ride him   *15*
not into the water.

Horse-courser. How sir, not into the water! Why, will
he not drink of all waters?°

Faustus. Yes, he will drink of all waters, but ride him not
into the water: o'er hedge and ditch or where thou   *20*
wilt, but not into the water. Go bid the hostler deliver him unto you, and remember what I say.

Horse-courser. I warrant you sir. O joyful day! Now
am I a made man forever.   *Exit.*

Faustus. What art thou, Faustus, but a man con-
demned to die?   *25*
Thy fatal time° draws to a final end;
Despair doth drive distrust into my thoughts.
Confound these passions with a quiet sleep.
Tush, Christ did call the thief upon the cross!°

---

10 **horse-flesh** (the possibility of a quibble on "whores' flesh" is increased
by "set me up" and "stand" in the ensuing dialogue)   12 **stand** hag-
gle   18 **drink of all waters** i.e., go anywhere   26 **fatal time** life span   29
Christ . . . cross (in Luke 23:39–43 Christ promised one of the thieves that
he would be with Christ in paradise)

30   Then rest thee Faustus, quiet in conceit.°

                                        He sits to sleep.

                    Enter the Horse-courser wet.

Horse-courser. O what a cozening° doctor was this!
        I riding my horse into the water, thinking some
        hidden mystery had been in the horse, I had noth-
        ing under me but a little straw and had much ado
35   to escape drowning. Well, I'll go rouse him and
        make him give me my forty dollars again. Ho,
        sirrah doctor, you cozening scab! Master doctor,
        awake and rise, and give me my money again, for
        your horse is turned to a bottle° of hay. Master
40   doctor!   *He pulls off his leg.*
        Alas, I am undone! What shall I do? I have
        pulled off his leg.

Faustus. O help, help! The villain hath murdered me!

Horse-courser. Murder or not murder, now he has
45   but one leg I'll outrun him, and cast this leg into
        some ditch or other.   [*Exit.*]

Faustus. Stop him, stop him, stop him!—Ha, ha, ha!
        Faustus hath his leg again, and the horse-courser
        a bundle of hay for his forty dollars.

                    Enter Wagner.

50   How now, Wagner? What news with thee?

Wagner. If it please you, the Duke of Vanholt doth
        earnestly entreat your company, and hath sent

---

30 **quiet in conceit** with a quiet mind   31 **cozening** deceiving   39 **bottle**
bundle

some of his men to attend you with provision fit
for your journey.

Faustus. The Duke of Vanholt's an honorable gentle-   55
man, and one to whom I must be no niggard of
my cunning. Come, away!   *Exeunt.*

[4.6] *Enter [Robin the] Clown, Dick, Horse-courser,
and a Carter.*

Carter. Come my masters, I'll bring you to the best
beer in Europe. What ho, hostess! Where be
these whores?

Enter Hostess.

Hostess. How now? What lack you? What, my old
guests, welcome.   5

Robin. [*aside*] Sirrah Dick, dost thou know why I
stand so mute?

Dick. [*aside*] No Robin, why is't?

Robin. [*aside*] I am eighteen pence on the score.°
But say nothing. See if she have forgotten me.   10

Hostess. Who's this that stands so solemnly by himself? What, my old guest!

Robin. O, hostess, how do you? I hope my score
stands still.

Hostess. Ay, there's no doubt of that, for methinks   15
you make no haste to wipe it out.

4.6.9 **on the score** in debt

Dick. Why hostess, I say, fetch us some beer!

Hostess. You shall, presently.—Look up into th' hall
there, ho!   *Exit.*

20 *Dick.* Come sirs, what shall we do now till mine hostess comes?

Carter. Marry sir, I'll tell you the bravest tale how
a conjurer served me. You know Doctor
Fauster?

Horse-courser. Ay, a plague take him! Here's some
25   on's have cause to know him. Did he conjure
thee too?

Carter. I'll tell you how he served me. As I was going
to Wittenberg t'other day with a load of hay, he
met me and asked me what he should give me
30   for as much hay as he could eat. Now sir, I thinking that a little would serve his turn, bad him
take as much as he would for three farthings.
So he presently gave me my money and fell to
eating; and as I am a cursen° man, he never left
35   eating till he had eat up all my load of hay.

All. O monstrous, eat a whole load of hay!

Robin. Yes yes, that may be, for I have heard of one
that has eat a load of logs.°

Horse-courser. Now sirs, you shall hear how villain-
40   ously he served me. I went to him yesterday to
buy a horse of him, and he would by no means
sell him under forty dollars. So sir, because I knew
him to be such a horse as would run over hedge
and ditch and never tire, I gave him his money.

34 **cursen** i.e., Christian (dialect form)   38 **eat a load of logs** been drunk

So, when I had my horse, Doctor Fauster bade   45
me ride him night and day and spare him no time.
"But," quoth he, "in any case ride him not into
the water." Now sir, I thinking the horse had had
some quality that he would not have me know
of, what did I but rid him into a great river—and   50
when I came just in the midst, my horse vanished
away and I sate straddling upon a bottle of hay.

All. O brave doctor!

Horse-courser. But you shall hear how bravely I
served him for it. I went me home to his house,   55
and there I found him asleep. I kept ahallowing
and whooping in his ears, but all could not wake
him. I seeing that, took him by the leg and never
rested pulling till I had pulled me his leg quite
off, and now 'tis at home in mine hostry.°   60

Dick. And has the doctor but one leg then? That's
excellent, for one of his devils turned me into
the likeness of an ape's face.

Carter. Some more drink, hostess!

Robin. Hark you, we'll into another room and drink   65
awhile, and then we'll go seek out the doctor.
                                Exeunt omnes.

[4.7] *Enter the Duke of Vanholt, his [Servants,]*
Duchess, Faustus, and Mephostophilis.

Duke. Thanks master doctor, for these pleasant sights.
Nor know I how sufficiently to recompense your

great deserts in erecting that enchanted castle in
the air, the sight whereof so delighted me,

5   As nothing in the world could please me more.

Faustus. I do think myself, my good lord, highly rec-
ompensed in that it pleaseth your Grace to think
but well of that which Faustus hath performed.—
But gracious lady, it may be that you have taken

10   no pleasure in those sights. Therefore I pray you
tell me what is the thing you most desire to have:
be it in the world it shall be yours. I have heard
that great-bellied° women do long for things are
rare and dainty.

15 *Duchess.* True master doctor, and since I find you so
kind, I will make known unto you what my heart
desires to have: and were it now summer, as it is
January, a dead time of the winter, I would request no better meat° than a dish of ripe grapes.

20 *Faustus.* This is but a small matter. Go Mephostophilis, away!   *Exit Mephostophilis.*
Madam, I will do more than this for your content.

Enter Mephostophilis again with the grapes.

Here, now taste ye these. They should be good,
For they come from a far country, I can tell you.

25 *Duke.* This makes me wonder more than all the rest,
that at this time of the year when every tree is
barren of his fruit, from whence you had these
ripe grapes.

Faustus. Please it your Grace, the year is divided into

4.7.13 **great-bellied** i.e., pregnant   19 **meat** food

two circles° over the whole world, so that when   30
it is winter with us, in the contrary circle it is
likewise summer with them, as in India, Saba,°
and such countries that lie far east, where they
have fruit twice a year. From whence, by means
of a swift spirit that I have, I had these grapes   35
brought as you see.

Duchess. And trust me, they are the sweetest grapes
that e'er I tasted.

The Clowns [*Robin, Dick, Carter, and Horse-courser*]
bounce° at the gate within.

Duke. What rude disturbers have we at the gate?
Go pacify their fury, set it ope,   40
And then demand of them what they would have.

They knock again and call out to talk with Faustus.

A Servant. Why, how now masters, what a coil° is
there!
What is the reason° you disturb the Duke?

Dick. We have no reason for it, therefore a fig for
him!

Servant. Why saucy varlets, dare you be so bold!   45

Horse-courser. I hope sir, we have wit enough to be
more bold than welcome.

30 **two circles** i.e., the northern and the southern hemispheres (though
later in the speech he talks of east rather than of north and
south) 32 **Saba** Sheba 38 s.d. **bounce** knock 42 **coil** turmoil 43 **reason** (pronounced like "raisin," leading to the quibble on "fig"; a "fig" here
is an obscene contemptuous gesture in which the hand is clenched and the
thumb is thrust between the first and second fingers, making the thumb
resemble the stem of a fig, or a penis)

Servant. It appears so. Pray be bold elsewhere
And trouble not the Duke.

50 *Duke.* What would they have?

Servant. They all cry out to speak with Doctor
Faustus.

Carter. Ay, and we will speak with him.

Duke. Will you sir? Commit° the rascals.

Dick. Commit with us! He were as good commit
55   with his father as commit with us!

Faustus. I do beseech your Grace, let them come in.
They are good subject for a merriment.

Duke. Do as thou wilt, Faustus, I give thee leave.

Faustus. I thank your Grace.

> *Enter [Robin] the Clown, Dick, Carter, and*
> *Horse-courser.*

Why, how now my good friends?
60 'Faith, you are too outrageous; but come near,
I have procured your pardons. Welcome all.

Robin. Nay sir, we will be welcome for our money,
and we will pay for what we take. What ho, give's
half a dozen of beer here, and be hanged!

Faustus. Nay, hark you, can you tell me where you
65   are?

Carter. Ay, marry can I, we are under heaven.

---

53 **Commit** imprison (Dick proceeds to quibble on the idea of committing adultery)

Servant. Ay, but Sir Sauce-box, know you in what
    place?

Horse-courser. Ay ay, the house is good enough
    to drink in. Zounds, fill us some beer, or we'll
    break all the barrels in the house and dash out   70
    all your brains with your bottles.

Faustus. Be not so furious. Come, you shall have beer.
    My lord, beseech you give me leave awhile;
    I'll gage° my credit 'twill content your Grace.

Duke. With all my heart, kind doctor, please thyself.   75
    Our servants and our court's at thy command.

Faustus. I humbly thank your Grace.—Then fetch
    some beer.

Horse-courser. Ay marry, there spake a doctor in-
    deed! And 'faith, I'll drink a health to thy
    wooden leg for that word.   80

Faustus. My wooden leg? What dost thou mean by
    that?

Carter. Ha, ha, ha, dost hear him Dick? He has forgot
    his leg.

Horse-courser. Ay ay, he does not stand much upon°   85
    that.

Faustus. No, 'faith, not much upon a wooden leg.

Carter. Good lord, that flesh and blood should be so
    frail with your worship! Do not you remember
    a horse-courser you sold a horse to?   90

Faustus. Yes, I remember I sold one a horse.

---

74 **gage** pledge   85 **stand much upon** (quibble on "attach much importance to")

Carter. And do you remember you bid he should not
ride into the water?

Faustus. Yes, I do very well remember that.

95 *Carter.* And do you remember nothing of your leg?

Faustus. No, in good sooth.

Carter. Then I pray remember your curtsy.°

Faustus. I thank you sir.

Carter. 'Tis not so much worth. I pray you tell me
100   one thing.

Faustus. What's that?

Carter. Be both your legs bedfellows every night
together?

Faustus. Would'st thou make a colossus° of me that
105   thou askest me such questions?

Carter. No, truly sir, I would make nothing of you,
but I would fain know that.

Enter Hostess with drink.

Faustus. Then I assure thee certainly they are.

Carter. I thank you, I am fully satisfied.

110 *Faustus.* But wherefore dost thou ask?

Carter. For nothing, sir, but methinks you should
have a wooden bedfellow of one of 'em.

---

97 **curtsy** (also called "a leg," hence there is a quibble on the Carter's previous speech)   104 **colossus** huge statue in the harbor at Rhodes, between
whose legs ships were said to have sailed

Horse-courser. Why, do you hear sir, did not I pull off
    one of your legs when you were asleep?

Faustus. But I have it again now I am awake. Look   *115*
    you here sir.

All. O horrible! Had the doctor three legs?

Carter. Do you remember sir, how you cozened me
    and eat up my load of—
                     Faustus charms him dumb.

Dick. Do you remember how you made me wear an   *120*
    ape's—   *[Faustus charms him.]*

Horse-courser. You whoreson conjuring scab! Do you
    remember how you cozened me with a ho—
                        [Faustus charms him.]

Robin. Ha' you forgotten me? You think to carry it
    away with your "hey-pass" and "re-pass"?° Do   *125*
    you remember the dog's fa—
        [Faustus charms him.] Exeunt Clowns.

Hostess. Who pays for the ale? Hear you master doc-
    tor, now you have sent away my guests, I pray
    who shall pay me for my a—
           [Faustus charms her.] Exit Hostess.

Duchess. My lord,   *130*
    We are much beholding to this learnèd man.

Duke. So are we madam, which we will recompense
    With all the love and kindness that we may:
    His artful sport drives all sad thoughts away.
                          Exeunt.

125 **hey-pass, re-pass** conjuring expressions

*[5.1] Thunder and lightning. Enter Devils with covered
dishes: Mephostophilis leads them into Faustus' study.
Then enter Wagner.*

Wagner. I think my master means to die shortly. He
has made his will and given me his wealth: his
house, his goods, and store of golden plate—
besides two thousand ducats ready coined. I
5   wonder what he means. If death were nigh, he
would not frolic thus. He's now at supper with the
scholars, where there's such belly-cheer as Wagner in his life ne'er saw the like! And see where
they come. Belike° the feast is done.°   *Exit.*

*Enter Faustus, Mephostophilis, and two or three
Scholars.*

10   *1 Scholar.* Master Doctor Faustus, since our conference about fair ladies, which was the beautiful-
est in all the world, we have determined with
ourselves that Helen of Greece was the admi-
rablest lady that ever lived. Therefore master
15   doctor, if you will do us so much favor as to let
us see that peerless dame of Greece, whom all
the world admires for majesty, we should think
ourselves much beholding unto you.

Faustus. Gentlemen,
20   For that I know your friendship is unfeigned,
It is not Faustus' custom to deny
The just request of those that wish him well:
You shall behold that peerless dame of Greece
No otherwise for pomp or majesty

5.1.9 **Belike** most likely   1–9 **I think . . . done** (though printed as prose in
the quarto, as here, perhaps this speech should be verse, the lines ending
shortly, wealth, plate, coined, nigh, supper, belly-cheer, like, done)

Than when Sir Paris crossed the seas with her   25
And brought the spoils° to rich Dardania.°
Be silent then, for danger is in words.

Music sounds. Mephostophilis brings in Helen:
she passeth over the stage.

2 Scholar. Was this fair Helen, whose admired worth
  Made Greece with ten years' wars afflict poor
    Troy?

3 Scholar. Too simple is my wit to tell her worth,   30
  Whom all the world admires for majesty.

1 Scholar. Now we have seen the pride of nature's
    work,
  We'll take our leaves, and for this blessèd sight
  Happy and blest be Faustus evermore.

Faustus. Gentlemen, farewell, the same wish I to you.   35
                       Exeunt Scholars.

Enter an Old Man.

Old Man. O gentle Faustus, leave this damnèd art,
  This magic that will charm thy soul to hell
  And quite bereave° thee of salvation.
  Though thou hast now offended like a man,
  Do not persever° in it like a devil.   40
  Yet, yet, thou hast an amiable soul°
  If sin by custom grow not into nature.
  Then, Faustus, will repentance come too late!
  Then, thou art banished from the sight of heaven!

---

26 **spoils** booty (including Helen)   26 **Dardania** Troy   38 **bereave** deprive   40 **persever** (accent on second syllable)   41 **an amiable soul** a soul
worthy of love

45   No mortal can express the pains of hell!
It may be this my exhortation
Seems harsh and all unpleasant. Let it not.
For gentle son, I speak it not in wrath
Or envy of thee but in tender love
50   And pity of thy future misery:
And so have hope that this my kind rebuke,
Checking° thy body, may amend thy soul.

Faustus. Where art thou, Faustus? Wretch, what hast
     thou done! *Mephostophilis gives him a dagger.*
55   Hell claims his right and with a roaring voice
Says "Faustus, come, thine hour is almost come!"
And Faustus now will come to do thee right!

Old Man. O stay, good Faustus, stay thy desperate
     steps!
I see an angel hover o'er thy head,
60   And with a vial full of precious grace
Offers to pour the same into thy soul:
Then call for mercy and avoid despair.

Faustus. O friend,
I feel thy words to comfort my distressèd soul:
65   Leave me awhile to ponder on my sins.

Old Man. Faustus, I leave thee, but with grief of heart,
Fearing the enemy of thy hapless soul.   *Exit.*

Faustus. Accursèd Faustus! Wretch, what hast thou
     done!
I do repent, and yet I do despair:
70   Hell strives with grace for conquest in my breast!
What shall I do to shun the snares of death?

Mephostophilis. Thou traitor Faustus, I arrest thy soul

52 **Checking** rebuking

For disobedience to my sovereign lord.
Revolt,° or I'll in piecemeal tear thy flesh.

Faustus. I do repent I e'er offended him.   75
   Sweet Mephostophilis, entreat thy lord
   To pardon my unjust presumption,
   And with my blood again I will confirm
   The former vow I made to Lucifer.

Mephostophilis. Do it then, Faustus, with unfeignèd
     heart   80
   Lest greater dangers do attend thy drift.

Faustus. Torment, sweet friend, that base and agèd
     man
   That durst dissuade me from thy Lucifer,
   With greatest torment that our hell affords.

Mephostophilis. His faith is great. I cannot touch his
     soul.   85
   But what I may afflict his body with
   I will attempt, which is but little worth.

Faustus. One thing, good servant, let me crave of thee
   To glut the longing of my heart's desire:
   That I may have unto my paramour   90
   That heavenly Helen which I saw of late,
   Whose sweet embraces may extinguish clear
   Those thoughts that do dissuade me from my vow,
   And keep mine oath I made to Lucifer.

Mephostophilis. This or what else my Faustus shall
     desire   95
   Shall be performed in twinkling of an eye.

Enter Helen again, passing over between two Cupids.

---

74 **Revolt** return (to your allegiance)

Faustus. Was this the face that launched a thousand
        ships
        And burnt the topless° towers of Ilium?°
        Sweet Helen, make me immortal with a kiss.
100   Her lips suck forth my soul. See where it flies!
        Come Helen, come, give me my soul again.
        Here will I dwell, for heaven is in these lips
        And all is dross that is not Helena.
        I will be Paris, and for love of thee
105   Instead of Troy shall Wittenberg be sacked;
        And I will combat with weak Menelaus°
        And wear thy colors on my plumèd crest.
        Yea, I will wound Achilles° in the heel
        And then return to Helen for a kiss.
110   O, thou art fairer than the evening's air
        Clad in the beauty of a thousand stars,
        Brighter art thou than flaming Jupiter
        When he appeared to hapless Semele,°
        More lovely than the monarch of the sky
115   In wanton Arethusa's° azure arms,
        And none but thou shalt be my paramour. *Exeunt.*

[5.2] *Thunder. Enter Lucifer, Belzebub, and*
            Mephostophilis.°

Lucifer. Thus from infernal Dis° do we ascend
        To view the subjects of our monarchy,

---

98 **topless** i.e., so tall their tops are beyond sight   98 **Ilium** Troy   106 **Menelaus** Greek king, deserted by Helen for Paris   108 **Achilles** greatest of
the Greek warriors   113 **Semele** beloved by Jupiter, who promised to do
whatever she wished; she asked to see him in his full splendor, and the
sight incinerated her   115 **Arethusa** a nymph, here apparently loved by
Jupiter, "the monarch of the sky"   5.2 s.d. **Enter Lucifer, Belzebub, and
Mephostophilis** (probably they rise out of a trapdoor and ascend to the
upper stage, Mephostophilis descending to the main stage at line 93)   1
infernal Dis the underworld (named for its ruler)

Those souls which sin seals the black sons of hell.
'Mong which as chief, Faustus, we come to thee,
Bringing with us lasting damnation   5
To wait upon thy soul. The time is come
Which makes it forfeit.

Mephostophilis.   And this gloomy night
Here in this room will wretched Faustus be.

Belzebub. And here we'll stay
To mark him how he doth demean himself.   10

Mephostophilis. How should he but in desperate
    lunacy?
Fond° worldling, now his heart blood dries with
    grief,
His conscience kills it, and his laboring brain
Begets a world of idle fantasies
To overreach the devil; but all in vain: 15
His store of pleasures must be sauced with pain!
He and his servant Wagner are at hand.
Both come from drawing Faustus' latest will.
See where they come.

Enter Faustus and Wagner.

Faustus. Say Wagner, thou hast perused my will;   20
How dost thou like it?

Wagner.   Sir, so wondrous well
As in all humble duty I do yield
My life and lasting service for your love.

Enter the Scholars.

12 **Fond** foolish

Faustus. Gramercies,° Wagner.—Welcome gentlemen.
    [*Exit Wagner.*]

1 Scholar. Now worthy Faustus, methinks your looks
25   are changed.

Faustus. O gentlemen!

2 Scholar. What ails Faustus?

Faustus. Ah my sweet chamber-fellow, had I lived
    with thee, then had I lived still!—But now must
30   die eternally. Look sirs, comes he not, comes he
    not?

1 Scholar. O my dear Faustus, what imports this
    fear?

2 Scholar. Is all our pleasure turned to melancholy?

3 Scholar. He is not well with being over-solitary.

35 *2 Scholar.* If it be so, we'll have physicians and Faus-
    tus shall be cured.

3 Scholar. 'Tis but a surfeit° sir, fear nothing.

Faustus. A surfeit of deadly sin that hath damned
    both body and soul!

40 *2 Scholar.* Yet Faustus, look up to heaven and re-
    member mercy is infinite.

Faustus. But Faustus' offense can ne'er be pardoned.
    The serpent that tempted Eve may be saved, but
    not Faustus! O gentlemen, hear with patience and
45   tremble not at my speeches. Though my heart
    pant and quiver to remember that I have been
    a student here these thirty years, O, would I had

24 **Gramercies** thank you   37 **a surfeit** indigestion

never seen Wittenberg, never read book.—And
what wonders I have done all Germany can wit-
ness, yea all the world, for which Faustus hath lost   *50*
both Germany and the world, yea heaven itself—
heaven, the seat of God, the throne of the blessèd,
the kingdom of joy—and must remain in hell
forever! hell, O hell forever! Sweet friends, what
shall become of Faustus being in hell forever?   *55*

2 Scholar. Yet Faustus, call on God.

Faustus. On God, whom Faustus hath abjured? On
God, whom Faustus hath blasphemed? O my
God, I would weep, but the devil draws in my
tears! Gush forth blood instead of tears, yea life   *60*
and soul! O, he stays my tongue! I would lift up
my hands, but see, they hold 'em, they hold 'em!

All. Who, Faustus?

Faustus. Why, Lucifer and Mephostophilis. O gentlemen, I gave them my soul for my cunning.   *65*

All. O, God forbid!

Faustus. God forbade it indeed, but Faustus hath
done it. For the vain pleasure of four and twenty
years hath Faustus lost eternal joy and felicity. I
writ them a bill with mine own blood. The date is   *70*
expired. This is the time. And he will fetch me.

1 Scholar. Why did not Faustus tell us of this before,
that divines might have prayed for thee?

Faustus. Oft have I thought to have done so, but the
devil threatened to tear me in pieces if I named   *75*
God —to fetch me body and soul if I once gave
ear to divinity; and now 'tis too late! Gentlemen, away, lest you perish with me.

2 Scholar. O, what may we do to save Faustus?

80 *Faustus.* Talk not of me but save yourselves and
          depart.

3 Scholar. God will strengthen me. I will stay with
          Faustus.

1 Scholar. Tempt not God, sweet friend, but let us
85   into the next room and pray for him.

Faustus. Ay, pray for me, pray for me. And what noise
          soever you hear, come not unto me, for nothing
          can rescue me.

2 Scholar. Pray thou, and we will pray that God may
90   have mercy upon thee.

Faustus. Gentlemen, farewell! If I live till morning,
          I'll visit you. If not, Faustus is gone to hell.

All. Faustus, farewell.

                              Exeunt Scholars.

Mephostophilis. Ay, Faustus, now thou hast no hope
          of heaven.
95   Therefore, despair! Think only upon hell,
          For that must be thy mansion, there to dwell.

Faustus. O thou bewitching fiend, 'twas thy tempta-
          tion
          Hath robbed me of eternal happiness.

Mephostophilis. I do confess it Faustus, and rejoice.
100   'Twas I, that when thou wert i' the way to heaven
          Dammed up thy passage. When thou took'st
          the book
          To view the Scriptures, then I turned the leaves
          And led thine eye.
          What, weep'st thou! 'Tis too late, despair, farewell!

Fools that will laugh on earth, most weep in hell.   *105*
                                                    Exit.

*Enter the Good Angel and the Bad Angel at
                several doors.*

Good Angel. O Faustus, if thou hadst given ear to
      me
Innumerable joys had followèd thee.
But thou did'st love the world.

Bad Angel.   Gave ear to me,
And now must taste hell's pains perpetually.

Good Angel. O, what will all thy riches, pleasures,
      pomps   *110*
Avail thee now?

Bad Angel.   Nothing but vex thee more,
To want in hell, that had on earth such store.
                    Music while the throne° descends.

Good Angel. O, thou hast lost celestial happiness,
Pleasures unspeakable, bliss without end.
Had'st thou affected° sweet divinity,   *115*
Hell or the devil had had no power on thee.
Had'st thou kept on that way, Faustus behold
In what resplendent glory thou had'st sat
In yonder throne, like those bright shining saints,
And triumphed over hell! That hast thou lost.   *120*
                        [*Throne ascends.*]
And now, poor soul, must thy good angel leave
      thee,
The jaws of hell are open to receive thee.   *Exit.*
                        Hell is discovered.

112 s.d. **throne** (symbolic of heaven)   115 **affected** preferred

Bad Angel. Now Faustus, let thine eyes with horror
   stare
   Into that vast perpetual torture-house.
125   There are the furies, tossing damnèd souls
   On burning forks. Their bodies boil in lead.
   There are live quarters° broiling on the coals,
   That ne'er can die: this ever-burning chair
   Is for o'er-tortured souls to rest them in.
130   These that are fed with sops of flaming fire
   Were gluttons and loved only delicates
   And laughed to see the poor starve at their gates.
   But yet all these are nothing. Thou shalt see
   Ten thousand tortures that more horrid be.

135   *Faustus.* O, I have seen enough to torture me.

   Bad Angel. Nay, thou must feel them, taste the smart
      of all:
   He that loves pleasure must for pleasure fall.
   And so I leave thee Faustus, till anon:
   Then wilt thou tumble in confusion.°   *Exit.*
                              The clock strikes eleven.

140   *Faustus.* O Faustus!
   Now hast thou but one bare hour to live
   And then thou must be damned perpetually.
   Stand still, you ever-moving spheres of Heaven
   That time may cease and midnight never come:
145   Fair nature's eye, rise, rise again and make
   Perpetual day, or let this hour be but a year,
   A month, a week, a natural day—
   That Faustus may repent and save his soul.
   O lente lente currite noctis equi!°

---

127 **quarters** bodies   139 **confusion** destruction   149 **O ... equi** slowly,
slowly run, O horses of the night (Latin, adapted from Ovid's *Amores*,
1.13.40, where a lover regretfully thinks of the coming of the dawn)

The stars move still, time runs, the clock will strike: *150*
The devil will come, and Faustus must be damned!
O, I'll leap up to my God! Who pulls me down?
See, see where Christ's blood streams in the fir-
    mament!
One drop of blood will save me. O my Christ!—
Rend not my heart for naming of my Christ!   *155*
Yet will I call on Him! O spare me, Lucifer!—
Where is it now? 'Tis gone: and see where God
Stretcheth out His arm and bends His ireful brows!
Mountains and hills, come, come and fall on me
And hide me from the heavy wrath of God!   *160*
No?
Then will I headlong run into the earth.
Gape earth! O no, it will not harbor me.
You stars that reigned at my nativity,
Whose influence hath allotted death and hell,   *165*
Now draw up Faustus like a foggy mist
Into the entrails of yon laboring cloud
That when you vomit forth into the air,
My limbs may issue from your smoky mouths—
But let my soul mount and ascend to heaven!   *170*
              The watch strikes.
O half the hour is passed! 'Twill all be passed anon!
O God,
If thou wilt not have mercy on my soul,
Yet for Christ's sake, whose blood hath ransomed
    me,
Impose some end to my incessant pain!   *175*
Let Faustus live in hell a thousand years,
A hundred thousand, and at last be saved!
No end is limited to° damnèd souls!
Why wert thou not a creature wanting soul?

178 **limited to** set for

180 Or why is this immortal that thou hast?
       O, Pythagoras' metempsychosis,° were that true
       This soul should fly from me and I be changed
       Into some brutish beast.
       All beasts are happy, for when they die
185 Their souls are soon dissolved in elements.
       But mine must live still° to be plagued in hell!
       Cursed be the parents that engendered me!
       No Faustus, curse thyself, curse Lucifer
       That hath deprived thee of the joys of heaven.
                                    The clock strikes twelve.
190 It strikes, it strikes! Now body, turn to air,
       Or Lucifer will bear thee quick° to hell!
       O soul, be changed into small water-drops
       And fall into the ocean, ne'er be found.

              Thunder, and enter the Devils.

       My God, my God! Look not so fierce on me!
195 Adders and serpents, let me breathe awhile!
       Ugly Hell, gape not! Come not Lucifer!
       I'll burn my books!—O Mephostophilis!
                        Exeunt [Devils with Faustus.]°

       [5.3] *Enter the Scholars.*

       1 Scholar. Come gentlemen, let us go visit Faustus,
         For such a dreadful night was never seen

181 **metempsychosis** transmigration of souls (a doctrine held by Pythagoras, philosopher of the sixth century B.C.) 186 **still** always 191 **quick**
alive 197 s.d. **Exeunt [Devils with Faustus]** (possibly the devils drag Faustus into the "hell" that was "discovered" at 5.2.122, and then toss his limbs
onto the stage, or possibly the limbs are revealed in 5.3.6 by withdrawing a
curtain at the rear of the stage)

Since first the world's creation did begin!
Such fearful shrieks and cries were never heard!
Pray heaven, the doctor have escaped the danger.   5

2 Scholar. O, help us heaven, see, here are Faustus'
    limbs
All torn asunder by the hand of death!

3 Scholar. The devils whom Faustus served have torn
    him thus:
For 'twixt the hours of twelve and one, methought
I heard him shriek and call aloud for help,   10
At which self° time the house seemed all on fire
With dreadful horror of these damnèd fiends.

2 Scholar. Well gentlemen, though Faustus' end be
    such
As every Christian heart laments to think on,
Yet for he was a scholar once admired   15
For wondrous knowledge in our German schools,
We'll give his mangled limbs due burial;
And all the students, clothed in mourning black,
Shall wait upon° his heavy° funeral.   *Exeunt.*

Enter Chorus.

Cut is the branch that might have grown full
    straight
And burnèd is Apollo's laurel bough°
That sometime grew within this learnèd man.
Faustus is gone: regard his hellish fall,
Whose fiendful fortune may exhort the wise   5

5.3.11 **self** same   19 **wait upon** attend   19 **heavy** sad   Chorus 2 **laurel
bough** symbol of wisdom, here associated with Apollo, god of divination

Only to wonder at° unlawful things,
Whose deepness doth entice such forward wits
To practice more than heavenly power permits.

[*Exit.*]

Terminat hora diem; terminat Author opus.°

FINIS

---

6 **Only to wonder at** i.e., merely to observe at a distance, with awe   9 **Terminat ... opus** the hour ends the day; the author ends his work (this Latin tag probably is not Marlowe's but the printer's, though it is engaging to believe Marlowe wrote it, ending his play at midnight, the hour of Faustus' death)

Textual Note

Although the play was probably written about 1590, the earliest edition, entitled *The Tragicall History of D. Faustus,* was not published until 1604, eleven years after Marlowe's death. It survives in only one copy. Possibly it had been preceded by an earlier edition, but because it is the first edition extant it is called the A-text. It was reprinted in 1609 (A2) and again in 1611 (A3), but these two editions have no independent authority, differing occasionally from A1 only by virtue of small errors that they introduce.

In 1616 a very different text was published, *The Tragicall History of the Life and Death of Doctor Faustus,* which, like the A-text of 1604, survives in only one copy. It is conventionally called the B-text, and it was reprinted several times in the seventeenth century. The B-text has:

some passages that are very close to A;

some episodes that are broadly parallel to A, but with little verbal similarity;

some deletions of A's material, especially of material that might be thought blasphemous;

six hundred and seventy-six more lines than A; the last act is notably fuller in B, which has a final visit of the angels, and the discovery of Faustus' mangled body. But although longer than A, B lacks a few passages—totaling 36 lines—found in A. (The A-text has 1,518 lines; the B-text has 2,122.)

Because it is known that Philip Henslowe, a theatrical entrepreneur, in 1602 paid William Birde and Samuel Rowley "for ther adicyones in doctor fostes," it is widely believed that B contains the un-Marlovian additions, and that A, the shorter text, is closer to Marlowe's own play. Something like this view, set forth with many thoughtful modifications, can be found in Roma Gill's edition (1989) and in the invaluable edition of both texts within one book by David Bevington and Eric Rasmussen (1993 and 1995). On the other hand, W. W. Greg, in *Marlowe's Doctor Faustus: 1604–1616: Parallel Texts* (Oxford, 1950), strongly argued that B is probably closer to Marlowe's play. The gist of Greg's view is that the A-text is based on a memorial reconstruction by actors who had performed an abridged version, perhaps while touring in the provinces. (The promptbook was a valuable theatrical possession, something that in general would not be given to a printer.) The B-text was prepared by someone who had access to the theater company's promptbook, which was derived from Marlowe's draft(s). In some places the material was damaged or illegible, and for these passages the editor was forced to rely on the A-text, which he did from the third edition of A (1611).

That the A-text shows signs of being an acting version can be seen, for example, in the relative abundance of connectives and ejaculations, such as "Tell me," "Tut," "Tush," and so forth. One cannot prove that Marlowe

did not write these, but when parallel sentences in B
lack them, one feels that they are an actor's additions.
Similarly, when in A we find repetitions where in B we
find variations, we seem to hear actors simplifying their
material. And, perhaps most important, A uses a simpler
stage than B, again evidence that A is an abridged and
provincial version. For example, A does not use a window in 4.2, or an upper stage in 5.2; nor in 5.2 is there
the descent of a throne from heaven and the discovery
of hell. In B, 5.3 apparently uses the inner stage, but A
lacks the scene.

But even if it is agreed that A is an abridged version
and that B may be closer to Marlowe's final manuscript,
or at least to Marlowe's play as it was performed in London around 1600, an editor today cannot rely only on B.
To repeat: There are places where B is unquestionably
indebted to A3 (1611). For example, A1 (1604) has:

> Fau. and what are you that liue with Lucifer?
> Me. Unhappy spirits that fel with Lucifer,

but A3 slipped, altering "fell" to "liue" as in the previous
line, and B follows the slip, printing

> Unhappy spirits that liue with Lucifer.

Moreover, the B text shows signs of compliance with
"An Acte to restraine Abuses of Players," which became
a law in 1607, i.e., fourteen years after Marlowe's death.
The Act prohibited references to God on the stage. It
held

> that if any tyme or tymes . . . any person or persons
> doe or shal in any Stage play . . . jestingly or pro-
> phanely speake or use the holy Name of God or of

Christ Jesus, or of the Holy ghoste or of the Trinitie,
which are not to be spoken but with feare and reverence, shall forfeite for everie such Offence by hym or
them committed Tenne Pounde.

The B-text prints, for example, "O mercy heauen," where
the A-text had printed, "My God, my God." The A-text,
then, surely contains words that the B-text inadvertently
lost and others that it censored. The A-text may have a
third value: If indeed it represents a performance (and
everyone grants this), it may contain some revisions made
by Marlowe at some time after he drafted the manuscript
that is behind B. But it is a tricky business to say that this
or that line in A sounds more Marlovian than the parallel line in B, and that therefore A sometimes supersedes
B because it contains Marlowe's second thoughts.

In short: The exact nature of B is uncertain, though it
certainly contains additions, playhouse annotations, and
revisions due to censorship. The precise degree to which
it is inferior to A is therefore a matter of argument. Still,
in the view of the present editor, plenty of evidence suggests that B gets us closer to Marlowe than A does. But
shall an editor relentlessly follow B? Of course not; it
has already been mentioned that B sometimes repeats
an error of A3, and that B sometimes gives a censored
version of A. I have therefore occasionally drawn upon
A, but have followed B whenever there was no compelling reason to depart from it. Take, for example, the very
first two lines of the play:

Not marching now in fields of Thracimene,
Where Mars did mate the Carthaginians   (A)

Not marching in the fields of Thrasimen,
Where Mars did mate the warlike Carthagens   (B)

I have assumed that since B makes excellent sense, that since it is not demonstrably derived from A or in need of anything that A offers, it is what should be printed. But elsewhere I have restored the "blasphemy" of A, which B toned down, and I have occasionally adopted a reading from A when there seemed to be cause to do so. For example, A speaks of "foure stately bridges," but B speaks of "two stately Bridges." Now, in this instance A agrees with the source, *The Damnable Life,* and it would be odd for the actors, in their memorial reconstruction, independently to come up with a version closer to Marlowe's source. Moreover, B's "two" is probably a compositor's slip, because the word "two" appears in the previous line:

> With winding bankes that cut it in two parts;
> Ouer the which two stately Bridges leane.

Given both of these arguments, it seems reasonable to depart from B and to follow A, printing "four" instead of "two," on the assumption that "four" is the word Marlowe wrote.

The present text, then, follows B quite closely; emendations have been made relatively sparingly, but spelling has been modernized. For example, "The fiery keele at Anwerpe bridge" is printed here as "The fiery keel at Antwerp bridge"; but note that unlike most editions, the present edition—though modernizing the spelling of "Anwerpe"—does not emend to "Antwerp's." The word here is an adjective, not genetive, and is comparable, for example, to "Verona streets" in *Romeo and Juliet* 3.1.90. In addition to modernizing the spelling, I have modernized the punctuation, regularized speech prefixes (e.g., "Good Angel" replaces "Good," and "Good A."), divided a few lines of verse differently from B, and corrected obvious typographical errors.

For convenience in reference, act and scene divisions
have been added, in square brackets [ ], though no edition of the play was so divided until the nineteenth century. The divisions here used are identical with those in
Greg's important edition, *Marlowe's Doctor Faustus:
1604–1616: Parallel Texts*. Greg for convenience followed
F. S. Boas' edition of 1932, which unfortunately begins a
new scene at 4.1.48 because at that point the stage is
cleared. But in fact Benvolio remains "above at a window," and he plays a part subsequently. Strictly speaking, then, we do not get a new scene here, but, again, the
divisions are merely a matter of convenience.

Other departures from B are listed below; the adopted reading is given first, in italic type, followed by the
original reading, in roman type. When the adopted reading comes from the A-text of 1604, that fact is indicated
in square brackets.

Prologue 12 *Rhode* Rhodes

1.1.7 *logices* Logicis 12 *on kai me on* [1604] Oeconomy 26–27
Si . . . et cetera [1616 prints as verse, with lines ending *duobus,
&c*] 26 *legatur* legatus 29 *Exhereditare* Exhereditari 37–43 *Stipendium . . . die* [1616 prints as verse, with lines ending *&c,
hard, veritas, sinne, vs. sinne, die*] 79 *India* [1604] Indian 87 *silk*
skill 102–3 *Divinity . . . vile* [1604; 1616 omits] 109 *Swarm* [1604]
Sworne 112 *shadows* [1604] shadow 126 *stuffs* [1604] stuff'd

1.2.1–2 [as in 1604; 1616 prints as verse, with lines ending *wont,
probo*]

1.3.12 *erring* [1604] euening 16 *dei* [1604] Dij 17 *aquatici* Aqua-
tani 20 *Mephostophilis . . . moraris* Mephostophilis Dragon,
quod tumeraris 21 *Gehennam* [1604] gehennan 24 *dicatus* di-
catis 45 *accidens* accident 52 *the Trinity* [1604] all godlinesse 69
fell [1604] liue 76 *who* [1604] that

1.4.3–4 *such pickadevants* [1604] beards 54 *vestigiis nostris* vestigias nostras

2.1.9 *Ay . . . again* [1604; 1616 omits] 10–11 *To . . . appetite* [as in 1604; 1616 prints as one line, with *Why* in place of *To God*] 20 *men* [1604] them 32 *Mephostophilis* [1604; 1616 omits] 54–56 *Lo . . . Lucifer's* [as in 1604; 1616 prints as two lines, ending *arme, Lucifers*] 79 *God* [1604] heauen 106 *form or shape* [1604] shape and forme 115 *or goods* [1604; 1616 omits] 121 *will I* [1604] I will 121 *with* [1604; 1616 omits]

2.2 s.d. [preceded in 1616 by the following passage, attributed to Wagner, which is an abbreviation of material that the Chorus speaks immediately preceding Act 3: Enter Wagner solns. Wag. Learned Faustus/To know the secrets of Astronomy/Grauen in the booke of Ioues high firmament,/Did mount himselfe to scale Olympus top,/Being seated in a chariot burning bright,/Drawne by the strength of yoaky Dragons necks,/He now is gone to proue Cosmography,/And as I gesse will first arriue at Rome,/To see the Pope and manner of his Court;/And take some part of holy Peters feast,/That to this day is highly solemnized. Exit Wagner] 42 *erring* [1604] euening 43–44 *But . . . tempore* [1616 prints as one line] 55 *suppositions* [1604] questions 83–84 *'Tis . . . late* [as in 1604; 1616 prints as one line] 94–95 *I . . . hell* [1616 prints as one line] 103–5 *Never . . . down* [1604; 1616 omits]

2.3.1 *Robin* [1616 omits]

3 Prologue 1–2 *Learnèd . . . astronomy* [as in 1604; 1616 prints as one line] 8 *tropics* Tropick

3.1.7 *Rhine* [1604] Rhines 12 *Quarters . . . equivalents* [1604; 1616 omits] 16 *rest* [1604] East 37 *four* [1604] two 43 *match* [1604] watch 77, 81 *cunning* comming 155 *keys* seales

3.2.70–71 *That . . . wine* [1616 prints as one line] 78 *I . . . banquet* [1616 prints as two lines, ending *this, banquet*] 90–91 *Now . . . candle* [1616 prints as verse, with lines ending *tell you, Candle*] 100 *on* [1604; 1616 omits] 107 s.d. *fireworks* [1604] fire worke

4 Prologue 1–17 *When . . . performed* [1604; 1616 omits]

4.2.25 *like a* like 74 *the* [1616 omits] 90 *is* [1616 omits]

4.3.71 *all* call

4.5 s.d. *Horse-courser* Horse-courser, and Mephostophilis

4.6.5 *guests* Guesse 60 *Dick* Clow[n, i.e., Robin]

4.7.38 s.d. *Clowns* Clowne 128 *guests* guesse

5.1.19–20 *Gentlemen . . . unfeigned* [1616 prints as one line] 27 s.d. *sounds* [1604] sound 62–63 *O . . . soul* [1616 prints as one line] 79 *Mephostophilis* [1604; 1616 omits] 81 *Faustus* [1604; 1616 omits] 93 *mine oath* [1604] my vow

5.2.28–30 *Ah . . . not* [1616 prints as verse, lines ending *thee, eternally, not*] 42–43 *But . . . saved* [1616 prints as verse, lines ending *pardoned, saued*] 118 *sat* set 126 *boil* broyle 152 *my God* [1604] heauen 153 *See . . . firmament* [1604; 1616 omits] 157–58 *gone . . . brows* [1604, which ends the lines with *gone, arme, browes*] gone./And see a threatning Arme, an angry Brow 160 *God* [1604] heauen 161–62 *No . . . earth* [1616 prints as one line] 172–73 *O . . . soul* [1604, which prints it as one line] O, if my soule must suffer for my sinne 174 *Yet . . . me* [1604; 1616 omits] 194 *My God, my God* [1604] O mercy heauen

The Source of
Doctor Faustus

The *Historia von D. Iohan Fausten* (1587), an anonymous German prose volume, describes the career of a man who gave the devil his soul in exchange for twenty-four years of earthly power, and who at last, after performing miraculous feats and low practical jokes, was carried off to hell. A translation of this book was published in 1592: *The Historie of the damnable life, and deserued death of Doctor Iohn Faustus, Newly imprinted, and in conuenient places imperfect matter amended . . . and translated into English by P. F. Gent[leman] . . . 1592.* Although the translation is fairly close, it is far from slavish, and some of its departures found their way into Marlowe's play. (If his play was written before 1592, Marlowe must have had access to a manuscript of the translation, or there must have been an edition—now lost—earlier than 1592. It is simplest, however, to assume that Marlowe wrote the play shortly after the edition of 1592 was printed.) This translation, commonly called the English Faust-book, or *The Damnable Life,* contains most of the narrative material for Marlowe's play, including the comic business of hitting the pope, making a fool of the horse-courser, etc. One episode in the play, however, where Pope Adrian humiliates Bruno, the rival pope who has the support of the emperor, has no parallel in *The Damnable Life,* and apparently is indebted to a passage in John Foxe's *Acts and Monuments.*

The following selection from P. F.'s *Damnable Life* includes all of the material that Marlowe used, and a few other portions that provide transitions and help to convey the flavor. The spelling has been modernized and the punctuation occasionally altered.

from *The History of the Damnable Life and
Deserved Death of Doctor John Faustus*

Of his parentage and birth. Chap. 1

John Faustus, born in the town of Rhode, lying in the province of Weimar in Germany, his father a poor husbandman and not able well to bring him up: but having an uncle at Wittenberg, a rich man and without issue, took this J. Faustus from his father and made him his heir, in so much that his father was no more troubled with him, for he remained with his uncle at Wittenberg where he was kept at the university in the same city to study divinity. But Faustus, being of a naughty mind and otherwise addicted, applied not his studies but took himself to other exercises, the which his uncle oftentimes hearing, rebuked him for it as Eli oft times rebuked his children for sinning against the Lord. Even so this good man labored to have Faustus apply his study of divinity that he might come to the knowledge of God and his laws. But it is manifest that many virtuous parents have wicked children, as Cain, Reuben, Absalom, and such like have been to their parents: so this Faustus having godly parents, and seeing him to be of a toward wit, were very desirous to bring him up in those virtuous studies, namely, of divinity. But he gave himself secretly to study necromancy and conjuration, in so much that few or none could perceive his profession.

But to the purpose. Faustus continued at study in the university and was by the rectors and sixteen masters afterwards examined how he had profited in his studies. And being found by them that none for his time were able to argue with him in divinity or for the excellency of his wisdom to compare with him, with one consent they made him Doctor of Divinity. But Doctor Faustus, within short time after he had obtained his degree, fell into such fantasies and deep cogitations that he was marked of many, and of the most part of the students was called the Speculator. And sometimes he would throw the Scriptures from him as though he had no care of his former profession, so that he began a very ungodly life, as hereafter more at large may appear. For the old proverb sayeth, Who can hold that will away? So, who can hold Faustus from the devil, that seeks after him with all his endeavor? For he accompanied himself with divers that were seen in those devilish arts and that had the Chaldean, Persian, Hebrew, Arabian, and Greek tongues, using figures, characters, conjurations, incantations, with many other ceremonies belonging to these infernal arts, as necromancy, charms, soothsaying, witchcraft, enchantment; being delighted with their books, words, and names so well that he studied day and night therein: in so much that he could not abide to be called Doctor of Divinity but waxed a worldly man and named himself an astrologian and a mathematician, and for a shadow sometimes a physician, and did great cures, namely with herbs, roots, waters, drinks, receipts, and clysters. And without doubt he was passing wise, and excellent perfect in the holy Scriptures; but he that knoweth his master's will and doth it not, is worthy to be beaten with many stripes. It is written, "No man can serve two masters," and "Thou shalt not tempt the Lord thy God." But Faustus threw all this in the wind and made his soul of no estimation, regarding more his worldly pleasure than the joys to come. Therefore at the day of judgment there is no hope of his redemption.

*How Doctor Faustus began to practice
in his devilish art, and how he
conjured the devil, making him to
appear and meet him on the morrow
at his own house. Chap. 2.*

You have heard before that all Faustus' mind was set to study the arts of necromancy and conjuration, the which exercise he followed day and night; and taking to him the wings of an eagle thought to fly over the whole world and to know the secrets of heaven and earth. For his speculation was so wonderful, being expert in using his vocabula, figures, characters, conjurations, and other ceremonial actions, that in all the haste he put in practice to bring the devil before him. And taking his way to a thick wood near to Wittenberg called in the German tongue Spisser Wald, that is in English the Spissers Wood (as Faustus would oftentimes boast of it among his crew being in his jollity), he came into the same wood toward evening into a crossway, where he made with a wand a circle in the dust, and within that many more circles and characters. And thus he passed away the time until it was nine or ten of the clock in the night. Then began Doctor Faustus to call for Mephostophiles the spirit, and to charge him in the name of Beelzebub to appear there personally without any long stay. Then presently the devil began so great a rumor in the wood as if heaven and earth would have come together with wind, the trees bowing their tops to the ground. Then fell the devil to blare as if the whole wood had been full of lions, and suddenly about the circle ran the devil as if a thousand wagons had been running together on paved stones. After this, at the four corners of the wood it thundered horribly with such lightnings as if the whole world, to his seeming, had been on fire. Faustus all this while half amazed at the devil's so long tarrying, and doubting whether he were best to abide any more such horrible conjurings, thought to leave his circle and depart. Whereupon the devil made him such music of all sorts as if the nymphs themselves had been in place, whereat Faustus was revived and stood stoutly in his circle aspecting his purpose and began again to conjure the spirit Mephostophiles in the name of the prince of devils to appear in his likeness, whereat suddenly over his head hung hovering in the air a mighty dragon. Then calls Faustus again after his devilish manner, at which there was a monstrous cry in the wood as if hell had been open and all the tormented souls crying to God for mercy. Presently not three fathoms above his head fell a flame in manner of a lightning and changed itself into a globe, yet Faustus feared it not but did persuade himself that the devil should give him his request before he would leave. Oftentimes after to his companions he would boast that he had the stoutest head (under the cope of heaven) at commandment, whereat they answered they knew none stouter than the Pope or Emperor. But Doctor Faustus said "The head that is my servant is above all on earth," and repeated certain words out of Saint Paul to the Ephesians to make his argument good: The prince of this world is upon earth and under heaven. Well, let us come again to his conjuration where we left him at his fiery globe. Faustus, vexed at the spirit's so long tarrying, used his charms with full purpose not to depart before he had his intent, and crying on Mephostophiles the spirit. Suddenly the globe opened and sprang up in height of a man; so burning a time, in the end it converted to the shape of a fiery man. This pleasant beast ran about the circle a great while and lastly appeared in manner of a gray friar, asking Faustus what was his request. Faustus commanded that the next morning at twelve of the clock he should appear to him at his house, but the devil would in no wise grant. Faustus began again to conjure him, in the name of Beelzebub, that he should fulfill his request, whereupon the spirit agreed, and so they departed each one his way.

The conference of Doctor Faustus
with the spirit Mephostophiles the
morning following at his own house. Chap. 3.

Doctor Faustus having commanded the spirit to be with him, at his hour appointed he came and appeared in his chamber, demanding of Faustus what his desire was. Then began Doctor Faustus anew with him to conjure him that he should be obedient unto him, and to answer him certain articles, and to fulfill them in all points.

1. That the spirit should serve him and be obedient unto him in all things that he asked of him from that hour until the hour of his death.

2. Farther, anything that he desired of him he should bring it to him.

3. Also, that in all Faustus' demands or interrogations, the spirit should tell him nothing but that which is true.

Hereupon the spirit answered and laid his case forth, that he had no such power of himself until he had first given his prince (that was ruler over him) to understand thereof and to know if he could obtain so much of his Lord. "Therefore speak farther that I may do thy whole desire to my prince, for it is not in my power to fulfill without his leave." "Show me the cause why," said Faustus. The spirit answered, "Faustus, thou shalt understand that with us it is even as well a kingdom as with you on earth. Yea, we have our rulers and servants, as I myself am one, and we name our whole number the legion; for although that Lucifer is thrust and fallen out of heaven through his pride and high mind, yet he hath notwithstanding a legion of devils at his command-ment that we call the oriental princes; for his power is great and infinite. Also there is an host in meridie, in septentrio, in occidente; and for that Lucifer hath his kingdom under heaven, we must change and give ourselves unto men to serve them at their pleasure. It is also certain, we have never as yet opened unto any man the truth of our dwelling, neither of our ruling, neither what our power is; neither have we given any man any gift or learned him anything except he prom-ise to be ours."

Doctor Faustus, upon this, arose where he sat and said, "I will have my request, and yet I will not be damned." The spirit answered, "Then shalt thou want thy desire, and yet art thou mine notwithstanding. If any man would detain thee it is in vain, for thine infidelity hath confounded thee."

Hereupon spake Faustus, "Get thee hence from me, and take Saint Valentine's farewell and Crisam with thee, yet I conjure thee that thou be here at evening, and bethink thyself on that I have asked thee, and ask thy prince's counsel therein." Mephostophiles the spirit, thus answered, vanished away, leaving Faustus in his study, where he sat pondering with himself how he might obtain his request of the devil without loss of his soul. Yet fully he was resolved in himself, rather than to want his pleasure, to do whatsoever the spirit and his lord should condition upon.

The second time of the spirit's appearing to Faustus in his house, and of their parley. Chap. 4.

Faustus continuing in his devilish cogitations, never moving out of the place where the spirit left him (such was his fervent love to the devil), the night approaching, this swift-flying spirit appeared to Faustus, offering himself with all submission to his service, with full authority from his prince to do whatsoever he would request if so be Faustus would promise to be his. "This answer I bring thee, and an answer must thou make by me again, yet will I hear what is thy desire because thou hast sworn me to be here at this time." Doctor Faustus gave him this answer, though faintly (for his soul's sake), that his request was none other but to become a devil, or at the least a limb of him, and that the spirit should agree unto these articles as followeth.

1. That he might be a spirit in shape and quality.

2. That Mephostophiles should be his servant and at his commandment.

3. That Mephostophiles should bring him anything, and do for him whatsoever.

4. That at all times he should be in his house, invisible to all men except only to himself, and at his commandment to show himself.

5. Lastly, that Mephostophiles should at all times appear at his command, in what form or shape soever he would.

Upon these points the spirit answered Doctor Faustus that all this should be granted him and fulfilled and more if he would agree unto him upon certain articles as followeth.

First, that Doctor Faustus should give himself to his Lord Lucifer, body and soul.

Secondly, for confirmation of the same he should make him a writing, written with his own blood.

Thirdly, that he would be an enemy to all Christian people.

Fourthly, that he would deny his Christian belief.

Fifthly, that he let not any man change his opinion, if so be any man should go about to dissuade or withdraw him from it.

Further, the spirit promised Faustus to give him certain years to live in health and pleasure, and when such years were expired that then Faustus should be fetched away; and if he should hold these articles and conditions that then he should have all whatsoever his heart would wish or desire; and that Faustus should quickly perceive himself to be a spirit in all manner of actions whatsoever. Hereupon Doctor Faustus' mind was so inflamed that he forgot his soul and promised Mephostophiles to hold all things as he had mentioned them. He thought the devil was not so black as they used to paint him, nor hell so hot as the people say, etc.

The third parley between Doctor Faustus and Mephostophiles about a conclusion. Chap. 5.

After Doctor Faustus had made his promise to the devil, in the morning betimes he called the spirit before him and commanded him that he should always come to him like a friar, after the order of Saint Francis, with a bell in his hand like Saint Anthony, and to ring it once or twice before he appeared, that he might know of his certain coming. Then Faustus demanded the spirit, what was his name? The spirit answered, "My name is as thou sayest, Mephostophiles, and I am a prince, but servant to Lucifer; and all the circuit from Septentrio to the Meridian I rule under him." Even at these words was this wicked wretch Faustus inflamed, to hear himself to have gotten so great a potentate to be his servant; forgot the Lord his maker and Christ his redeemer; became an enemy unto all mankind. Yea, worse than the giants whom the poets feign to climb the hills to make war with the gods, not unlike that enemy of God and his Christ that for his pride was cast into hell, so likewise Faustus forgot that the high climbers catch the greatest falls and that the sweetest meat requires the sourest sauce.

After a while, Faustus promised Mephostophiles to write and make his obligation, with full assurance of the articles in the chapter before rehearsed. A pitiful case, Christian reader, for certainly this letter of obligation was found in his house after his most lamentable end, with all the rest of his damnable practices used in his whole life. Therefore I wish all Christians to take an example by this wicked Faustus and to be comforted in Christ, contenting themselves with that vocation whereunto it hath pleased God to call them, and not to esteem the vain delights of this life, as did this unhappy Faustus in giving his soul to the devil. And to confirm it the more assuredly, he took a small penknife and pricked a vein in his left hand, and for certainty thereupon were seen on his hand these words written as if they had been written with blood, *O homo fuge*: whereat the spirit vanished, but Faustus continued in his damnable mind, and made his writing as followeth.

How Doctor Faustus set his blood in a saucer on
warm ashes, and writ as followeth. Chap. 6.

I, Johannes Faustus, Doctor, do openly acknowledge with mine own hand, to the greater force and strengthening of this letter, that since I began to study and speculate the course and order of the elements I have not found through the gift that is given me from above any such learning and wisdom that can bring me to my desires. And for that I find that men are unable to instruct me any farther in the matter, now have I, Doctor John Faustus, unto the hellish prince of Orient and his messenger Mephostophiles given both body and soul upon such condition that they shall learn me and fulfill my desire in all things as they have promised and vowed unto me, with due obedience unto me, according unto the articles mentioned between us.

Further, I covenant and grant with them by these presents that at the end of twenty-four years next ensuing the date of this present letter, they being expired, and I in the meantime during the said years be served of them at my will, they accomplishing my desires to the full in all points as we are agreed, that then I give them full power to do with me at their pleasure, to rule, to send, fetch, or carry me or mine, be it either body, soul, flesh, blood, or goods, into their habitation, be it wheresoever. And hereupon I defy God and his Christ, all the host of heaven, and all living creatures that bear the shape of God, yea all that lives; and again I say it, and it shall be so. And to the more strengthening of this writing, I have written it with mine own hand and blood, being in perfect memory, and hereupon I subscribe to it with my name and title, calling all the infernal, middle, and supreme powers to witness of this my letter and subscription.

> John Faustus, approved in the elements,
> and the spiritual doctor.

*The manner how Faustus proceeded with his damnable
life, and of the diligent service that Mephostophiles used
towards him. Chap. 8.*

Doctor Faustus having given his soul to the devil,
renouncing all the powers of heaven, confirming this
lamentable action with his own blood, and having already delivered his writing now into the devil's hand,
the which so puffed up his heart that he had forgot the
mind of a man and thought rather himself to be a spirit.
This Faustus dwelt in his uncle's house at Wittenberg,
who died and bequeathed it in his testament to his
cousin Faustus. Faustus kept a boy with him that was his
scholar, an unhappy wag called Christopher Wagner, to
whom this sport and life that he saw his master follow
seemed pleasant. Faustus loved the boy well, hoping to
make him as good or better seen in his devilish exercise than himself, and he was fellow with Mephostophiles. Otherwise Faustus had no more company in his
house but himself, his boy, and his spirit, that ever was
diligent at Faustus' command, going about the house
clothed like a friar with a little bell in his hand, seen of
none but Faustus. For his victual and other necessaries,
Mephostophiles brought him at his pleasure from the
Duke of Saxon, the Duke of Bavaria, and the Bishop
of Salzburg; for they had many times their best wine
stolen out of their cellars by Mephostophiles. Likewise
their provision for their own table, such meat as Faustus wished for, his spirit brought him in. Besides that,
Faustus himself was become so cunning that when he
opened his window, what fowl soever he wished for
came presently flying into his house, were it never so
dainty. Moreover, Faustus and his boy went in sumptuous apparel, the which Mephostophiles stole from

the mercers at Nuremberg, Augsburg, Frankfort, and Leipzig; for it was hard for them to find a lock to keep out such a thief. All their maintenance was but stolen and borrowed ware; and thus they lived an odious life in the sight of God, though as yet the world were unacquainted with their wickedness. It must be so, for their fruits be none other, as Christ saith through John where he calls the devil a thief and a murderer; and that found Faustus, for he stole him away both body and soul.

How Doctor Faustus would have married, and how the Devil had almost killed him for it. Chap. 9.

Doctor Faustus continued thus in his epicurish life day and night and believed not that there was a God, hell, or devil. He thought that body and soul died together and had quite forgotten divinity or the immortality of his soul, but stood in his damnable heresy day and night. And bethinking himself of a wife, called Mephostophiles to counsel, which would in no wise agree, demanding of him if he would break the covenant made with him or if he had forgot it. "Hast not thou," quoth Mephostophiles, "sworn thyself an enemy to God and all creatures? To this I answer thee, thou canst not marry; thou canst not serve two masters, God and my prince. For wedlock is a chief institution ordained of God, and that hast thou promised to defy, as we do all, and that hast thou also done; and moreover thou hast confirmed it with thy blood. Persuade thyself that what thou dost in contempt of wedlock, it is all to thine own delight. Therefore, Faustus, look well about thee and bethink thyself better, and I wish thee to change thy mind; for if thou keep not what thou hast promised in thy writing, we will tear thee in pieces like the dust under thy feet. Therefore, sweet Faustus, think with what unquiet life, anger, strife, and debate thou shalt live in when thou takest a wife; therefore change thy mind."

Doctor Faustus was with these speeches in despair; and as all that have forsaken the Lord can build upon no good foundation, so this wretched Faustus, having forsook the rock, fell in despair with himself, fearing if he should motion matrimony any more that the devil would tear him in pieces. "For this time," quoth he to Mephostophiles, "I am not minded to marry." "Then you do well," answered his spirit. But shortly, and that within two hours after, Faustus called his spirit, which came in his old manner like a friar. Then Faustus said unto him, "I am not able to resist nor bridle my fantasy; I must and will have a wife, and I pray thee give thy consent to it." Suddenly upon these words came such a whirlwind about the place that Faustus thought the whole house would come down; all the doors in the house flew off the hooks. After all this, his house was full of smoke and the floor covered over with ashes, which when Doctor Faustus perceived, he would have gone up the stairs. And flying up, he was taken and thrown into the hall, that he was not able to stir hand nor foot. Then round about him ran a monstrous circle of fire, never standing still, that Faustus fried as he lay and thought there to have been burned. Then cried he out to his spirit Mephostophiles for help, promising him he would live in all things as he had vowed in his handwriting. Hereupon appeared unto him an ugly devil, so fearful and monstrous to behold that Faustus durst not look on him. The devil said, "What wouldst thou have, Faustus? How likest thou thy wedding? What mind art thou in now?" Faustus answered, he had forgot his promise, desiring him of pardon, and he would talk no more of such things. The devil answered, "Thou were best so to do," and so vanished.

After appeared unto him his friar Mephostophiles with a bell in his hand, and spake to Faustus: "It is no jesting with us. Hold thou that which thou hast vowed and we will perform as we have promised; and more than that, thou shalt have thy heart's desire of what woman soever thou wilt, be she alive or dead, and so long as thou wilt thou shalt keep her by thee."

These words pleased Faustus wonderfully well, and repented himself that he was so foolish to wish himself married that might have any woman in the whole city brought to him at his command, the which he practiced and persevered in a long time.

Questions put forth by Doctor Faustus unto his spirit Mephostophiles. Chap. 10.

Doctor Faustus, living in all manner of pleasure that his heart could desire, continuing in his amorous drifts, his delicate fare, and costly apparel, called on a time his Mephostophiles to him: which being come, brought with him a book in his hand of all manner of devilish and enchanted arts, the which he gave Faustus, saying "Hold, my Faustus, work now thy heart's desire." The copy of this enchanting book was afterwards found by his servant, Christopher Wagner. "Well," quoth Faustus to his spirit, "I have called thee to know what thou canst do if I have need of thy help." Then answered Mephostophiles and said, "My Lord Faustus, I am a flying spirit, yea, so swift as thought can think, to do whatsoever." Here Faustus said, "But how came thy Lord and master Lucifer to have so great a fall from heaven?" Mephostophiles answered, "My Lord Lucifer was a fair angel, created of God as immortal, and being placed in the seraphins, which are above the cherubins, he would have presumed unto the throne of God, with intent to have thrust God out of his seat. Upon this presumption the Lord cast him down headlong, and where before he was an angel of light, now dwells he in darkness, not able to come near his first place without God send for him to appear before him as Raphael. But unto the lower degree of angels that have their conversation with men he was come, but not unto the second degree of heavens that is kept by the archangels, namely Michael and Gabriel, for these are called angels of God's wonders: yet are these far inferior places to that from whence my Lord and Master Lucifer fell. And thus far, Faustus, because thou art one of the beloved children of my Lord Lucifer, following and feeding thy mind in manner as he did his, I have shortly resolved thy request, and more I will do for thee at thy pleasure." "I thank thee, Mephostophiles," quoth Faustus. "Come let us now go rest, for it is night." Upon this, they left their communication.

How Doctor Faustus dreamed that he had seen hell in his sleep, and how he questioned with his spirit of matters as concerning hell, with the spirit's answer. Chap. 11.

The night following, after Faustus his communication had with Mephostophiles as concerning the fall of Lucifer, Doctor Faustus dreamed that he had seen a part of hell; but in what manner it was or in what place he knew not, whereupon he was greatly troubled in mind and called unto him Mephostophiles his spirit, saying to him, "My Mephostophiles, I pray thee resolve me in this doubt. What is hell, what substance is it of, in what place stands it, and when was it made?" Mephostophiles answered, "My Faustus, thou shalt know that before the fall of my Lord Lucifer there was no hell, but even then was hell ordained. It is of no substance, but a confused thing. For I tell thee that before all elements were made, and the earth seen, the Spirit of God moved on the waters and darkness was over all; but when God said, 'Let it be light,' it was so at his word, and the light was on God's right hand, and God praised the light. Judge thou further: God stood in the middle, the darkness was on his left hand, in the which my Lord was bound in chains until the day of judgment: in this confused hell is nought to find but a filthy, sulphurish, fiery, stinking mist or fog. Further, we devils know not what substance it is of, but a confused thing. For as a bubble of water flieth before the wind, so doth hell before the breath of God. Further, we devils know not how God hath laid the foundation of our hell, nor whereof it is: but to be short with thee, Faustus, we know that hell hath neither bottom nor end."

Another question put forth by Doctor Faustus to his spirit concerning his Lord Lucifer, with the sorrow that Faustus fell afterwards into. Chap. 13.

Doctor Faustus began again to reason with Mephostophiles, requiring him to tell him in what form and shape and in what estimation his Lord Lucifer was when he was in favor with God. Whereupon his spirit required him of three days' respite, which Faustus granted. The three days being expired, Mephostophiles gave him this answer: "Faustus, my Lord Lucifer (so called now, for that he was banished out of the clear light of heaven) was at the first an angel of God, he sat on the cherubins, and saw all the wonderful works of God, yea he was so of God ordained, for shape, pomp, authority, worthiness, and dwelling, that he far exceeded all other the creatures of God, yea our gold and precious stones: and so illuminated that he far surpassed the brightness of the sun and all other stars; wherefore God placed him on the cherubins, where he had a kingly office, and was always before God's seat, to the end he might be the more perfect in all his beings: but when he began to be high minded, proud, and so presumptuous that he would usurp the seat of his Majesty, then was he banished out from amongst the heavenly powers, separated from their abiding into the manner of a fiery stone that no water is able to quench but continually burneth until the end of the world."

Doctor Faustus, when he had heard the words of his spirit, began to consider with himself, having diverse and sundry opinions in his head: and very pensively (saying nothing) unto his spirit, he went into his chamber and laid him on his bed, recording the words of Mephostophiles; which so pierced his heart that he fell into sighing and great lamentation, crying out "Alas, ah, woe is me! What have I done? Even so shall it come to pass with me. Am not I also a creature of God's making, bearing his own image and similitude, into whom he hath breathed the spirit of life and immortality, unto whom he hath made all things living subject? But woe is me; mine haughty mind, proud aspiring stomach, and filthy flesh hath brought my soul into perpetual damnation. Yea, pride hath abused my understanding, in so much that I have forgot my maker; the Spirit of God is departed from me. I have promised the devil my soul, and therefore it is but a folly for me to hope for grace, but it must be even with me as with Lucifer, thrown into perpetual burning fire. Ah, woe is me that ever I was born." In this perplexity lay this miserable Doctor Faustus, having quite forgot his faith in Christ, never falling to repentance truly, thereby to attain the grace and Holy

Spirit of God again, the which would have been able to have resisted the strong assaults of Satan. For although he had made him a promise, yet he might have remembered through true repentance sinners come again into the favor of God; which faith the faithful firmly hold, knowing they that kill the body are not able to hurt the soul. But he was in all his opinions doubtful, without faith or hope, and so he continued.

Here followeth the second part of Doctor Faustus, his life and practices, until his end. Chap. 17.

Doctor Faustus, having received denial of his spirit to be resolved any more in such like questions propounded, forgot all good works and fell to be a calendar maker by help of his spirit, and also in short time to be a good astronomer or astrologian. He had learned so perfectly of his spirit the course of the sun, moon, and stars, that he had the most famous name of all the mathematics that lived in his time, as may well appear by his works dedicated unto sundry dukes and lords; for he did nothing without the advice of his spirit, which learned him to presage of matters to come, which have come to pass since his death. The like praise won he with his calendars and almanacs making, for when he presaged upon any change, operation, or alteration of the weather or elements—as wind, rain, fogs, snow, hail, moist, dry, warm, cold, thunder, lightning—it fell so duly out as if an angel of heaven had forewarned it. He did not like the unskillful astronomers of our time, that set in winter cold, moist, airy, frosty; and in the dog days hot, dry, thunder, fire, and such like; but he set in all his works day and hour, when, where, and how it should happen. If anything wonderful were at hand, as death, famine, plague, or wars, he would set the time and place in true and just order when it should come to pass.

How Doctor Faustus fell into despair with himself: for having put forth a question unto his spirit, they fell at variance, whereupon the whole rout of devils appeared unto him, threatening him sharply. Chap. 19.

Doctor Faustus revolving with himself the speeches of his spirit, he became so woeful and sorrowful in his cogitations that he thought himself already frying in the hottest flames of hell; and lying in his muse, suddenly there appeared unto him his spirit, demanding what thing so grieved and troubled his conscience, whereat Doctor Faustus gave no answer: yet the spirit very earnestly lay upon him to know the cause, and if it were possible, he would find remedy for his grief and ease him of his sorrows. To whom Faustus answered, "I have taken thee unto me as a servant to do me service, and thy service will be very dear unto me; yet I cannot have any diligence of thee farther than thou list thyself, neither dost thou in anything as it becometh thee." The spirit replied, "My Faustus, thou knowest that I was never against thy commandments as yet, but ready to serve and resolve thy questions, although I am not bound unto thee in such respects as concern the hurt of our kingdom, yet was I always willing to answer thee, and so I am still: therefore, my Faustus, say on boldly, what is thy will and pleasure?" At which words, the spirit stole away the heart of Faustus, who spake in this sort: "Mephostophiles, tell me how and after what sort God made the world, and all the creatures in them, and why man was made after the image of God."

The spirit, hearing this, answered, "Faustus, thou

knowest that all this is in vain for thee to ask. I know
that thou art sorry for that thou hast done, but it availeth
thee not, for I will tear thee in thousands of pieces if
thou change not thine opinions," and hereat he vanished
away. Whereat Faustus, all sorrowful for that he had put
forth such a question, fell to weeping and to howling bit-
terly, not for his sins towards God but for that the devil
was departed from him so suddenly and in such a rage.
And being in this perplexity, he was suddenly taken in
such an extreme cold as if he should have frozen in the
place where he sat, in which the greatest devil in hell appeared unto him with certain of his hideous and infernal
company in the most ugliest shapes that it was possible
to think upon, and traversing the chamber round about
where Faustus sat, Faustus thought to himself, now are
they come for me though my time be not come, and that
because I have asked such questions of my servant Mephostophiles. At whose cogitations, the chiefest devil
which was his lord, unto whom he gave his soul, that
was Lucifer, spake in this sort: "Faustus, I have seen thy
thoughts, which are not as thou hast vowed unto me
by virtue of this letter," and showed him the obligation
that he had written with his own blood, "wherefore I am
come to visit thee and to show thee some of our hellish
pastimes, in hope that will draw and confirm thy mind
a little more steadfast unto us." "Content," quoth Faustus, "go to; let me see what pastime you can make." At
which words, the great devil in his likeness sat him down
by Faustus, commanding the rest of the devils to appear
in their form as if they were in hell. First entered Belial
in form of a bear, with curled black hair to the ground,
his ears standing upright. Within the ear was as red as
blood, out of which issued flames of fire. His teeth were
a foot at least long, as white as snow; with a tail three ells
long (at the least); having two wings, one behind each

arm. And thus one after another they appeared to Faustus in form as they were in hell. Lucifer himself sat in manner of a man, all hairy but of a brown color like a squirrel, curled, and his tail turning upwards on his back as the squirrels use; I think he could crack nuts too, like a squirrel. After him came Beelzebub in curled hair of horse flesh color, his head like the head of a bull with a mighty pair of horns and two long ears down to the ground, and two wings on his back, with pricking stings like thorns; out of his wings issued flames of fire; his tail was like a cow. Then came Astaroth in form of a worm, going upright on his tail; he had no feet, but a tail like a slow-worm; under his chaps grew two short hands, and his back was coal black, his belly thick in the middle and yellow like gold, having many bristles on his back like a hedgehog. . . . The rest of the devils were in form of unsensible beasts, as swine, harts, bears, wolves, apes, buffaloes, goats, antelopes, elephants, dragons, horses, asses, lions, cats, snakes, toads, and all manner of ugly, odious serpents and worms: yet came in such sort that every one at his entry into the hall made their reverence unto Lucifer, and so took their places, standing in order as they came, until they had filled the whole hall. . . . Then said Faustus, "I like not so many of you together," whereupon Lucifer commanded them to depart except seven of the principal. Forthwith they presently vanished, which Faustus perceiving, he was somewhat better comforted, and spake to Lucifer, "Where is my servant Mephostophiles? Let me see if he can do the like." Whereupon came a fierce dragon, flying and spitting fire round about the house, and coming towards Lucifer, made reverence, and then changed himself to the form of a friar, saying "Faustus, what wilt thou?" Saith Faustus, "I will that thou teach me to transform myself in like sort as thou and the rest have done." Then Lucifer put forth his paw and gave Faustus a book, saying "Hold. Do what thou wilt." Which he looking upon, straightway changed himself into a hog, then into a worm, then into a dragon, and finding this for his purpose, it liked him well. . . .

How Doctor Faustus was carried through the air up to the heavens to see the world, and how the sky and planets ruled: after the which he wrote one letter to his friend of the same to Leipzig, how he went about the world in eight days. Chap. 21.

This letter was found by a freeman and citizen of Wittenberg, written with his own hand, and sent to his friend at Leipzig a physician named Jove Victori, the contents of which were as followeth. . . . I being once laid on my bed, and could not sleep for thinking on my calendar and practice, I marveled with myself how it were possible that the firmament should be known and so largely written of men, or whether they write true or false, by their own opinions, or supposition, or by due observations and true course of the heavens. Behold, being in these my muses, suddenly I heard a great noise, in so much that I thought my house would have been blown down, so that all my doors and chests flew open, whereas I was not a little astonished, for withal I heard a groaning voice which said "Get up. The desire of thy heart, mind, and thought shalt thou see." At the which I answered "What my heart desireth, that would I fain see, and to make proof, if I shall see I will away with thee." "Why then," quoth he, "look out at thy window. There cometh a messenger for thee." That did I, and behold, there stood a wagon, with two dragons before it to draw the same, and all the wagon was of a light burning fire, and for that the moon shone I was the willinger at that time to depart. But the voice spake again, "Sit up and let us away." "I will," said I, "go with thee, but upon this condition, that I may ask after all things that I see, hear, or think on." The voice answered, "I am content for this time." Hereupon I got me into the wagon, so that the dragons carried me upright into the air. The wagon had also four wheels which rattled so and made such a noise as if we had been all this while running on the stones. And round about us flew out flames of fire, and the higher that I came the more the earth seemed to be darkened, so that methought I came out of a dungeon; and looking down from heaven, behold, Mephostophiles my spirit and servant was behind me. And when he perceived that I saw him, he came and sat by me, to whom I said, "I pray thee, Mephostophiles, whither shall I go now?" "Let not that trouble thy mind," said he, and yet they carried us higher up. And now will I tell thee, good friend and schoolfellow, what things I have seen and proved; for on the Tuesday went I out, and on Tuesday seven-nights following I came home again, that is eight days, in which time I slept not, no, not one wink came in mine eyes, and we went invisible of any man. And as the day began to appear, after our first night's journey, I said to my spirit Mephostophiles, "I pray thee how far have we now ridden? I am sure thou knowest: for methinks that we are ridden exceeding far, the world seemeth so little." Mephostophiles answered me, "My Faustus, believe me, that from the place from whence thou camst unto this place where we are now is already forty-seven leagues right in height." And as the day increased I looked down upon the world. There saw I many kingdoms and provinces; likewise the whole world, Asia, Europe, and Africa, I had a sight of. . . . Then looked I up to the heavens, and behold, they went so swift that

I thought they would have sprung in thousands. Likewise it was so clear and so hot that I could not long gaze into it, it so dimmed my sight: and had not my spirit Mephostophiles covered me as it were with a shadowing cloud, I had been burnt with the extreme heat thereof; for the sky the which we behold here when we look up from the earth is so fast and thick as a wall, clear and shining bright as a crystal, in the which is placed the sun, which casteth forth his rays or beams over the universal world to the uttermost confines of the earth. But we think that the sun is very little: no, it is altogether as big as the world. Indeed the body substantial is but little in compass, but the rays or stream that it casteth forth, by reason of the thing wherein it is placed, maketh him to extend and show himself over the whole world. And we think that the sun runneth his course and that the heavens stand still: no, it is the heavens that move his course and the sun abideth perpetually in his place. He is permanent and fixed in his place, and although we see him beginning to ascend in the orient or east, at the highest in the meridian or south, setting in the occident or west, yet is he at the lowest in septentrio or north, and yet he moveth not. It is the axle of the heavens that moveth the whole firmament, being a chaos or confused thing, and for that proof, I will show thee this example: like as thou seest a bubble made of water and soap blown forth of a quill, is in form of a confused mass or chaos, and being in this form, is moved at pleasure of the wind, which runneth round about that chaos, and moveth him also round; even so is the whole firmament or chaos, wherein are placed the sun, and the rest of the planets turned and carried at the pleasure of the Spirit of God, which is wind. . . . And like as I showed before of the bubble or confused chaos made of water and soap, through the wind and breath of man is turned round and carried with every wind; even so the firmament wherein the sun and the rest of the planets are fixed, moved, turned, and carried with the wind, breath, or Spirit of God; for the heavens and firmament are movable as the chaos, but the sun is fixed in the firmament. And farther, my good schoolfellow, I was thus nigh the heavens, where methought every planet was but as half the earth, and under the firmament ruled the spirits in the air, and as I came down I looked upon the world and the heavens, and methought that the earth was enclosed in comparison within the firmament as the yolk of an egg within the white, and methought that the whole length of the earth was not a span long. . . .

How Doctor Faustus made his journey through the principal and most famous lands in the world. Chap. 22.

Doctor Faustus having overrun fifteen years of his appointed time, he took upon him a journey, with full pretence to see the whole world; and calling his spirit Mephostophiles unto him, he said, "Thou knowest that thou art bound unto me upon conditions, to perform and fulfill my desire in all things, wherefore my pretence is to visit the whole face of the earth visible and invisible when it pleaseth me: wherefore, I enjoin and command thee to the same." Whereupon Mephostophiles answered, "I am ready, my lord, at thy command," and forthwith the spirit changed himself into the likeness of a flying horse, saying "Faustus, sit up, I am ready." Doctor Faustus loftily sat upon him, and forward they went. Faustus came through many a land and province. . . . He took a little rest at home, and burning in desire to see more at large and to behold the secrets of each kingdom, he set forward again on his journey upon his swift horse Mephostophiles, and came to Trier, for that he chiefly desired to see this town and the monuments thereof; but there he saw not many wonders except one fair palace that belonged unto the bishop, and also a mighty large castle that was built of brick, with three walls and three great trenches, so strong that it was impossible for any prince's power to win it. Then he saw a church wherein was buried Simeon and the Bishop Popo; their tombs are of most sumptuous large marble stone closed and joined together with great bars of iron. From whence he departed to Paris, where he liked well the Academy; and what place or kingdom soever fell in his mind, the same he visited. He came from Paris to Mentz, where the river of Main falls into the Rhine; notwithstanding he tarried not long there, but went to Campania in the kingdom of Naples, in which he saw an innumerable sort of cloisters, nunneries, and churches, great and high houses of stone, the streets fair and large, and straight forth from one end of the town to the other as a line; and all the pavement of the city was of brick, and the more it rained in the town the fairer the streets were. There saw he the tomb of Vergil and the highway that he cut through that mighty hill of stone in one night, the whole length of an English mile. Then he saw the number of galleys and argosies that lay there at the city head, the windmill that stood in the water, the castle in the water, and the houses above the water where under the galleys might ride most safely from rain or wind. Then he saw the castle on the hill over the town and many monuments within, also the hill called Vesuvius, whereon groweth all the Greekish wine and most pleasant sweet olives. From thence he came to Venice, whereas he wondered not a little to see a city so famously built standing in the sea, where through every street the water ran in such largeness that great ships and barks might pass from one street to another, having yet a way on both sides the water whereon men and horse might pass. He marveled also how it was possible for so much victual to be found in the town and so good cheap, considering that for a whole league off nothing grew near the same. He wondered not a little at the fairness of Saint Mark's place and the sumptuous church standing therein called Saint Mark's: how all the pavement was set with colored stones and all the rood or loft of the church doubly gilded over. Leaving this, he came to Padua, beholding the manner of their Academy, which is called the mother or nurse of Christendom. There he heard the doctors and saw the most monuments in the town, entered his name into the university of the German nation, and wrote himself Doctor Faustus, the insatiable speculator. Then saw he the worthiest monument in the world for a church, named Saint Anthony's Cloister, which for the pinnacles thereof and the contriving of the church hath not the like in Christendom. This town is fenced about with three mighty walls of stone and earth, betwixt the which runneth goodly ditches of water. Twice every twenty-four hours passeth boats betwixt Padua and Venice with passengers as they do here betwixt London and Gravesend, and even so far they differ in distance. Faustus beheld likewise the council house and the castle with no small wonder. Well, forward he went to Rome, which lay and doth yet lie on the river Tiber, the which divideth the city in two parts: over the river are four great stone bridges, and upon the one bridge called Ponte S. Angelo is the Castle of S. Angelo, wherein are so many great cast pieces as there are days in a year, and such pieces that will shoot seven bullets off with one fire; to this castle cometh a privy vault from the church and palace of Saint Peter, through the which the Pope (if any danger be) passeth from his palace to the castle for safegard. The city hath eleven gates, and a hill called Va-ticinium whereon Saint Peter's church is built. In that church the holy fathers will hear no confession without the penitent bring money in his hand. Adjoining to this church is the Campo Santo, the which Carolus Magnus built, where every day thirteen pilgrims have their din-ners served of the best: that is to say, Christ and his twelve Apostles. Hard by this he visited the churchyard of Saint Peter's, where he saw the pyramid that Julius Caesar brought out of Africa. It stood in Faustus' time leaning against the church wall of Saint Peter's, but now Papa Sixtus hath erected it in the middle of Saint Peter's churchyard. It is twenty-four fathom long and at the lower end six fathom foursquare, and so forth smaller upwards; on the top is a crucifix of beaten gold; the stone standeth on four lions of brass. Then he visited the seven churches of Rome, that were Saint Peter's, Saint Paul's, Saint Sebastian's, Saint John Lateran, St. Laurence, Saint Mary Magdalen, and Saint Marie Majora. Then went he without the town, where he saw the conduits of water that run level through hill and dale, bringing water into the town fifteen Italian miles off. Other monuments he saw, too many to recite, but amongst the rest he was de-sirous to see the pope's palace, and his manner of ser-vice at his table. Wherefore, he and his spirit made themselves invisible and came into the pope's court and privy chamber where he was. There saw he many ser-vants attendant on his holiness, with many a flattering sycophant carrying of his meat, and there he marked the pope and the manner of his service, which he seeing to be so unmeasurable and sumptuous, "Fie," quoth Faus-tus, "why had not the devil made a pope of me?" Faustus saw notwithstanding in that place those that were like to himself, proud, stout, willful, gluttons, drunkards, whore-mongers, breakers of wedlock, and followers of all man-

ner of ungodly exercises. Wherefore he said to his spirit,
"I thought that I had been alone a hog or pork of the
devil's, but he must bear with me yet a little longer, for
these hogs of Rome are already fattened and fitted to
make his roast meat. The devil might do well now to spit
them all and have them to the fire, and let him summon
the nuns to turn the spits. For as none must confess the
nun but the friar, so none should turn the roasting friar
but the nun." Thus continued Faustus three days in the
pope's palace, and yet had no lust to his meat, but stood
still in the pope's chamber and saw everything whatsoever it was. On a time the pope would have a feast prepared for the Cardinal of Pavia, and for his first welcome
the cardinal was bidden to dinner, and as he sat at meat
the pope would ever be blessing and crossing over his
mouth. Faustus could suffer it no longer, but up with his
fist and smote the pope on the face, and withall he
laughed that the whole house might hear him, yet none
of them saw him nor knew where he was. The pope persuaded his company that it was a damned soul, commanding a mass presently to be said for his delivery out
of purgatory, which was done. The pope sat still at meat,
but when the latter mess came in to the pope's board,
Doctor Faustus laid hands thereon, saying "This is mine."
And so he took both dish and meat and fled unto the
Capitol or Campadolia, calling his spirit unto him, and
said, "Come, let us be merry, for thou must fetch me
some wine and the cup that the pope drinks of, and here
upon Monte Caval will we make good cheer in spite of
the pope and all his fat abbey lubbers." His spirit, hearing this, departed towards the pope's chamber, where he
found them yet sitting and quaffing: wherefore he took
from before the pope the fairest piece of plate or drinking goblet and a flagon of wine, and brought it to Faustus. But when the pope and the rest of his crew perceived

they were robbed, and knew not after what sort, they persuaded themselves that it was the damned soul that before had vexed the pope so and that smote him on the face; wherefore he sent commandment through all the whole city of Rome that they should say mass in every church and ring all the bells for to lay the walking spirit, and to curse him with bell, book, and candle, that so invisibly had misused the pope's holiness, with the Cardinal of Pavia and the rest of their company. But Faustus notwithstanding made good cheer with that which he had beguiled the pope of, and in the midst of the order of Saint Barnard's barefooted friars, as they were going on procession through the market place called Campa de Fiore, he let fall his plate dishes and cup, and withall for a farewell he made such a thunderclap and a storm of rain as though heaven and earth should have met together, and so he left Rome. . . .

How the Emperor Carolus Quintus requested
of Faustus to see some of his cunning,
whereunto he agreed. Chap. 29.

The Emperor Carolus, the fifth of that name, was personally with the rest of his nobles and gentlemen at the town of Innsbruck where he kept his court; unto the which also Doctor Faustus resorted, and being there well known of divers nobles and gentlemen, he was invited into the court to meat, even in the presence of the emperor: whom when the emperor saw, he looked earnestly on him, thinking him by his looks to be some wonderful fellow, wherefore he asked one of his nobles whom he should be, who answered that he was called Doctor Faustus. Whereupon the emperor held his peace until he had taken his repast, after which he called unto him

Faustus, into the privy chamber. Whither being come, he said unto him, "Faustus, I have heard much of thee, that thou art excellent in the black art, and none like thee in mine empire, for men say that thou hast a familiar spirit with thee and that thou canst do what thou list. It is therefore," saith the emperor, "my request of thee that thou let me see a proof of thine experience, and I vow unto thee by the honor of mine imperial crown, none evil shall happen unto thee for so doing." Hereupon Doctor Faustus answered his majesty that upon those conditions he was ready in anything that he could to do his highness's commandment in what service he would appoint him. "Well, then hear what I say," quoth the emperor. "Being once solitary in my house, I called to mind mine elders and ancestors, how it was possible for them to attain unto so great a degree of authority, yea so high that we the successors of that line are never able to come near. As for example, the great and mighty monarch of the world Alexander Magnus was such a lantern and spectacle to all his successors, as the chronicles make mention of so great riches, conquering, and subduing so many kingdoms, the which I and those that follow me (I fear) shall never be able to attain unto. Wherefore, Faustus, my hearty desire is that thou wouldst vouchsafe to let me see that Alexander, and his paramour, the which was praised to be so fair; and I pray thee show me them in such sort that I may see their personages, shape, gesture and apparel as they used in their lifetime, and that here before my face; to the end that I may say I have my long desire fulfilled and to praise thee to be a famous man in thine art and experience." Doctor Faustus answered, "My most excellent lord, I am ready to accomplish your request in all things, so far forth as I and my spirit are able to perform. Yet your majesty shall know that their dead bodies are not able substantially to be brought before you, but such spirits as have seen Alexander and his paramour alive shall appear unto you in manner and form as they both lived in their most flourishing time; and herewith I hope to please your imperial majesty." Then Faustus went a little aside to speak to his spirit, but he returned again presently, saying "Now if it please your majesty you shall see them, yet upon this condition that you demand no question of them nor speak unto them," which the emperor agreed unto. Wherewith Doctor Faustus opened the privy chamber door, where presently entered the great and mighty Emperor Alexander Magnus, in all things to look upon as if he had been alive, in proportion a strong thick-set man of a middle stature, black hair and that both thick and curled head and beard, red cheeks, and a broad face, with eyes like a basilisk; he had on a complete harness burnished and graven exceeding rich to look upon. And so passing towards the Emperor Carolus, he made low and reverent curtsy, whereat the Emperor Carolus would have stood up to receive and greet him with the like reverence, but Faustus took hold of him and would not permit him to do it. Shortly after, Alexander made humble reverence and went out again, and coming to the door his paramour met him, she coming in. She made the emperor likewise reverence; she was clothed in blue velvet wrought and embroidered with pearl and gold; she was also excellent fair like milk and blood mixed, tall and slender, with a face round as an apple. And thus she passed certain times up and down the house, which the emperor marking, said to himself, "Now have I seen two persons which my heart hath long wished for to behold, and sure it cannot otherwise be," said he to himself, "but that the spirits have changed themselves into these forms and have not deceived me," calling to his mind the woman that raised the prophet Samuel. And for that the emperor would be the more satisfied in the matter, he thought, "I have heard say that behind her neck she had a great wart or wen," wherefore he took Faustus by the hand without any words and went to see if it were also to be seen on her or not; but she, perceiving that he came to her, bowed down her neck, where he saw a great wart, and hereupon she vanished, leaving the emperor and the rest well contented.

How Doctor Faustus in the sight of the emperor conjured a pair of hart's horns upon a knight's head that slept out of a casement. Chap. 30.

When Doctor Faustus had accomplished the emperor's desire in all things as he was requested, he went forth into a gallery, and leaning over a rail to look into the privy garden he saw many of the emperor's courtiers walking and talking together. And casting his eyes now this way, now that way, he espied a knight leaning out at a window of the great hall, who was fast asleep (for in those days it was hot) but the person shall be nameless that slept, for that he was a knight, although it was done to a little disgrace of the gentleman. It pleased Doctor Faustus, through the help of his spirit Mephostophiles, to firm upon his head as he slept a huge pair of hart's horns; and as the knight awoke, thinking to pull in his head he hit his horns against the glass that the panes thereof flew about his ears. Think here how this good gentleman was vexed, for he could neither get backward nor forward: which when the emperor heard all the courtiers laugh, and came forth to see what was happened, the emperor also, when he beheld the knight with so fair a head, laughed heartily thereat and was therewithal well pleased. At last Faustus made him quit of his horns again, but the knight perceived how they came, etc.

How the above-mentioned knight went about to be revenged of Doctor Faustus. Chap. 31.

Doctor Faustus took his leave of the emperor and the rest of the courtiers, at whose departure they were sorry, giving him many rewards and gifts. But being a league and a half from the city he came into a wood, where he beheld the knight that he had jested with at the court with other in harness, mounted on fair palfreys, and running with full charge towards Faustus. But he, seeing their intent, ran toward the bushes, and before he came amongst the bushes he returned again, running as it were to meet them that chased him; whereupon suddenly all the bushes were turned into horsemen which also ran to encounter with the knight and his company; and coming to them, they closed the knight and the rest and told them that they must pay their ransom before they departed. Whereupon the knight, seeing himself in such distress, besought Faustus to be good to them, which he denied not, but let them loose; yet he so charmed them that every one, knight and other, for the space of a whole month did wear a pair of goat's horns on their brows, and every palfrey a pair of ox horns on their head; and this was their penance appointed by Faustus, etc.

How Doctor Faustus deceived an Horse-courser. Chap. 34.

In like manner he served an horse-courser at a fair called Pheiffring, for Doctor Faustus through his cunning had gotten an excellent fair horse, whereupon he rode to the fair, where he had many chapmen that offered him money. Lastly, he sold him for forty dollars, willing him that bought him that in any wise he should not ride him over any water. But the horse-courser marveled with himself that Faustus bade him ride him over no water, but quoth he, "I will prove," and forthwith he rode him into the river. Presently the horse vanished from under him, and he sat on a bundle of straw, in so much that the man was almost drowned. The horse-courser knew well where he lay that had sold him his horse, wherefore he went angrily to his inn, where he found Doctor Faustus fast asleep and snorting on a bed. But the horse-courser could no longer forbear him, took him by the leg and began to pull him off the bed; but he pulled him so that he pulled his leg from his body, in so much that the horse-courser fell down backward in the place. Then began Doctor Faustus to cry with an open throat, "He hath murdered me!" Hereat the horse-courser was afraid and gave the flight, thinking none other with himself but that he had pulled his leg from his body. By this means Doctor Faustus kept his money.

How Doctor Faustus ate a load of hay. Chap. 35.

Doctor Faustus being in a town of Germany called Zwickau, where he was accompanied with many doctors and masters, and going forth to walk after supper, they met with a clown that drove a load of hay. "Good even, good fellow," said Faustus to the clown, "what shall I give thee to let me eat my belly full of hay?" The clown thought with himself, what a mad man is this to eat hay; thought he with himself, thou wilt not eat much. They agreed for three farthings he should eat as much as he could: wherefore Doctor Faustus began to eat, and that so ravenously that all the rest of his company fell a-laughing, blinding so the poor clown that he was sorry at his heart, for he seemed to have eaten more than the half of his hay. Wherefore the clown began to speak him fair, for fear he should have eaten the other half also. Faustus made as though he had had pity on the clown, and went his way. When the clown came in place where he would be, he had his hay again as he had before, a full load.

How Faustus served the drunken clowns. Chap. 37.

Doctor Faustus went into an inn wherein were many tables full of clowns, the which were tippling can after can of excellent wine, and to be short, they were all drunken. And as they sat, they so sung and hallooed that one could not hear a man speak for them. This angered Doctor Faustus, wherefore he said to those that had called him in, "Mark, my masters, I will show you a merry jest." The clowns continuing still hallooing and singing, he so conjured them that their mouths stood as wide open as it was possible for them to hold them, and never a one of them was able to close his mouth again. By and by the noise was gone; the clowns notwithstanding looked earnestly one upon another and wist not what was happened; wherefore one by one they went out, and so soon as they came without, they were as well as ever they were. But none of them desired to go in any more.

How Doctor Faustus played a merry jest with the Duke of Anholt in his court. Chap. 39.

Doctor Faustus on a time came to the Duke of Anholt, the which welcomed him very courteously, this was

in the month of January, where sitting at the table he
perceived the duchess to be with child. And forbear-
ing himself until the meat was taken from the table and
that they brought in the banqueting dishes, said Doctor Faustus to the duchess, "Gracious lady, I have always
heard that the great bellied women do always long for
some dainties. I beseech therefore your grace hide not
your mind from me, but tell me what you desire to eat."
She answered him, "Doctor Faustus now truly I will not
hide from you what my heart doth most desire, namely,
that if it were now harvest, I would eat my belly full of
ripe grapes, and other dainty fruit." Doctor Faustus answered hereupon, "Gracious lady, this is a small thing
for me to do, for I can do more than this." Wherefore he
took a plate and made open one of the casements of the
window, holding it forth, where incontinent he had his
dish full of all manner of fruits, as red and white grapes,
pears, and apples, the which came from out of strange
countries. All these he presented the duchess, saying
"Madame, I pray you vouchsafe to taste of this dainty
fruit, the which came from a far country, for there the
summer is not yet ended." The duchess thanked Faustus
highly, and she fell to her fruit with full appetite. The
Duke of Anholt notwithstanding could not withhold to
ask Faustus with what reason there were such young
fruit to be had at that time of the year. Doctor Faustus
told him, "May it please your grace to understand that
the year is divided into two circles over the whole world,
that when with us it is winter, in the contrary circle it
is notwithstanding summer; for in India and Saba there
falleth or setteth the sun so that it is so warm that they
have twice a year fruit. And, gracious lord, I have a swift
spirit, the which can in the twinkling of an eye fulfill my
desire in anything, wherefore I sent him into those coun-

tries, who hath brought this fruit as you see." Whereat the duke was in great admiration.

How Doctor Faustus through his charms made a great castle in presence of the Duke of Anholt. Chap. 40.

Doctor Faustus desired the Duke of Anholt to walk a little forth of the court with him, wherefore they went both together into the field, where Doctor Faustus through his skill had placed a mighty castle, which when the duke saw, he wondered thereat. So did the duchess, and all the beholders, that on that hill, which was called the Rohumbuel, should on the sudden be so fair a castle. At last Doctor Faustus desired the duke and the duchess to walk with him into the castle, which they denied not. This castle was so wonderfully strong, having about it a great and deep trench of water, the which was full of fish and all manner of water fowl as swans, ducks, geese, bitterns, and such like. About the wall was five stone doors and two other doors; also within was a great open court wherein were enchanted all manner of wild beasts, especially such as were not to be found in Germany, as apes, bears, buffalos, antelopes, and such like strange beasts. Furthermore, there were other manner of beasts, as hart, hind, and wild swine, roe, and all manner of land fowl that any man could think on, the which flew from one tree to another. After all this, he set his guests to the table, being the duke and duchess with their train, for he had provided them a most sumptuous feast, both of meat and all manner of drinks. For he set nine messes of meat upon the board at once, and all this must his Wagner do, place all things on the board, the which was brought unto him by the spirit invisibly of all things that their heart could desire, as wild fowl and venison with all manner of dainty fish that could be thought on; of wine also great plenty, and of divers sorts, as French wine, Cullin wine, Crabatsher wine, Rhenish wine, Spanish wine, Hungarian wine, Watzburg wine, malmsey and sack: in the whole, there were a hundred cans standing round about the house. This sumptuous banquet the duke took thankfully, and afterwards he departed homewards, and to their thinking they had neither eaten nor drunk, so were they blinded the while that they were in the castle. But as they were in their palace they looked toward the castle, and behold, it was all in a flame of fire, and all those that beheld it wondered to hear so great a noise, as if it were great ordnance should have been shot off; and thus the castle burned and consumed away clean. Which done, Doctor Faustus returned to the duke, who gave him great thanks for showing them of so great courtesy, giving him a hundred dollars and liberty to depart or use his own discretion therein.

How Doctor Faustus showed the fair Helena unto the students upon the Sunday following. Chap. 45.

The Sunday following came these students home to Doctor Faustus' own house and brought their meat and drink with them. These men were right welcome guests unto Faustus, wherefore they all fell to drinking of wine smoothly; and being merry, they began some of them to talk of the beauty of women, and everyone gave forth his verdict what he had seen and what he had heard. So one among the rest said, "I never was so desirous of anything in this world as to have a sight (if it were possible) of fair Helena of Greece for whom the worthy town of Troy was destroyed and razed down to the ground, therefore" sayth he, "that in all men's judgment she was more than commonly fair, because that when she was stolen away from her husband there was for her recovery so great bloodshed."

Doctor Faustus answered, "For that you are all my friends and are so desirous to see that famous pearl of Greece, fair Helena, the wife of King Menelaus and daughter of Tindalus and Laeda, sister to Castor and Pollux, who was the fairest lady in all Greece, I will therefore bring her into your presence personally and in the same form of attire as she used to go when she was in her chiefest flower and pleasantest prime of youth. The like have I done for the Emperor Carolus Quintus; at his desire I showed him Alexander the Great and his paramour. But," said Doctor Faustus, "I charge you all that upon your peril you speak not a word nor rise up from the table so long as she is in your presence." And so he went out of the hall, returning presently again, after whom immediately followed the fair and beautiful Helena, whose beauty was such that the students were all amazed to see her, esteeming her rather to be a heavenly than an earthly creature. This lady appeared before them in a most sumptuous gown of purple velvet, richly embroidered; her hair hung down loose as fair as the beaten gold and of such length that it reached down to her hams; with amorous coal-black eyes, a sweet and pleasant round face, her lips red as a cherry, her cheeks of rose all color, her mouth small, her neck as white as the swan, tall and slender of personage; and in sum, there was not one imperfect part in her. She looked round-about her with a rolling hawk's eye, a smiling and wanton countenance, which nearly had inflamed the hearts of the students but that they persuaded themselves she was a spirit, wherefore such fantasies passed away lightly with them. And thus fair Helena and Doctor Faustus went out again one with another. But the students at Doctor Faustus' entering again into the hall requested of him to let them see her again the next day, for that they would bring with them a painter and so take her counterfeit, which he denied, affirming that he could not always raise up her spirit, but only at certain times. "Yet," said he, "I will give you her counterfeit, which shall be always as good to you as if yourselves should see the drawing thereof," which they received according to his promise but soon lost it again. The students departed from Faustus' home everyone to his house, but they were not able to sleep the whole night for thinking on the beauty of fair Helena. Wherefore a man may see that the devil blindeth and inflameth the heart with lust oftentimes, that men fall in love with harlots, nay even with furies, which afterward cannot lightly be removed.

How an old man, the neighbor of Faustus,
sought to persuade him to amend his evil life
and to fall unto repentance. Chap. 48.

A good Christian, an honest and virtuous old man, a lover of the holy Scriptures, who was neighbor unto Doctor Faustus, when he perceived that many students had their recourse in and out unto Doctor Faustus, he suspected his evil life. Wherefore like a friend he invited Doctor Faustus to supper unto his house, unto the which he agreed. And having ended their banquet, the old man began with these words. "My loving friend and neighbor Doctor Faustus, I have to desire of you a friendly and Christian request, beseeching you that you will vouchsafe not to be angry with me but friendly resolve me in my doubt and take my poor inviting in good part." To whom Doctor Faustus answered, "My loving neighbor, I pray you say your mind." Then began the old patron to say: "My good neighbor, you know in the beginning how that you have defied God and all the host [of] heaven and given your soul to the devil, wherewith you have incurred God's high displeasure and are become from a Christian far worse than a heathen person. Oh, consider what you have done. It is not only the pleasure of the body but the safety of the soul that you must have respect unto, of which if you be careless then are you cast away and shall remain in the anger of almighty God. But yet is it time enough, Doctor Faustus, if you repent and call unto the Lord for mercy, as we have example in the Acts of the Apostles, the eighth chapter of Simon in Samaria, who was led out of the way, affirming that he was Simon Homo Sanctus. This man was notwithstanding in the end converted, after that he had heard the sermon of Philip, for he was baptized and saw his sins and repented. Likewise I beseech you, good brother Doctor Faustus, let my rude sermon be unto you a conversion, and forget the filthy life that you have led, repent, ask mercy, and live. For Christ saith, 'Come unto me all ye that are weary and heavy laden, and I will refresh you.' And in Ezekiel, 'I desire not the death of a sinner, but rather that he convert and live.' Let my words, good brother Faustus, pierce into your adamant heart, and desire God for his Son Christ's sake to forgive you. Wherefore have you so long lived in your devilish practices, knowing that in the Old and New Testament you are forbidden, and that men should not suffer any such to live, neither have any conversation with them, for it is an abomination unto the Lord, and that such persons have no part in the Kingdom of God." All this while Doctor Faustus heard him very attentively, and replied: "Father, your persuasions like me wondrous well, and I thank you with all my heart for your good will and counsel, promising you so far as I may to follow your discipline." Whereupon he took his leave. And being come home, he laid him very pensive on his bed, bethinking himself of the words of the good old man, and in a manner began to repent that he had given his soul to the devil, intending to deny all that he had promised unto Lucifer. Continuing in these cogitations, suddenly his spirit appeared unto him clapping him upon the head, and wrung it as though he would have pulled the head from the shoulders, saying unto him "Thou knowest, Faustus, that thou has given thyself body and soul unto my lord Lucifer, and has vowed thyself an enemy unto God and unto all men; and now thou beginnest to harken to an old doting fool which persuadeth thee as it were unto God, when indeed it is too late, for that thou art the devil's, and he hath good power presently to fetch thee: wherefore he hath sent me unto thee to tell thee, that seeing thou hast sorrowed for that thou hast done, begin again and write another writing with thine own blood; if not, then will I tear thee all to pieces." Hereat Doctor Faustus was sore afraid, and sayd, "My Mephostophiles, I will write again what thou wilt." Wherefore he sat him down and with his own blood he wrote as followeth, which writing was afterwards sent to a dear friend of the said Doctor Faustus being his kinsman.

How Doctor Faustus wrote the second time with his own blood and gave it to the Devil. Chap. 49.

I, Doctor John Faustus, acknowledge by this my deed and handwriting, that sith my first writing, which is seventeen years, that I have right willingly held, and have been an utter enemy unto God and all men, the which I once again confirm, and give fully and wholly my self

unto the devil both body and soul, even unto the great
Lucifer. And that at the end of seven years ensuing after
the date of this letter, he shall have to do with me according as it pleaseth him, either to lengthen or shorten
my life as liketh him. And hereupon I renounce all per-
suaders that seek to withdraw me from my purpose by
the word of God, either ghostly or bodily. And further, I
will never give ear unto any man, be he spiritual or tem-
poral, that moveth any matter for the salvation of my
soul. Of all this writing, and that therein contained, be
witness, my own blood, the which with mine own hands
I have begun and ended.

Dated at Wittenberg the 25 of July.

And presently upon the making of this letter, he became so great an enemy unto the poor old man that he
sought his life by all means possible; but this godly man
was strong in the Holy Ghost, that he could not be van-
quished by any means. For about two days after that he
had exhorted Faustus, as the poor man lay in his bed,
suddenly there was a mighty rumbling in the chamber
the which he was never wont to hear, and he heard as
it had been the groaning of a sow, which lasted long.
Whereupon the good old man began to jest and mock,
and said "Oh, what barbarian cry is this, oh fair bird,
what foul music is this of a fair angel that could not tarry
two days in his place? Beginnest thou now to run into a
poor man's house where thou hast no power and wert
not able to keep thine own two days?" With these and
such like words the spirit departed. And when he came
home Faustus asked him how he had sped with the old
man: to whom the spirit answered, the old man was har-
nessed, and that he could not once lay hold upon him.
But he would not tell how the old man had mocked him,
for the devils can never abide to hear of their fall. Thus

doth God defend the hearts of all honest Christians that betake themselves under his tuition.

How Doctor Faustus gathered together a great army of men in his extremity against a knight that would have injured him on his journey. Chap. 52.

Doctor Faustus traveled towards Eisleben, and when he was nigh half the way he espied seven horsemen, and the chief of them he knew to be the knight to whom he had played a jest in the emperor's court, for he had set a huge pair of hart's horns upon his head. And when the knight now saw that he had fit opportunity to be revenged of Faustus, he ran upon him himself, and those that were with him, to mischief him, intending privily to shoot at him. Which when Doctor Faustus espied, he vanished away into the wood which was hard by them. But when the knight perceived that he was vanished away, he caused his men to stand still, where as they remained they heard all manner of warlike instruments of music, as drums, flutes, trumpets, and such like, and a certain troup of horsemen running towards them. Then they turned another way and there also were assaulted on the same side; then another way and yet they were freshly assaulted; so that which way soever they turned themselves he was encountered, in so much that when the knight perceived that he could escape no way, but that they his enemies laid on him which way soever he offered to fly, he took a good heart and ran amongst the thickest, and thought with himself better to die than to live with so great an infamy. Therefore, being at handy-blows with them, he demanded the cause why they should so use them; but none of them would give him answer until Doctor Faustus showed himself unto the knight, where withal they enclosed him round and Doctor Faustus said unto him, "Sir, yield your weapon and yourself; otherwise it will go hardly with you." The knight, that knew none other but that he was environed with a host of men (where indeed they were none other than devils), yielded. Then Faustus took away his sword, his piece, and horse, with all the rest of his companions. And further he said unto him, "Sir, the chief general of our army hath commanded to deal with you according to the law of arms; you shall depart in peace whither you please." And then he gave the knight a horse after the manner and set him thereon so he rode. The rest went on foot until they came to their inn, where being alighted his page rode on his horse to the water, and presently the horse vanished away, the page being almost sunk and drowned, but he escaped. And coming home, the knight perceived his page so bemired and on foot, asked where his horse was become. Who answered that he was vanished away; which when the knight heard, he said, "Of a truth, this is Faustus' doing, for he serveth me now as he did before at the court, only to make me a scorn and a laughingstock."

How Doctor Faustus caused Mephostophiles to bring him seven of the fairest women that he could find in all those countries he had traveled in, in the twentieth year. Chap. 53.

When Doctor Faustus called to mind that his time from day to day drew nigh, he began to live a swinish and epicurish life, wherefore he commanded his spirit Mephostophiles to bring him seven of the fairest women that he had seen in all the time of his travel. Which being brought, first one and then another he lay with them all, insomuch that he liked them so well that he continued with them in all manner of love and made them to travel with him in all his journeys. These women were two Netherlanders, one Hungarian, one English, two Walloons, one Franklander; and with these sweet personages he continued long, yea even to his last end.

How Doctor Faustus made the spirit of fair Helena of Greece his own paramour and bedfellow in his twenty-third year. Chap. 55.

To the end that this miserable Faustus might fill the lust of his flesh and live in all manner of voluptuous pleasures, it came in his mind after he had slept his first sleep and in the twenty-third year past of his time, that he had a great desire to lie with fair Helena of Greece, especially her whom he had seen and showed unto the students of Wittenberg, wherefore he called unto him his spirit Mephostophiles, commanding him to bring him the fair Helena, which he also did. Whereupon he fell in love with her and made her his common concubine and bedfellow, for she was so beautiful and delightful a piece that he could not be one hour from her if he should therefore have suffered death, she had so stolen away his heart. And to his seeming, in time she was with child and in the end brought him a man child whom Faustus named Justus Faustus. This child told Doctor Faustus many things that were to come and what strange matters were done in foreign countries; but in the end when Faustus lost his life, the mother and the child vanished away both together.

How Doctor Faustus made his will, in the which he named
his servant Wagner to be his heir. Chap. 56.

Doctor Faustus was now in his twenty-fourth and last
year, and he had a pretty stripling to his servant, the
which had studied also at the University of Wittenberg.
This youth was very well acquainted with his knaveries
and sorceries, so that he was hated as well for his own
knaveries as also for his master's, for no man would give
him entertainment into his service, because of his un-
happiness, but Faustus. This Wagner was so well beloved
with Faustus that he used him as his son, for do what
he would his master was always therewith well content.
And when the time drew nigh that Faustus should end,
he called unto him a notary and certain masters the
which were his friends and often conversant with him, in
whose presence he gave this Wagner his house and garden. Item, he gave him in ready money sixteen hundred
guilders. Item, a farm. Item, a gold chain, much plate,
and other household stuff. This gave he all to his servant,
and the rest of his time he meant to spend in inns and
students' company, drinking and eating, with other jollity. And thus he finished his will for that time.

How Doctor Faustus having but one month of his
appointed time to come, fell to mourning and sorrow with
himself for his devilish exercise. Chap. 58.

Time ran away with Faustus, as the hourglass, for he
had but one month to come of his twenty-four years, at
the end whereof he had given himself to the devil body
and soul, as is before specified. Here was the first token,
for he was like a taken murderer or a thief, the which
findeth himself guilty in conscience before the judge

have given sentence, fearing every hour to die; for he was grieved, and wailing spent the time, went talking to himself, wringing of his hands, sobbing and sighing; he fell away from flesh and was very lean, and kept himself close. Neither could he abide to see or hear of his Mephostophiles any more.

How Doctor Faustus complained that he should in his lusty time and youthful years die so miserably. Chap. 59.

This sorrowful time drawing near so troubled Doctor Faustus that he began to write his mind, to the end he might peruse it often and not forget it, and is in manner as followeth.

Ah Faustus, thou sorrowful and woeful man, now must thou go to the damned company in unquenchable fire, whereas thou mightest have had the joyful immortality of the soul, the which thou now hast lost. Ah gross understanding and willful will, what seizeth on my limbs other than a robbing of my life? Bewail with me my sound and healthful body, wit and soul, bewail with me my senses, for you have had your part and pleasure as well as I. Oh envy and disdain, how have you crept both at once into me, and now for your sakes I must suffer all these torments? Ah whither is pity and mercy fled? Upon what occasion hath heaven repaid me with this reward by sufferance to suffer me to perish? Wherefore was I created a man? The punishment that I see prepared for me of myself now must I suffer. Ah miserable wretch, there is nothing in this world to show me comfort: then woe is me, what helpeth my wailing.

Another complaint of Doctor Faustus. Chap. 60.

Oh poor, woeful and weary wretch, oh sorrowful soul of Faustus, now art thou in the number of the damned. For now must I wait for unmeasurable pains of death, yea far more lamentable than ever yet any creature hath suffered. Ah senseless, willful and desperate forgetfulness! O cursed and unstable life! O blind and careless wretch, that so hast abused thy body, sense and soul! O foolish pleasure, into what a weary labyrinth hast thou brought me, blinding mine eyes in the clearest day! Ah weak heart! O troubled soul, where is become thy knowledge to comfort thee? O pitiful weariness! Oh desperate hope, now shall I never more be thought upon! Oh, care upon carefulness, and sorrows on heaps; ah grievous pains that pierce my panting heart, whom is there now that can deliver me? Would God that I knew where to hide me, or into what place to creep or fly. Ah, woe, woe is me, be where I will, yet am I taken. Herewith poor Faustus was so sorrowfully troubled that he could not speak or utter his mind any further.

How Doctor Faustus bewailed to think on hell, and of the miserable pains therein provided for him. Chap. 61.

Now thou Faustus, damned wretch, how happy wert thou if as an unreasonable beast thou mightest die without soul, so shouldst thou not feel any more doubts! But now the devil will take thee away both body and soul and set thee in an unspeakable place of darkness. For although other souls have rest and peace, yet I, poor damned wretch, must suffer all manner of filthy stench, pains, cold, hunger, thirst, heat, freezing, burning, hissing, gnashing, and all the wrath and curse of God, yea all the creatures that God hath created are enemies to me. And now too late I remember that my spirit Mephostophiles did once tell me there was a great difference amongst the damned, for the greater the sin, the greater the torment. For as the twigs of the tree make greater flame than the trunk thereof, and yet the trunk continueth longer in burning, even so the more that a man is rooted in sin the greater is his punishment. Ah thou perpetual damned wretch, now art thou thrown into the everlasting fiery lake that never shall be quenched; there must I dwell in all manner of wailing, sorrow, misery, pain, torment, grief, howling, sighing, sobbing, blubbering, running of eyes, stinking at nose, gnashing of teeth, fear to the ears, horror to the conscience, and shaking both of hand and foot. Ah that I could carry the heavens on my shoulders, so that there were time at last to quit me of this everlasting damnation! Oh who can deliver me out of these fearful tormenting flames, the which I see prepared for me? Oh there is no help, nor any man that can deliver me, nor any wailing of sins can help me, neither is there rest to be found for me day nor night. Oh woe is me, for there is no help for me, no shield, no defense, no comfort. Where is my hold? Knowledge dare I not trust, and for a soul to God wards that have I not, for I shame to speak unto him. If I do, no answer shall be made me, but he will hide his face from me, to the end that I should not behold the joys of the chosen. What mean I then to complain where no help is? No, I know no hope resteth in my groanings. I have desired that it should be so, and God hath said Amen to my misdoings: for now I must have shame to comfort me in my calamities.

An oration of Faustus to the students. Chap. 63.

My trusty and well beloved friends, the cause why I
have invited you into this place is this: Forasmuch as you
have known me this many years, in what manner of life
I have lived, practicing all manner of conjurations and
wicked exercises, the which I have obtained through the
help of the devil, into whose devilish fellowship they
have brought me, the which use the like art and practice, urged by the detestable provocation of my flesh, my
stiff-necked and rebellious will, with my filthy infernal
thoughts, the which were ever before me, pricking me
forward so earnestly that I must perforce have the consent of the devil to aid me in my devices. And to the end
I might the better bring my purpose to pass, to have the
devil's aid and furtherance, which I never have wanted
in mine actions, I have promised unto him at the end and
accomplishing of twenty-four years, both body and soul,
to do therewith at his pleasure. And this day, this dismal
day, those twenty-four years are fully expired, for night
beginning my hourglass is at an end, the direful finish-
ing whereof I carefully expect. For out of all doubt this
night he will fetch me, to whom I have given myself in
recompense of his service, both body and soul, and twice
confirmed writings with my proper blood. Now have I
called you, my well beloved lords, friends, brethren, and
fellows, before that fatal hour to take my friendly farewell, to the end that my departing may not hereafter be
hidden from you; beseeching you herewith courteous
and loving lords and brethren, not to take in evil part
anything done by me, but with friendly commendations
to salute all my friends and companions wheresoever,
desiring both you and them, if ever I have trespassed
against your minds in anything, that you would all heartily forgive me. And as for those lewd practices the which

this full twenty-four years I have followed, you shall hereafter find them in writing. And I beseech you let this my lamentable end to the residue of your lives be a sufficient warning, that you have God always before your eyes, praying unto him that he would ever defend you from the temptation of the devil and all his false deceits, not falling altogether from God as I, wretched and ungodly damned creature, have done, having denied and defied baptism, the sacraments of Christ's body, God himself, all heavenly powers, and earthly men, yea, I have denied such a God that desireth not to have one lost. Neither let the evil fellowship of wicked companions mislead you as it hath done me. Visit earnestly and oft the church, war and strive continually against the devil with a good and steadfast belief on God and Jesus Christ, and use your vocation in holiness. Lastly, to knit up my troubled oration, this is my friendly request, that you would to rest, and let nothing trouble you. Also, if you chance to hear any noise or rumbling about the house, be not therewith afraid, for there shall no evil happen unto you. Also, I pray you, arise not out of your beds. But above all things I entreat you, if you hereafter find my dead carcass, convey it unto the earth, for I die both a good and bad Christian: a good Christian for that I am heartily sorry and in my heart always pray for mercy that my soul may be delivered; a bad Christian for that I know the devil will have my body, and that would I willingly give him so that he would leave my soul in quiet. Wherefore I pray you that you would depart to bed, and so I wish you a quiet night, which unto me notwithstanding will be horrible and fearful.

This oration or declaration was made by Doctor Faustus, and that with a hearty and resolute mind, to the end he might not discomfort them. But the students wondered greatly thereat, that he was so blinded, for knavery, conjuration, and such like foolish things, to give his body and soul unto the devil; for they loved him entirely and never suspected any such thing before he had opened his mind to them. Wherefore one of them said unto him, "Ah, friend Faustus, what have you done to conceal this matter so long from us? We would by the help of good divines and the grace of God have brought you out of this net and have torn you out of the bondage and chains of Satan, whereas now we fear it is too late, to the utter ruin of your body and soul." Doctor Faustus answered, "I durst never do it, although I often minded, to settle myself unto godly people, to desire counsel and help, as once mine old neighbor counselled me that I should follow his learning and leave all my conjurations. Yet when I was minded to amend and to follow that good man's counsel, then came the devil and would have had me away, as this night he is like to do, and said so soon as I turned again to God he would dispatch me altogether. Thus, even thus, good gentlemen and my dear friends, was I enthralled in that Satanical band, all good desires drowned, all piety banished, all purpose of amendment utterly exiled by the tyrannous threatenings of my deadly enemy." But when the students heard his words, they gave him counsel to do naught else but call upon God, desiring him for the love of his sweet Son Jesus Christ's sake, to have mercy upon him, teaching him this form of prayer: O God be merciful unto me, poor and miserable sinner, and enter not into judgment with me, for no flesh is able to stand before thee. Although, O Lord, I must leave my sinful body unto the devil, being by him deluded, yet thou in mercy mayest preserve my soul.

This they repeated unto him, yet it could take no hold, but even as Cain he also said his sins were greater than God was able to forgive; for all his thought was on his writing, he meant he had made it too filthy in writing it with his own blood. The students and the others that were there, when they had prayed for him they wept and so went forth, but Faustus tarried in the hall. And when the gentlemen were laid in bed, none of them could sleep for that they attended to hear if they might be privy of his end. It happened between twelve and one o'clock at midnight; there blew a mighty storm of wind against the house as though it would have blown the foundation thereof out of his place. Hereupon the students began to fear, and got out of their beds, comforting one another, but they would not stir out of the chamber; and the host of the house ran out of doors, thinking the house would fall. The students lay near unto that hall wherein Doctor Faustus lay, and they heard a mighty noise and hissing as if the hall had been full of snakes and adders. With that, the hall door flew open wherein Doctor Faustus was; then he began to cry for help, saying "Murder, murder," but it came forth with half a voice hollowly. Shortly after, they heard him no more. But when it was day, the students that had taken no rest that night arose and went into the hall in the which they left Doctor Faustus, where notwithstanding they found no Faustus, but all the hall lay besprinkled with blood, his brains cleaving to the wall. For the devil had beaten him from one wall against another: in one corner lay his eyes, in another his teeth, a pitiful and fearful sight to behold. Then began the students to bewail and weep for him and sought for his body in many places. Lastly they came into the yard, where they found his body lying on the horse dung, most monstrously torn and fearful to behold, for his head and all his joints were dashed in pieces.

The forenamed students and masters that were at his death, have obtained so much, that they buried him in the village where he was so grievously tormented. After

the which, they returned to Wittenberg, and coming into
the house of Faustus, they found the servant of Faustus
very sad, unto whom they opened all the matter, who
took it exceeding heavily. There found they also this
history of Doctor Faustus noted, and of him written as
is before declared, all save only his end, the which was
after by the students thereto annexed; further, what his
servant had noted thereof was made in another book.
And you have heard that he held by him in his life the
spirit of fair Helena, the which had by him one son, the
which he named Justus Faustus. Even the same day of
his death they vanished away, both mother and son. The
house before was so dark that scarce anybody could
abide therein. The same night Doctor Faustus appeared
unto his servant lively, and showed unto him many secret things the which he had done and hidden in his
lifetime. Likewise there were certain which saw Doctor
Faustus look out of the window by night as they passed
by the house.

And thus ended the whole history of Doctor Faustus
his conjuration and other acts that he did in his life, out
of the which example every Christian may learn. But
chiefly the stiff-necked and high-minded may thereby
learn to fear God, and to be careful of their vocation,
and to be at defiance with all devilish works, as God
hath most precisely forbidden, to the end we should
not invite the devil as a guest nor give him place as that
wicked Faustus hath done. For here we have a fearful
example of his writing, promise, and end, that we may
remember him: that we go not astray, but take God
always before our eyes, to call alone upon him, and to
honor him all the days of our life with heart and hearty
prayer, and with all our strength and soul to glorify his
holy name, defying the devil and all his works, to the end

we remain with Christ in all endless joy. Amen, amen, that wish I unto every Christian heart, and God's name to be glorified. Amen.

FINIS

Commentaries

Richard B. Sewall
The Tragic Form

A discussion of tragedy is confronted at the outset with
the strenuous objections of Croce, who would have no
truck with the genres. "Art is one," he wrote in his famous *Britannica* article,[1] "and cannot be divided." For
convenience, he would allow the division of Shakespeare's plays into tragedies, comedies, and histories,
but he warned of the dogmatism that lay in any further
refining of distinctions. He made a special point of tragedy, which as usual was the fighting issue. No artist, he
said, will submit to the servitude of the traditional definition: that a tragedy must have a subject of a certain
kind, characters of a certain kind, and a plot of a certain
kind and length. Each work of art is a world in itself, "a
creation, not a reflection, a monument, not a document."
The concepts of aesthetics do not exist "in a transcendent region" but only in innumerable specific works. To
ask of a given work "is it a tragedy?" or "does it obey the
laws of tragedy?" is irrelevant and impertinent.

Although this may be substituting one dogmatism for

From *Essays in Criticism*, IV (1954), 345–58. Reprinted by permission of *Essays
in Criticism: A Quarterly Journal of Literary Criticism*. This essay includes no
specific comment on Marlowe's play, but its examination of the tragic cosmos,
tragic man, and tragic society provides much relevant material. The footnotes
have been renumbered consecutively.
[1]Eleventh edition, article "Aesthetics."

another, there is sense in it. Nothing is more dreary than the textbook categories; and their tendency, if carried too far, would rationalize art out of existence. The dilemma is one of critical means, not ends: Croce would preserve tragedy by insuring the autonomy of the artist; the schoolmen would preserve it by insuring the autonomy of the form.

But the dilemma is not insurmountable, as Eliot and a number of others have pointed out. There is a life-giving relationship between tradition and the individual talent, a "wooing both ways" (in R. P. Blackmur's phrase) between the form which the artist inherits and the new content he brings to it. This wooing both ways has been especially true of the development of tragedy, where values have been incremental, where (for instance) each new tragic protagonist is in some degree a lesser Job and each new tragic work owes an indispensable element to the Greek idea of the chorus. So I should say that, provided we can get beyond the stereotypes Croce seems to have had in mind, we should continue to talk about tragedy, to make it grow in meaning, impel more artists, and attract a greater and more discerning audience.

But we must first get a suitable idea of form. Blackmur's article[2] from which I have just quoted provides, I think, a useful suggestion. It is the concept of "theoretic form," which he distinguishes from technical or "executive" form. "Technical form," he writes, "is our means of getting at . . . and then making something of, what we feel the form of life itself is: the tensions, the stresses, the deep relations and the terrible disrelations that inhabit them. . . . This is the form that underlies the forms we merely practice. . . ." This (and here Croce's full concept

[2]"The Loose and Baggy Monsters of Henry James: Notes on the Underlying Classic Form in the Novel," *Accent,* Summer 1951; see also Eliseo Vivas, "Literature and Knowledge," *Sewanee Review,* Autumn 1952.

of form is more adequately represented) is "what Croce means by theoretic form for feeling, intuition, insight, what I mean by the theoretic form of life itself." Discussion of the "form" of tragedy in this sense need be neither prescriptive nor inhibiting, but it may define a little more precisely a vital area of thought and feeling.

Here is the kind of situation in which such a discussion might be helpful: Two years ago, in *Essays in Criticism* (October 1952), Miss K. M. Burton defended what she called the "political tragedies" of Ben Jonson and George Chapman as legitimate tragedies, although non-Aristotelian. *Sejanus* was perhaps the clearest case in point. Herford and Simpson, in their commentary, had set the play down as at best "the tragedy of a satirist" a "proximate" tragedy, with no tragic hero and with no cathartic effect. "Whatever effect [Jonson] aimed at," they wrote, "it was not the purifying pity excited by the fatal errors of a noble nature." Miss Burton's reply lay in her concept of political tragedy. She saw Jonson's tragic theme as "the manner in which evil penetrates the political structure." The "flaw" that concerned him lay "within the social order," and whatever purifying pity we feel would come from contemplating the ordeal of society, not the fatal errors of a noble nature. The play for her had "tragic intensity"; it was both "dramatic, and a tragedy."

Whether one agrees with her or not, the question, despite Croce, is out: "Is the play a tragedy?" And many others follow. Can there be a tragedy without a tragic hero? Can "the social order" play his traditional role? Is catharsis the first, or only, or even a reliable test? In a recent article, Professor Pottle wrote, "I shall be told Aristotle settled all that." And added, "I wish he had." The disagreement on *Sejanus* is symptomatic. F. L. Lucas once pointed out that (on much the same issues) Hegel thought only the Greeks wrote true tragedy; and I. A. Richards, only Shakespeare. Joseph Wood Krutch ruled out the moderns, like Hardy, Ibsen and O'Neill; and Mark Harris ruled them in.[3] The question arises about every new "serious" play or novel; we seem to care a great deal about whether it is, or is not, a tragedy.

I have little hope of settling all this, but I am persuaded that progress lies in the direction of theoretic form, as Blackmur uses the term. Is it not possible to bring the dominant feelings, intuitions, insights that we meet in so-called tragic writings into some coherent relationship to which the word "form" could be applied without too great violence? This is not to tell artists what to do, nor to set up strict *a priori* formulae, nor to legislate among the major genres. The problem of evaluating the total excellence of a given work involves much more than determining its status as a tragedy, or as a "proximate" tragedy, or as a non-tragedy. It involves, among other things, the verbal management within the work and the ordering of the parts. Furthermore, our discussion need not imply the superiority of tragedy over comedy (certainly not as Dante conceived of comedy) or over epic, although, if we look upon these major forms as presenting total interpretations of life, the less inclusive forms (lyric, satire) would seem to occupy inferior categories. But as we enter the world of any play or novel to which the term "tragedy" is at all applicable, we may well judge it by what we know about the possibilities of the form, without insisting that our judgment is absolute. If, set against the full dimensions of the tragic form, Jonson's *Sejanus* or Hemingway's *A Farewell to Arms* (for instance) reveal undeveloped possibilities or

[3]F. A. Pottle, "Catharsis," *Yale Review,* Summer 1951; F. L. Lucas, *Tragedy in Relation to Aristotle's Poetics,* N.Y., 1928; Joseph Wood Krutch, *The Modern Temper,* N.Y., 1929; Mark Harris, *The Case for Tragedy,* N.Y., 1932.

contrary elements, we can still respect their particular modes of expression.

In indicating these dimensions of tragedy, I shall be mindful of Unamuno's warning[4] that tragedy is not a matter, ultimately, to be systematized. He speaks truly, I think, about "the tragic sense of life." He describes it as a sub-philosophy, "more or less formulated, more or less conscious," reaching deep down into temperament, not so much "flowing from ideas as determining them." It is the sense of ancient evil, of the mystery of human suffering, of the gulf between aspiration and achievement. It colours the tragic artist's vision of life (his theoretic form) and gives his works their peculiar shade and tone. It speaks, not the language of systematic thought, but through symbolic action, symbol and figure, diction and image, sound and rhythm. Such a recognition should precede any attempt to talk "systematically" about tragedy, while not denying the value of the attempt itself.

Two more comments remain to be made about method. The first is the problem of circular evidence,[5] the use of tragedies to define tragedy. I am assuming that we can talk meaningfully about a body of literature which reveals certain generic qualities and which can be distinguished from the body of literature called comedy, epic, satire, or the literature of pathos. My purpose is to isolate these qualities and to refer to the works themselves as illustrations rather than proof.

The second comment involves the problem of affectivism, which is the problem of catharsis: "This play is a tragedy because it makes me feel thus and so." As Max Scheler puts it, this method would bring us ultimately to the contemplation of our own ego. Thus, I would reverse

[4] *The Tragic Sense of Life,* tr. J. E. C. Flitch, London, 1921, pp. 17–18.
[5] Cf. Max Scheler, "On the Tragic," *Cross Currents,* Winter 1954. This is a selection from Scheler's *Vom Umsturz der Werte,* vol. I (1923), tr. Bernard Stambler.

the order of F. L. Lucas's discussion, which assumes that we must know what tragedy does before we can tell what it is: "We cannot fully discuss the means," Lucas wrote, "until we are clear about the ends." It is true that the usual or "scientific" way is to define natures by effects, which are observable. But rather than found a definition of tragedy on the infinite variables of an audience's reactions, I would consider first the works themselves as the "effects" and look in them for evidences of an efficient cause: a world-view, a form that "underlies the forms we merely practice." What are the generic qualities of these effects? Do they comprise a "form"? I think they do; and for convenience I shall use the term from the start as if I had already proved its legitimacy.

Basic to the tragic form is its recognition of the inevitability of paradox, of unresolved tensions and ambiguities, of opposites in precarious balance. Like the arch, tragedy never rests—or never comes to rest, with all losses restored and sorrows ended. Problems are put and pressed, but not solved. An occasional "happy ending," as in *The Oresteia* or *Crime and Punishment,* does not mean a full resolution. Though there may be intermittences, there is no ultimate discharge in that war. Although this suggests formlessness, as it must in contrast with certain types of religious orthodoxy or philosophical system, it would seem the essence of the tragic form. Surely it is more form than chaos. For out of all these tensions and paradoxes, these feelings, intuitions, insights, there emerges a fairly coherent attitude towards the universe and man. Tragedy makes certain distinguishable and characteristic affirmations, as well as denials, about (I) the cosmos and man's relation to it; (II) the nature of the individual and his relation to himself; (III) the individual in society.

(I) *The tragic cosmos.* In using the term "cosmos" to

signify a theory of the universe and man's relation to it, I have, of course, made a statement about tragedy: that tragedy affirms a cosmos of which man is a meaningful part. To be sure, the characteristic locale of tragedy is not the empyrean. Tragedy is primarily humanistic. Its focus is an event in this world; it is uncommitted as to questions of ultimate destiny, and it is nonreligious in its attitude toward revelation. But it speaks, however vaguely or variously, of an order that transcends time, space and matter.[6] It assumes man's connection with some supersensory or supernatural, or metaphysical being or principle, whether it be the Olympians, Job's Jehovah or the Christian God; Fate, Fortune's Wheel, the "elements" that Lear invoked, or Koestler's "oceanic sense," which comes in so tentatively (and pathetically) at the end of *Darkness at Noon*. The first thing that tragedy says about the cosmos is that, for good or ill, it *is*; and in this respect tragedy's theoretic opposite is naturalism or mechanism. Tragedy is witness (secondly) to the cosmic mystery, to the "wonderful" surrounding our lives; and in literature the opposite of tragedy is not only writing based upon naturalistic theory but also upon the four-square, "probable"[7] world of satire and rationalistic comedy. Finally, what distinguishes tragedy from other forms which bespeak this cosmic sense—for tragedy of course is not unique in this—is its peculiar and intense preoccupation with the *evil* in the universe, whatever it is in the stars that compels, harasses, and bears man down. Tragedy wrestles with the evil of the mystery—and the mystery of the evil. And the contest never ends.

---

[6] Cf. Susan Taubes, "The Nature of Tragedy," *Review of Metaphysics,* December 1953.
[7] The "wonderful" and the "probable" are the basic categories in Albert Cook's distinction between tragedy and comedy. (*The Dark Voyage and the Golden Mean,* Cambridge, Mass., 1949, chap. 1.)

But, paradoxically, its view of the cosmos is what sustains tragedy. Tragedy discerns a principle of goodness that coexists with the evil. This principle need be nothing so pat as The Moral Order, the "armies of unalterable law," and it is nothing so sure as the orthodox Christian God. It is nearer the folk sense that justice exists somewhere in the universe, or what Nietzsche describes as the orgiastic, mystical sense of oneness, of life as "indestructibly powerful and pleasurable." It may be a vision of some transcendent beauty and dignity against which the present evil may be seen as evil and the welter as welter. This is what keeps tragedy from giving up the whole human experiment, and in this respect its opposite is not comedy or satire but cynicism and nihilism, as in Schopenhauer's theory of resignation. The "problem of the good" plays as vital a part in tragedy as the "problem of evil." It provides the living tension without which tragedy ceases to exist.

Thus tragedy contemplates a universe in which man is not the measure of all things. It confronts a mystery. W. Macneile Dixon[8] pointed out that tragedy started as "an affair with the gods"; and the extent to which literature has become "secularized and humanized," he wrote, is a sign of its departure from (to use our present term)

[8] *Tragedy,* London, 1924. The extent of my indebtedness to this book, and to the other discussions of tragedy mentioned in this paper, is poorly indicated by such passing references as this. Since observations on tragedy and the theory of tragedy appear in innumerable discussions of particular authors, eras, and related critical problems, a complete list would be far too cumbersome. Among them would be, surely, the standard work of A. C. Bradley and Willard Farnham on Shakespearean tragedy; C. M. Bowra and Cedric Whitman on Sophocles; W. L. Courtney (*The Idea of Tragedy,* London, 1900); Maxwell Anderson, *The Essence of Tragedy,* Washington, 1939; Northrop Frye, "The Archetypes of Literature," *Kenyon Review,* Winter 1951; Moody Prior, *The Language of Tragedy,* N.Y., 1947; and Herbert Weisinger, *Tragedy and the Paradox of the Fortunate Fall,* Michigan State College Press, 1953, which makes rich use of the archaeological and mythographic studies of the origin of tragedy (Cornford, Harrison, Murray). I am indebted, also, to my colleague Laurence Michel, for frequent conversations and helpful criticism.

the tragic form. While agreeing with him as to the tendency, one may question the wholesale verdict which he implies. The affair with the gods has not, in the minds of all our artists, been reduced to an affair with the social order, or the environment, or the glands. But certainly where it becomes so, the muse of tragedy walks out; the universe loses its mystery and (to invoke catharsis for a moment) its terror.

The terms "pessimism" and "optimism" in the view of the universe as conceived in the tragic form, do not suggest adequate categories, as Nietzsche first pointed out.[9] Tragedy contains them both, goes beyond both, illuminates both, but comes to no conclusion. Tragedy could, it is true, be called pessimistic in its view of the evil in the universe as unremitting and irremediable, the blight man was born for, the necessary condition of existence. It is pessimistic, also, in its view of the overwhelming proportion of evil to good and in its awareness of the mystery of why this should be—the "unfathomable element" in which Ahab foundered. But it is optimistic in what might be called its vitalism, which is in some sense mystical, not earthbound; in its faith in a cosmic good; in its vision, however fleeting, of a world in which all questions could be answered.

(II) *Tragic man.* If the tragic form asserts a cosmos, some order behind the immediate disorder, what does it assert about the nature of man, other than that he is a being capable of cosmic affinities? What is tragic man as he lives and moves on this earth? Can he be distinguished meaningfully from the man of comedy, satire, epic or lyric? How does he differ from "pathetic man" or "religious man"—or from man as conceived by the materialistic psychologies? Tragic man shares some

[9] See also Reinhold Niebuhr, *Beyond Tragedy,* London, 1938.

qualities, of course, with each of these. I shall stress differences in the appropriate contexts.

Like the cosmos which he views, tragic man is a paradox and a mystery. He is no child of God; yet he feels himself more than a child of earth. He is not the plaything of Fate, but he is not entirely free. He is "both creature and creator" (in Niebuhr's phrase)—"fatefully free and freely fated" (in George Schrader's). He recognizes "the fact of guilt" while cherishing the "dream of innocence" (Fiedler), and he never fully abandons either position. He is plagued by the ambiguity of his own nature and of the world he lives in. He is torn between the sense in common sense (which is the norm of satire and rationalistic, or corrective, comedy) and his own uncommon sense. Aware of the just but irreconcilable claims within and without, he is conscious of the immorality of his own morality and suffers in the knowledge of his own recalcitrance.

The dynamic of this recalcitrance is pride. It sustains his belief, however humbled he may become by later experience, in his own freedom, in his innocence, and in his uncommon sense. Tragic man is man at his most prideful and independent, man glorying in his humanity. Tragic pride, like everything else about tragedy, is ambiguous; it can be tainted with arrogance and have its petty side; but it is not to be equated with sin or weakness. The Greeks feared it when it threatened the gods or slipped into arrogance, but they honoured it and even worshipped it in their heroes. It was the common folk, the chorus, who had no pride, or were "flawless."[10] The chorus invariably argue against pride, urging caution and moderation, because they know it leads to suffering; but tragedy as such does not prejudge it.

---

[10]Cf. Arthur Miller, "Tragedy and the Common Man," *New York Times,* February 27th, 1949.

While many of these things, again, might be said of other than tragic man, it is in the peculiar nature of his suffering, and in his capacity for suffering and appropriating his suffering, that his distinguishing quality lies. For instance (to ring changes on the Cartesian formula), tragic man would not define himself, like the man of corrective comedy or satire, "I think, therefore I am"; nor like the man of achievement (epic): "I act, or conquer, therefore I am"; nor like the man of sensibility (lyric): "I feel, therefore I am"; nor like the religious man: "I believe, therefore I am." Although he has all these qualities (of thought, achievement, sensibility, and belief) in various forms and degrees, the essence of his nature is brought out by suffering: "I suffer, I will to suffer, I learn by suffering; therefore I am." The classic statement, of course, is Aeschylus's: "Wisdom comes alone through suffering" (Lattimore's translation); perhaps the most radical is Dostoevski's: "Suffering is the sole origin of consciousness."[11]

This is not to say that only tragic man suffers or that he who suffers is tragic. Saints and martyrs suffer and learn by suffering; Odysseus suffered and learned; Dante suffered and learned on his journey with Virgil. But tragic man, I think, is distinguishable from these others in the nature of his suffering as conditioned by its source and locus, in its characteristic course and consequences (that is, the ultimate disaster and the "knowledge" it leads to), and in his intense preoccupation with his own suffering.

But to consider these matters in turn and to illustrate them briefly:

I have already suggested the main sources and locus of tragic man's suffering. He suffers because he is more

[11] *Notes from Underground,* tr. B. G. Guerney.

than usually sensitive to the "terrible disrelations" he
sees about him and experiences in himself. He is more
than usually aware of the mighty opposites in the universe and in man, of the gulf between desire and fulfil-
ment, between what is and what should be. This kind
of suffering is suffering on a high level, beyond the
reach of the immature or brutish, and forever closed
to the extreme optimist, the extreme pessimist,[12] or
the merely indifferent. It was Job on the ash heap, the
prototype of tragic man, who was first struck by the
incongruity between Jehovah's nature and His actions,
between desert and reward in this life; and it was he
who first asked, not so much for a release from physical
suffering as a reasonable explanation of it. But above
all, the source of tragic suffering is the sense, in the
consciousness of tragic man, of simultaneous guilt and
guiltlessness. Tillich called tragedy "a mixture of guilt
and necessity." If tragic man could say, "I sinned, therefore I suffer" or "He (or They or God) sinned, therefore I suffer," his problem would be resolved, and the
peculiar poignancy of his suffering would be removed.
If he felt himself entirely free or entirely determined,
he would cease to be tragic. But he is neither—he is,
in short, a paradox and mystery, the "riddle of the
world."

To draw further distinctions: The element of guilt in
tragic suffering distinguishes it from the pathetic suffering of the guiltless and from the suffering of the
sentimentalist's bleeding heart. On the other hand,
tragic man's sense of fate, and of the mystery of fate,
distinguishes his suffering from the suffering (which is
little more than embarrassment) of the man of corrective comedy and satire. The suffering of the epic hero

[12]Cf. William Van O'Connor, *Climates of Tragedy,* Baton Rouge, La., 1943.

has little of the element of bafflement or enigma; it is
not, characteristically, spiritual suffering. The Christian
in his suffering can confess *total* guilt and look to the
promise of redemption through grace.[13] The martyr
seeks suffering, accepts it gladly, "glories in tribulation."
Tragic man knows nothing of grace and never glories in
his suffering. Although he may come to acquiesce in it
partly and "learn" from it (a stage I shall discuss below),
his characteristic mood is resentment and dogged en-
durance. He has not the stoic's patience, although this
may be part of what he learns. Characteristically, he is
restless, intense, probing and questioning the universe
and his own soul (Job, Lear, Ahab). It is true that, from
Greek tragedy to tragedy written in the Christian era
(Shakespeare and beyond) emphasis shifts from the
universe to the soul, from the cosmic to the psychological. But Prometheus had an inner life; Antigone, for all
her composure, suffered an ultimate doubt; Oedipus
suffered spiritually as he grew to understand the dark
ambiguities in his own nature. And we should be mistaken if we tried to interpret the divine powers in the
plays of Shakespeare simply as "allegorical symbols for
psychological realities."[14]

Tragic man, then, placed in a universe of irreconcil-
ables, acting in a situation in which he is both innocent
and guilty, and peculiarly sensitive to the "cursèd spite"
of his condition, suffers. What in the tragic view is the
characteristic course of this suffering and what further
aspects of tragic man are revealed by it? The tragic form
develops, not only the partial outlines of a cosmology
and a psychology, but of an ethic.

(III) *Tragic man and society.* The tragic sufferer may

[13]Cf. Karl Jaspers, *Tragedy Is Not Enough,* tr. Reiche, Moore, Deutsch; Boston,
1952.
[14]Susan Taubes, op. cit., p. 196.

now be viewed in his social and moral relationships. In the tragic world there are several alternatives. A man can default from the human condition—"Curse God and die"—and bring his suffering to an end: he can endure and be silent; he can turn cynic. Tragic man understands these alternatives, feels their attractions, but chooses a different way. Rising in his pride, he protests: he pits himself in some way against whatever, in the heavens above and in the earth beneath, seems to him to be wrong, oppressive, or personally thwarting. This is the hero's commitment, made early or late, but involving him necessarily in society and in action—with Prometheus and Antigone early, with Hamlet late. What to the orthodox mind would appear to be the wisdom or folly, the goodness or badness, of the commitment is not, in the beginning, the essence of the matter. In the first phase of his course of suffering, the hero's position may be anarchic, individual, romantic. Herein tragedy tests all norms—as, by contrast, satire,[15] comedy, or epic tend to confirm them. The commitment may even be expressed in what society knows as a crime, but, as with tragic pride (of which the commitment is in part the expression) tragedy does not prejudge it. Thus it is said that tragedy studies "the great offenders," and Dostoevski sought among criminals and outcasts for his greatest spiritual discoveries. But the commitment must grow in meaning to include the more-than-personal. Ultimately, and ideally, the tragic hero stands as universal man, speaking for all men. The tragic sufferer, emerging from his early stage of lament or rebellion (Job's opening speech; the first scenes of Prometheus; Lear's early bursts of temper), moves beyond the "intermittences" of

---

[15]Cf. Maynard Mack, "The Muse of Satire," *Yale Review,* Spring 1952.

his own heart and makes a "pact with the world that is unremitting and sealed."[16]

Since the commitment cannot lead in the direction of escape or compromise, it must involve head-on collision with the forces that would oppress or frustrate. Conscious of the ambiguities without and within, which are the source of his peculiar suffering, tragic man accepts the conflict. It is horrible to do it, he says, but it is more horrible to leave it undone. He is now in the main phase of his suffering—the "passion."[17]

In his passion he differs from the rebel, who would merely smash; or the romantic hero, who is not conscious of guilt; or the epic hero, who deals with emergencies rather than dilemmas. Odysseus and Aeneas, to be sure, face moral problems, but they proceed in a clear ethical light. Their social norms are secure. But the tragic hero sees a sudden, unexpected evil at the heart of things that infects all things. His secure and settled world has gone wrong, and he must oppose his own ambiguous nature against what he loves. Doing so involves total risk, as the chorus and his friends remind him. He may brood and pause, like Hamlet, or he may proceed with Ahab's fury; but proceed he must.

He proceeds, suffers, and in his suffering "learns." This is the phase of "perception." Although it often culminates in a single apocalyptic scene, a moment of "recognition," as in *Oedipus* and *Othello,* it need not be separate in time from the passion phase. Rather, perception is all that can be summed up in the spiritual and

[16]Wallace Fowlie, "Swann and Hamlet: A Note on the Contemporary Hero," *Partisan Review,* 1942.
[17]Cf. Francis Fergusson, *The Idea of a Theatre,* Princeton, N.J., 1949, chap. 1, "The Tragic Rhythm of Action." Fergusson translates Kenneth Burke's formulation "*Poiema, Pathema, Mathema*" into "Purpose, Passion, Perception." (See *A Grammar of Motives,* pp. 38ff.) Cf. also Susan Taubes, op. cit., p. 199.

moral change that the hero undergoes from first to last and in the similar change wrought by his actions or by his example in those about him.

For the hero, perception may involve an all-but-complete transformation in character, as with Lear and Oedipus; or a gradual development in poise and self-mastery (Prometheus, Hamlet); or the softening and humanizing of the hard outlines of a character like Antigone's. It may appear in the hero's change from moody isolation and self-pity to a sense of his sharing in the general human condition, of his responsibility for it and to it. This was one stage in Lear's pilgrimage ("I have ta'en too little care of this") and as far as Dostoevski's Dmitri Karamazov ever got. In all the manifestations of this perception there is an element of Hamlet's "readiness," of an acceptance of destiny that is not merely resignation. At its most luminous it is Lear's and Oedipus's hard-won humility and new understanding of love. It may transform or merely inform, but a change there must be.

And it is more, of course, than merely a moral change, just as the hero's problem is always more than a moral one. His affair is still with the gods. In taking up arms against the ancient cosmic evil, he transcends the human situation, mediating between the human and the divine. It was Orestes's suffering that, in the end, made the heavens more just. In the defeat or death which is the usual lot of the tragic hero, he becomes a citizen of a larger city, still defiant but in a new mood, a "calm of mind," a partial acquiescence. Having at first resented his destiny, he has lived it out, found unexpected meanings in it, carried his case to a more-than-human tribunal. He sees his own destiny, and man's destiny, in its ultimate perspective.

But the perception which completes the tragic form

is not dramatized solely through the hero's change, although his pilgrimage provides the traditional tragic structure.[18] The full nature and extent of the new vision is measured also by what happens to the other figures in the total symbolic situation—to the hero's antagonists (King Creon, Claudius, Iago); to his opposites (the trimmers and hangers-on, the Osrics); to his approximates (Ismene, Horatio, Kent, the Chorus). Some he moves, some do not change at all. But his suffering must make a difference somewhere outside himself. After Antigone's death the community (even Creon) re-forms around her; the "new acquist" at the end of *Samson Agonistes* is the common note, also, at the end of the Shakespearean tragedies. For the lookers-on there is no sudden rending of the veil of clay, no triumphant assertion of The Moral Order. There has been suffering and disaster, ultimate and irredeemable loss, and there is promise of more to come. But all who are involved have been witness to new revelations about human existence, the evil of evil and the goodness of good. They are more "ready." The same old paradoxes and ambiguities remain, but for the moment they are transcended in the higher vision.

[18]Indeed, it has been pointed out that, in an age when the symbol of the hero as the dominating centre of the play seems to have lost its validity with artist and audience, the role is taken over by the artist himself, who is his own tragic hero. That is, "perception" is conveyed more generally, in the total movement of the piece and through all the parts. The "pact with the world" and the suffering are not objectified in a hero's ordeal but seem peculiarly the author's. This quality has been noted in Joyce's *Ulysses*; Berdiaev saw it in Dostoevski; Hardy, Conrad, Faulkner are examples that come to mind. At any rate, the distinction may be useful in determining matters of tone, although it is not clear-cut, as distinctions in tone seldom are. But it is one way of pointing to the difference between the tragic tone and the Olympian distance of Meredithian comedy, the harmony of the final phase of Dantesque comedy, or the ironic detachment of satire. Nietzsche spoke of the difference between the Dionysian (or tragic) artist and "the poet of the dramatized epos . . . the calm, unmoved embodiment of Contemplation, whose wide eyes see the picture before them." (*Birth of Tragedy* in *Works*, ed. O. Levy, Edinburgh and London, 1909, III, p. 96.)

G. K. Hunter
Five-Act Structure in *Doctor Faustus*

The original and substantive texts of Marlowe's *Doctor Faustus* (the Quartos of 1604 and 1616) present the play completely without the punctuation of act division or scene enumeration. This is common enough in the play-texts of the period. Indeed it is much the commonest form in plays written for the public theatres.[1] Shakespeare's *Henry V* and *Pericles* are without divisions in their quarto texts, but we know that they were written with a five-act structure in mind—the choruses tell us that.

What is exceptional in the textual history of *Doctor Faustus* is not the lack of division in the original texts; it is rather the reluctance of modern editors to impose an act-structure on the modern texts. This is curious, but it seems possible to discern why the reluctance exists and a survey of the modern editions of *Faustus* throws some interesting light on critical attitudes to the subject matter of the play.

Marlowe (like other Elizabethan dramatists) was "re-discovered" by the educated English public in an atmo-

First published in the *Tulane Drama Review*, Vol. 8, No. 4 (T24 Summer 1964). Copyright © 1964, *Tulane Drama Review*; Copyright © 1967, *The Drama Review*. Reprinted by permission of the publisher and author.
[1]W. T. Jewkes notes that "of the 134 plays written for the public stage [*and printed before 1616*], 30 are divided, as against 104 undivided." (*Act division in Elizabethan and Jacobean Plays, 1583–1616,* [Hamden, Conn.: 1958], p. 96.)

sphere which played down his specifically dramatic and theatrical powers. Charles Lamb's *Specimens of the English dramatic poets who lived about the time of Shakespeare* (1808) established him primarily as a poet. This, as I say, did not distinguish him from other dramatists of the period. But the attitudes implied by Lamb's volume were more difficult to shake off in the case of *Doctor Faustus* than in other Elizabethan plays; for here they were reinforced, later in the century, by a second wave of anti-theatrical (or at least a-theatrical) influence. In 1887 the young Havelock Ellis (then a medical student) suggested to Henry Vizetelly, well known in "advanced" circles as a courageous though rather *risqué* publisher, that he should put out a series of unexpurgated (key word!) texts of the Elizabethan dramatists—the famous "Mermaid" series. The *Marlowe,* the first volume in the series, was edited by Ellis himself, and may be taken as a manifesto of the whole new movement. It bore proudly on the title-page the legend *Unexpurgated,* not simply because the usual casual indecencies of clown conversations were preserved, but rather because an appendix carried the full testimony of the informer Richard Baines "concernynge [Marlowe's] damnable opinions and judgment of Religion and scorne of Gods worde," to which Ellis added the even more offensive comment that such "damnable opinions . . . have, without exception, been substantially held, more or less widely, by students of science and the Bible in our own days." To say this of remarks like "Moses was but a juggler," "that Christ better deserved to die than Barabas," etc., was to push Marlowe into the front line of the late Victorian battle against bourgeois values. Marlowe appears as a social rebel and religious freethinker (like Ellis himself) and this comes to reinforce the earlier view that he was primarily a poet. The two attitudes join together, in fact, to suggest that he was a poet *because* he was a free-thinker, rejecting social conventions in order to achieve his individual and personal vision. He becomes the morning-star of the nineties, a harder and more gemlike Oscar Wilde.

In order to preserve the image of Marlowe as a cult-figure of this kind it is necessary to discount the theatrical, and so popular, provenance of his work. If he was the laureate of the atheistical imagination, he must have stood at a considerable distance from his rudely Christian audience; and this assumption presses especially heavily upon *Doctor Faustus*, whose hero is himself a freethinker and (by implication at least) a poet. It is not surprising therefore to find Ellis saying in his headnote to *Faustus*: "I have retained the excellent plan introduced by Professor Ward and adopted by Mr. Bullen, of dividing the play into scenes only; it is a dramatic poem rather than a regular drama." In the face of this critical assurance, and with the *Zeitgeist* exerting the kind of pressure that I have described, the earlier editorial practice of presenting the play in five acts, derived from the 1663 Quarto by Robinson (1826) and continued in Cunningham (1870), Wagner (1877), and Morley (1883), withered away. It was not until the bibliographical breakthrough[2] of Boas, Kirschbaum, and Greg (1932, 1946, 1950) that the play reappeared in the five-act form.

---

[2] I mean the perception that the 1616 text must be the basis of any modern recension. In this text the nature of the structure is much clearer; and it was, in fact, the reading of Greg's *editio minor* that first made clear to me the precision with which the play moved. Greg himself, however, hedges his bets. He finds the act division "convenient in discussing the construction of the play" (parallel text edition, p. 153) and so presents it to the reader; but he confides to us in a footnote that "I see no reason to suppose that any act division was originally contemplated" (p. 153 n.5). His argument is that there is too great a disproportion between the numbers of lines to be found in the different acts for these to make just divisions. A rereading of *The Winter's Tale*, in which Act 4 is two and a half times as long as Act 3, ought to convince us of the insignificance of this mode of assessment.

Even after their labors the old attitudes persist. The edition by Kocher (1950) is divided into scenes only, and the recent replacement of Boas by the "Revels" edition of J. D. Jump (1962) avoids the act divisions: "Neither A1 [1604] nor B1 [1616] makes any attempt to divide the play into acts and scenes, so no such distribution is given prominence in the present edition" (xxxv). It may be sufficient reply to this to quote the recent comment of W. T. Jewkes, who has analyzed the act structure of all the plays in the period:

> The plays of the "University wits," however, appear both undivided and divided. On a closer inspection it was evident that the clearly divided texts from this group were those which showed least sign of playhouse annotation, while those which retained fragmentary division, or none at all, showed signs of adaptation for performance. It is evident then that these dramatists divided their plays originally, but that adaptation for the stage resulted in either the total or partial loss of act headings.[3]

This argument might well be augmented, in the particular case of *Doctor Faustus,* by reference to the choruses which mark the beginnings of some of the acts, or by repeating Boas' observations about the material taken from the Faustbook. But it is not my purpose here to argue the textual or theatrical probability that *Faustus* is in five-act form. I rather wish to look at the developing movement of the play to see if the act divisions accepted by Boas and others correspond to anything in the inner economy of the work, marking progressive stages in an organized advance through the material. Since Goethe remarked, "How greatly is it all planned" in 1829,[4] many

[3]*Op. cit.,* p. 97.
[4]Recorded in the *Diary* of H. Crabb Robinson, for 2nd August, 1829.

have been found to repeat his encomium, but few to jus-
tify it. I would suggest that the play *is* planned greatly,
even precisely, in five clear stages (or acts), moving forward continuously in a single direction. I am assuming,
when I say this, that the text as we have it in the 1616
Quarto is the product of a unified organizing intelligence. Marlowe *may* have had a collaborator, but I do
not believe that we can detect his work—and a stroke of
Occam's razor makes him disappear.

The first point I should like to make is that the action
(I deal only with the main plot at the moment) moves
through clearly separable stages. Act 1 is concerned (as
is usual) with setting up the situation and introducing
the principal characters. Here we learn the nature of
Faustus' desires, set against the limiting factor of his nature; we meet Mephostophilis and the contrast between
the two is made evident. Act 2 begins with a prelimi-
nary reminder (found before each act of the play) of the
stage at which the action has arrived:

> Now, Faustus, must thou needs be damned;
> Canst thou not be saved!
> What boots it then to think on God or heaven?
>
> (2.1.1–3)

In Act 1, the temptation to think of heaven is hardly
present; but the subject here announced is the warp on
which much of the main-plot action of Act 2 is woven.
The conflict is entered upon in real earnest. The introductory note to Act 3 is more obvious, being handled
by the "Chorus." He tells us that "Learned Faustus,"
having searched into the secrets of Astronomy, now is
gone to prove Cosmography. He is in fact completing his
Grand Tour when we meet him, having taken in Paris,
Mainz, Naples, Venice, and Padua, and is newly arrived

in Rome, "Queen of the Earth" as Milton calls it,[5] and the summation of worldly grandeur. Mephostophilis describes the sights, and then conducts his master into the highest social circles in the city, and so in the world.

Act 3 is spent in Rome; Act 4 in the courts of Germany. The introductory Chorus makes clear the distinction between "the view/Of rarest things" which is the substance of Act 3 and the "trial of his art" which is what we are to see in Act 4. The introductory speech to Act 5 is spoken by Wagner, Faustus' servant, who is confused in one text with the Chorus, and who is exercising here what is clearly a choric function. His first line marks the change of key: "I think my master means to die shortly." Act 5 is concerned with preparations and prevarications in the face of death.

It is obvious enough, I suggest, that each act handles a separate stage in Faustus' career. But it is not obvious from what I have said that the stages move forward in any single and significant line of development. To see that they do requires a fairly laborious retracing of the action, seen now in the light of what was more obvious to Marlowe and his audience than to us—the supposed hierarchy of studies.

The opening lines of the play show us Faustus trying to *settle his studies*; the opening speech, with this aim in mind, moves in an orthodox direction through the academic disciplines, beginning with logic, here representative of the whole undergraduate course of Liberal Arts, through the *Noble Sciences* of Medicine and Law and so to the *Queen of Sciences*, Divinity. So far, the movement has been, as I say, completely orthodox, and a frame of reference has been neatly established. But, having

[5] Cf. William Thomas, who calls Rome "the onelie jewell, myrrour, maistres, and beautie of the worlde" (*Historie of Italie* [1549]).

reached Divinity, Faustus still hopes to advance, and can only do so in reverse:

> ... Divinity, adieu!
> These metaphysics of magicians
> And negromantic books are heavenly.[6]
>
>   (1.1.46–48)

At this point he passes, as it were, through the looking glass; he goes on trying to evaluate experience, but his words of value (like "heavenly") now mean the opposite of what they should. The "profit and delight ... power ... honor ... omnipotence" that he promises himself through the practice of magic are all devalued in advance. By embracing negromancy he ensures that worthwhile ends cannot be reached; and the rest of the play is a demonstration of this, moving as it does in a steadily downward direction.

The route taken by Faustus in his descent through human activities was, I think, intended to be easily understood by the original audience, and again I suggest that it is the structure of knowledge as at that time understood that provides the key. Divinity was, as I have noted, the "Queen of the Sciences." Not only so, but it was the discipline which gave meaning to all other knowledge and experience. Hugh of St. Victor expresses the idea succinctly: "all the natural arts serve divine science, and the lower order leads to the higher."[7] In Marlowe's own day the same point is made, more elaborately, in the popular *French Academy* of La Primaudaye:

---

[6]I preserve the original form *negromantic,* though most modernizing editors change it to *necromantic.* This seems to me to be a greater change than is warranted by a licence to modernize. It is the "black art" in general that Faustus is welcoming, not the power to raise the dead.

[7]*De Sacramentis* (Prologue), in Migne's *Patrologia Latina* Vol. CLXXVI, col. 185.

What would it availe or profit us to have and at-
taine unto the knowledge and understanding of all
humane and morall Philosophy, Logicke, Phisicke,
Metaphisicke, and Mathematick . . . not to bee ignorant of any thing, which the liberall arts and sciences
teach us, therewith to content the curious minds of
men and by that means to give them a tast, and to
make them enjoy some kind of transitory good in
this life: and in the meane time to be altogether and
wholy ignorant, or badly instructed, in the true and
onely science of divine Philosophy, whereat all the
rest ought to aime.

(Preface to Book IV)

But if one rejects the final cause here supposed, what
happens to the rest of knowledge? This is the question
that the play asks and pursues. In what direction does
the Icarus of learning fall when he abandons the orthodox methods of flight? The order of topics in the medieval encyclopaedias gives one some clue here. These
regularly begin with God and divine matters. Vincent of
Beauvais' *Speculum* starts from the Creator, then moves
to "the empyrean heaven and the nature of angels," then
to "the formless material and the making of the world;
the nature and the properties of things created," then
to the human state and its ramifications. The *De Rerum
Natura* attributed to Bede and William of Conches'
Philosophia Mundi[8] have the same four-book order.
Book I deals with God; Book II with the heavens; Book
III with the lower atmosphere; Book IV with the earth,
so down to man and his human activities. The *Proem* to
Book IV (identical in both works) gives a fair indication
of the nature of the movement assumed:

[8]The first is to be found in *Patrologia Latina* XC, cols. 1127 ff., and the second (attributed to Honorius Augustodunensis) in vol. CLXXII, cols. 39 ff. I am indebted
to Dr. Hans Liebeschütz for pointing these out to me.

The series of books which began with the First Cause has now descended to The Earth, not catering for itching ears nor loitering in the minds of fools, but dealing with what is useful to the reader. For now is that verse fulfilled: "For the time will come when they will not endure sound doctrine; but after their own lusts shall they heap to themselves teachers, having itching ears." (2 Timothy, IV, 3). But since the mind of the honest man does not turn after wickedness, but conforms itself to the better way, let us turn to the remaining subjects, in the interest of a mind of this kind, estranged from wickedness and conformable to virtue.

In Marlowe's own day this order of topics appeared in works as popular as the Baldwin-Palfreyman *Treatise of Moral Philosophy* (innumerable editions from 1557 to 1640), in Palfreyman's companion *Treatise of Heavenly Philosophy,* and in William Vaughan's *The Golden Grove* (1600; 1608). *The French Academy,* which Marlowe has been supposed to have known, uses the same organization of topics but treats them in reverse order, upwards from (1) "the institution of manners and callings of all estates," through (2) "concerning the soule and body of man," and (3) "a notable description of the whole world ... Angels ... the foure elements ... fowles, fishes, beasts ... etc." to (4) "Christian philosophy, instructing the true and onely meanes to eternal life." It seems reasonable to suppose that Marlowe knew this system of knowledge; and it is my assertion that he used it to plan the relationship of the parts of *Doctor Faustus.*

When Faustus has signed away his soul, the first fruits of his new "power ... honor ... omnipotence" appear in the knowledge of astronomy that he seeks. Astronomy is a heavenly art, no doubt—it appears early in the encyclopaedias—but it is one that is not obviously dependent on divinity. Yet here it leads by the natural process

that the encyclopaedists describe to the question of first
cause. If the heavens involve more than the tedium of
mechanics ("these slender questions Wagner can decide") then astronomy leads straight back to the funda-
mental question: Who made the world? But, under the
conditions of knowledge that Faustus has embraced, this
basic question cannot be answered, for it is "against our
kingdom." The trap closes on the pseudo-scholar and
forces him backwards and downwards.

This is the movement—backwards into ever more
superficial shallows of knowledge and experience—
which continues inexorably throughout the whole play,
as it must, given the initial choice. Balked in Act 2 from
the full pursuit of astronomy, in Act 3 Faustus turns to
cosmography, from the heavens to the earth. But the
charms of sightseeing pall, and a magical entrée even to
the "best" society in the world involves only a tediously
superficial contact. Marlowe's age had serious doubts
about the importance of cosmography (or geography)
as an object of human endeavor. *The French Academy*
treats it under the heading of "curiosity and novelty," as
a destructively unserious pursuit. The drop in the status
of Faustus' activities is nicely caught by the change of
tone between the Chorus at the beginning of Act 3 and
that introducing Act 4. The first tells us that

> Learnèd Faustus,
> To find the secrets of astronomy
> Graven in the book of Jove's high firmament,
> Did mount him up to scale Olympus' top.

> (3.Prol.1–4)

We seem here still to be dealing with a genuine search
for knowledge. But in the second chorus we hear only
that:

When Faustus had *with pleasure*[9] ta'en the view
Of rarest things and royal courts of kings,
He stayed his course and so returnèd home
                                        (4.Prol.1–3)

The emphasis is no longer on the search after knowledge, with discovery, presumably, as the aimed-for end,
but with what is more appropriate to the diabolical
premise ("that is not against our kingdom"), with pleasure taken and then given up, without reaching forward
to the final causes. Faustus' merry japes among the cardinals are enjoyed by the protagonist, and are clearly
meant to be enjoyed by the audience; but nothing more
than pleasure is involved, and given the giant pretensions of the first act, the omission is bound to be a factor
in our view of the Roman scenes.

Faustus not only views Rome. He also dabbles in
statecraft, rescuing the Antipope Bruno and transport-
ing him back to his supporters in Germany. The step
from cosmography to statecraft is similar to that from
astronomy to cosmography. In each case we have a reduction in the area covered, an increasing remoteness
from first causes. The panoply of state is not here (as it
usually is in Shakespeare) an awesome and a righteous
thing. It is not approached through the lives of those
who must live and suffer inside the system, but via the
structure of knowledge, so that it is the relationship to
divinity rather than the power over individual lives that
is the determining factor in our attitude. The ludicrous
antics at the papal court have usually been seen as a
simple piece of Protestant propaganda, pleasing to the
groundlings and inserted for no better reason. Yet one
can see that this episode (placed where it is) has its own

[9]My italics.

unique part to play in the total economy of the work. It is proper to start Faustus' descent through the world from the highest point, in Rome; it is equally proper to begin his social and political descent with the Vicar of Christ (and so down to Emperor, to Duke, and back to private life). By turning the conduct of the papal court into farce Marlowe devalues *all* sovereignty and political activity in advance. Bruno (and his tiara) are saved; but there is no suggestion that *he* has any more virtue to recommend him; he has no real function in the play except to reduce the title and state of the Pope to a mere name.

There is no suggestion in this act that Faustus himself is aware of the startling discrepancy between the actual happenings and the promises he made to himself (and to us) at the beginning of the play. The audience, however, can hardly forget so soon; and our memory is reinforced in the papal palace by the ritual threats of damnation uttered by the Pope and friars. It is no doubt comic that the Pope should be boxed on the ear and exclaim, "Damn'd be this soul for ever for this deed," but we should not fail to notice the sinister echo reverberating behind the horseplay; the curse is comic at this point, but sinister in the context of the whole action.

Act 4 carries the descent of Faustus one more clear step, by still further reducing the importance of the area in which he operates. I have mentioned the social descent to the secular courts of Emperor and Duke of Vanholt. At the same time there is a descent in terms of the kind of activity that the magic procures. Faustus' anti-papal activities can be seen as political action of a kind, and this aspect would be more obvious to the Elizabethans than it is to us (involved, as they were, in the kind of struggle depicted). But in Act 4 he is presented quite frankly as a court entertainer or hired conjurer. In the court of Charles V, of course, there is still some intellectual dignity in his activities. Charles's longing, to see "that famous conqueror, Great Alexander, and his paramour," is a kingly interest in a paragon of kingship. But when Faustus goes on to the court of the Duke of Vanholt he is reduced to satisfying nothing more dignified than the pregnant "longings" of the duchess for out-of-season grapes. At the same time his side activities are brought down by a parallel route. At the court of the Emperor he was matched against the disbelieving knights, Frederick, Benvolio, etc.; at Vanholt his opponents are clowns, the Horse-courser, the Hostess.[10]

The last act of *Faustus* is often thought of as involving restoration of dignity and brilliance to the sadly tarnished magician. In terms of poetic power there is something to be said on this side; but the poetry that Faustus is given in this act serves to do more than simply glorify the speaker. The fiery brilliance of the Helen speech is lit by the Fire of Hell (as has been pointed out by Kirschbaum[11] and others). The imminence of eternal damnation gives strength and urgency to the action, but the actions that Faustus himself can initiate are as trivial and as restricted as one would expect, given the moral development that I have described as operating throughout the rest of the play. There is no change of direction. In Acts 3 and 4 we saw Faustus sink steadily from political intrigue at the Curia to fruit-fetching for a longing duchess. The last act shows a consistent extension of this movement. It picks up the role of Faustus as entertainer, but reduces the area of its exercise still further; it is now confined to the enjoyment of some "two or three" pri-

[10]I find that this general point has been made by Kirschbaum in his paperback *The Plays of Christopher Marlowe* (New York: Meridian, 1962): "Surely Marlowe means to stress the magician's continuing degradation by showing him first playing his tricks with the spiritual head of all Roman Christendom and then ultimately declining, to play them with the clowns" (p. 119).
[11]"Marlowe's Faustus: a Reconsideration," *R.E.S.* XIX (1943).

vate friends, and as an epilogue to what Wagner charac-
terizes by "banquet ... carouse ... swill ... belly-cheer."
Helen appears, in short, at the point where one might
have expected dancing-girls.

The nature of the object conjured in Act 5, no less
than the occasion of the conjuring, shows the same logical development of the movement in the preceding acts.
Charles V had longed to satisfy an intellectual interest;
the Duchess of Vanholt longed for the satisfaction of
a carnal but perfectly natural appetite; but the desire
to view Helen of Troy is both carnal and (as the ironic
word *blessed* should warn us) reprehensible, and leads
logically to the further and final depravity of:

> One thing, good servant, let me crave of thee
> To glut the longing of my heart's desire:
> That I may have unto my paramour
> That heavenly Helen which I saw of late,
> Whose sweet embraces may extinguish clear
> Those thoughts that do dissuade me from my vow,
> And keep mine oath I made to Lucifer.
>
> (5.1.87–93)

The circle in which Faustus conjures has now shrunk
from the *urbs et orbis* of Rome to the smallest circle of
all—that which contains only himself. When the dream
of power was lost, the gift of entertainment remained;
but even this has now faded. The conjuring here exists for an exclusively self-interested and clearly damnable purpose. The loneliness of the damned, summed
up in Mephostophilis' cryptic "*Solamen miseris socios
habuisse doloris,*" this now is clearly Faustus' lot. Left
alone with himself and the mirror of his own damnation[12] in Helen ("Her lips suck forth my soul: see where

[12]See W. W. Greg, "The Damnation of Faustus," *M.L.R.* XLI (1946).

it flies"), he is in a situation that cannot be reached by either the Old Man or the students. His descent has taken him below the reach of human aid; and there is a certain terrible splendor in this, as the poetry conveys, but the moral level of this splendor is never in doubt; it is something that the whole weight of the play's momentum presses on our attention, moving steadily as it does, through the clearly defined stages of its act-structure, away from the deluded dream of power and knowledge and downward, inevitably, coherently, and logically, into the sordid reality of damnation.

I have sought to show that the movement of the main plot of *Faustus* is controlled and splendidly meaningful. It moves in a single direction (downwards) through a series of definite stages which it would be wilfully obscurantist not to call acts. Indeed it conforms, by and large, to the strict form of five-act structure which was taught in Tudor grammar schools, out of the example of Terence. The structural paradigm was, of course, concerned with comedy, and especially the comedy of intrigue, and could not be applied very exactly to a moralistic tragedy like *Faustus*. But it is easy to see that Act 1 of *Faustus* gives us the introductory materials, Act 2 the first moves in the central conflict (Faustus versus the Devil), Acts 3 and 4 the swaying back and forward of this conflict, and Act 5 the catastrophe.

What is more, these stages of the main plot are reinforced or underlined by a parallel movement going on simultaneously in the subplot. The general relation between the two levels of the plot, the level of spiritual struggle and that of carnal opportunism, is one of parody—a mode of connection that was common in the period. And I should state that by "parody" I do not mean the feeble modern reduction of characteristics to caricature, but rather that multiple presentation of serious themes[13] which relates them both to the man of affairs and to the light-minded clown.

It is not only in the detail of individual scenes that the subplot parodies the main plot: the whole movement of the subplot mirrors that social and intellectual descent that I have traced in the career of Faustus. The first subplot scene concerns Wagner, a man close to Faustus himself. The second comic scene involves Wagner and *his* servants, Robin and Dick. The third and subsequent scenes show Robin and Dick by themselves, Wagner having disappeared (he reappears—though not as part of the subplot—in 5.1). It has been argued that this very descent, and the disappearance of Wagner, "suggests a different hand" [*not Marlowe's*] for the Robin and Dick scenes.[14] This provides an interesting parallel to the assumption that Marlowe cannot be responsible for the main plot scenes in the middle of the play. At both levels the action descends to trivialities, and the critics close their eyes in dissent. But if the movement is deliberate at one level it seems likely that it is so at the other level also.

Even more impressive than this general movement in the subplot is the accumulation of details in which the action of the subplot scene mirrors that of the contiguous main plot. Thus Act 1, scene one shows us Faustus using his virtuosity in logic to deceive himself. Scene two shows us Wagner as no less able to chop logic and so to avoid the plain meaning of words. As a development from this we see Faustus raising Mephostophilis and arranging that he should be his servant. The following scene shows us Wagner trying to control Robin, who

---

[13]See G. K. Hunter, *John Lyly* (Cambridge: Harvard University Press, 1962), pp. 135–40. The significance of the parody in *Faustus* is denied by Jump (*op. cit.* lix–lx).
[14]*Doctor Faustus,* ed. F. S. Boas (London: Methuen, 1932), p. 27.

would not "give his soul to the devil for a shoulder of mutton," unless it were "well roasted, and good sauce to it, if I pay so dear." Wagner too has learned how to raise spirits and makes Robin his servant by a parody compact, promising to teach him "to turn thyself to a dog, or a cat, or a mouse, or a rat, or anything." It may be noted that the general effect of this and the preceding comic scene is to reduce in status and to "place" for us Faustus' pretensions to have conquered a new art by the force of his learning, and to have gained important new powers. When such as Wagner can raise Banio and Belcher, and all for the sake of terrifying Robin, then neither the means nor the ends of magic can be considered sufficient, by themselves, to make the magician a hero.

In Act 2, scenes one and two, Faustus signs his pact with the Devil and has the first fruits of his "new" knowledge. In scene three we meet Robin again. The power of raising spirits has declined from Faustus' servant Wagner to Wagner's servant, Robin. He and his fellow, Dick, plan to use one of the conjuring books to get free drink. In Act 3 the first two scenes show Doctor Faustus surveying the great cities of Europe and conjuring at Rome. The third scene shows Robin and Dick enjoying *themselves* in their own clownish way; but it is not now a way that is so remote from that of Faustus. He "took away his Holiness' wine," "stole his Holiness' meat from the table," "took Friar Sandelo a blow on the pate"; they stole the Vintner's cup, and when pursued for it they rely (as Faustus does) on magic, as a rescue from their scape.

The play began with Faustus and Robin at opposite ends of the spectrum. One was "glutted with learning's golden gifts," powerful and renowned; the other was ignorant, "out of service," and "hungry." But the process of logical development in the main plot, as I have described it, has by the end of Act 3 brought Faustus down through the diminishing circles of his capacity to the point where his powers and Robin's are no longer incommensurate. Up to this point, of course, Faustus and the clowns have never appeared together in any one scene. Such a conjunction would be unthinkable at the beginning of the play. But by Act 4 Faustus has himself sunk to the level of a comic entertainer. His relationship to Frederick, Martino, and Benvolio is entirely without dignity or intellectual pretension, and the intrusion of the clowns, Robin, Dick, Carter, Horse-courser, Hostess, into the court of the Duke of Vanholt marks a natural and inevitable climax in the downward movement of the main plot. The comic "Doctor Fustian" is now all the figure that Faustus can cut in the world; the "success" that he has bought so dearly is to be the leader of a troupe of clowns.

There is no doubt a *frisson* intended between the last line of Act 4 and the first line of Act 5—between the duchess's appreciation of Faustus' powers: "His artful sport drives all sad thoughts away," and (set against that) Wagner's "I think my master means to die shortly." The contrast between the two lines catches much of the movement from Act 4 to Act 5. Act 4 is the climax of the subplot interest. Almost the whole act is taken up with triviality of one kind or another, and it ends with the confrontation of main plot and subplot characters, reducing them to one level. Act 5, on the other hand, is without comic relief; and one can see why, in the terms I have outlined, this should be so. Through Act 4 we see Faustus' life enmeshed in the triviality that was inherent in the original stipulation of "any thing . . . that is not against our kingdom." Act 5, as it begins with the mention of death, so continues to move in the shadow of a tragic conclusion. Faustus has now fallen *beneath* the level of the clowns and horse-courser:

Why wert thou not a creature wanting soul?
....

O, Pythagoras' metempsychosis, were that true
This soul should fly from me and I be changed
Into some brutish beast.
All beasts are happy, for when they die
Their souls are soon dissolved in elements.

(5.2.179, 181–85)

The movement of the subplot helps to confirm this
view of the general direction of Faustus' development.
The constant looming presence of the clownish common man, with his attention set on immediate comforts,
serves as a norm against which we may observe and
judge the splendors and the miseries of the overween-
ing intellectual.

David Bevington and Eric Rasmussen
Faustus' Tragedy

Is *Doctor Faustus* a "Christian tragedy"? The very phrase is a contradiction in terms, as has often been pointed out,[1] since tragedy cannot constrict itself within the parameters of a Christian story that is, in Dante's terms, a divine comedy. Despite the contradictions, however, Richard Sewall argues that the term "is permissible and, I think, useful, to indicate the new dimensions and tensions introduced into human life by Christianity and which perforce entered into the Elizabethan tragic synthesis."[2] Sewall calls to his aid W. H. Auden's distinction between the Greek "tragedy of necessity" and the Christian "tragedy of possibility": at the end of a Greek tragedy we say, "What a pity it had to be this way," whereas at the end of a Christian tragedy we say, "What a pity it had to be this way when it might have been otherwise."[3] In this sense, argues Sewall, Faustus is close to Dostoevsky's tragic heroes in being torn between the desire to exploit a new mastery over the world and

From Christopher Marlowe, *Doctor Faustus: A- and B-Texts,* eds. David Bevington and Eric Rasmussen (Manchester University Press, 1993), pp. 36–38.
[1] Laurence Michel, "The Possibility of a Christian Tragedy," *Thought,* XXXI (Autumn 1956), 403–28. See also Richard Sewall, *The Vision of Tragedy* (New Haven: Yale University Press, 1959), p. 159, n. 58.
[2] Sewall, *The Vision of Tragedy,* pp. 57–67, 159.
[3] W. H. Auden, "The Christian Tragic Hero," *New York Times Book Review,* 16 December 1945, p. 1.

guilt-ridden allegiance to traditional values. Faustus is, like many of Dostoevsky's protagonists, a criminal in the eyes of society, "the first modern tragic man, part believer, part unbeliever, vacillating between independence and dependence upon God, now arrogant and confident, now anxious and worried, justified yet horribly unjustified." He does not abase himself, as a Christian might, but resists his fate and clings to a doomed life.[4] The "tragedy of possibility" mocks him with the illusion of a new freedom he may not have, but it also defines what is generically new in Marlowe's play. If we understand "Christian tragedy" in this ironic sense, the concept is critically useful.

On what does the unity of such a tragedy depend, or does it in fact have a unity? Since the play is manifestly nonclassical in the way it organises its material, juxtaposing and inverting what Marlowe found in his sources as Faustus veers back and forth from serious inquiry to frivolity, unity must be sought paradoxically in the contradictions and struggles of the play's protagonist, in what Nicholas Brooke calls the bitter irony of Faustus' blasphemous protest "against the monstrous nature of a world where man is created to want to be at his finest precisely what he is not allowed to be." The play's unity of vision lies in its perception that man's nature "is in direct opposition to his fate."[5]

Yet even those critics who respond to Faustus' tragedy as a whole are often troubled by the play's seeming lack of a proper middle. In Cleanth Brooks' view, Faustus appears to have little to do after he has signed his fateful bargain "except to fill in the time before the

[4]Sewall, *The Vision of Tragedy,* pp. 63–67.
[5]Nicholas Brooke, "The Moral Tragedy of *Doctor Faustus,*" *Cambridge Journal,* VII (1952), 662–87, rpt. in *Critics on Marlowe,* ed. Judith O'Neill (Coral Gables: University of Miami Press, 1969), pp. 93–114.

mortgage falls due and the devil comes to collect the forfeited soul." The lack of any fixed tragic structure allows the playwright (or his collaborator and later revisers) to "stuff in comedy and farce" at this point "more or less *ad libitum*." Faustus is a man "all dressed up with no place to go."[6] Can answers be found to this key structural problem?

One persuasive reply looks to the practicalities of theatre, especially as theatre evolved in late medieval England. Morality drama experimented extensively in the sixteenth century with formulas of contrast between serious action and burlesque parody. Moreover, as Nigel Alexander notes, in any age a good comedian knows "that it matters a great deal what he puts in as filler." The middle of the play is needed to make clear to the audience the nature of Faustus's danger and folly. It does so by generating what Alexander calls the "logic of suspense," making use of rapid transitions to sharpen the audience's awareness of Faustus's approaching destiny. The Seven Deadly Sins entertain Faustus with "a representation of the bonds which will fetter him until his destruction at the end of the play." The low comedy scenes are much more than parody; they are tied together by a symbolic imagery of evil that suspensefully reminds us of the "consequences of following passion wherever it leads."[7] They give objective form to the dilemma in which Faustus is caught, between his knowledge that grace is truly offered to the penitent and his own conviction that he cannot repent.

---

[6]Cleanth Brooks, "The Unity of Marlowe's *Doctor Faustus*," in *To Nevill Coghill from Friends*, ed. J. Lawlor and W. H. Auden (London: Faber, 1966), pp. 109–24.
[7]Nigel Alexander, "The Performance of Christopher Marlowe's *Dr. Faustus*," *PBA* (1971), 331–49. On structure in morality drama, see David Bevington, *From "Mankind" to Marlowe* (Cambridge, Mass.: Harvard University Press, 1962), passim. See also Richard Levin, *The Multiple Plot in English Renaissance Drama* (University of Chicago Press, 1971), pp. 119–23.

Equally persuasive is the argument that *Doctor Faustus,* for all its mix of comic and tragic, moves (in both its A- and B-texts) through a regular five-act structure. The B-text is in fact divided into five acts; the A-text, though obscured by textual difficulties and the decision of most modern editors to present the A-text in scenes, lends itself to the five-act division employed in Keefer's and this present edition. Act 1 is expository; Act 2 centres on the signing of the contract that sets the tragedy on its inexorable course; Act 3 is spent in Rome, Act 4 in the courts of Germany; Act 5 is the dénouement. As George Hunter argues, a "single and significant line of development" connects these points as we move from initial excitement in Act 1 to Faustus' being balked from his pursuit of astronomy in Act 2 to his being distracted into sightseeing and sensual indulgence as his intellectual quest falters. The subplot material meantime operates through parody, not in a feeble modern sense but through the "multiple presentation of serious themes."[8] All in all, then, the genre and structure of *Doctor Faustus* are most clearly evident when they are measured sympathetically against the traditions of a native English theatre rather than being subjected to a superimposed Aristotelian analysis.

[8]G. K. Hunter, "Five-Act Structure in *Doctor Faustus," TDR,* VIII.iv (1964), 77–91. The objection to merely scenic division on the part of most editors was made earlier by Boas. See also Susan Snyder, "Marlowe's *Doctor Faustus* as an Inverted Saint's Life," *SP,* LXIII (1966), 571–74; Robert Ornstein, "The Comic Synthesis in *Doctor Faustus," ELH,* XXII (1955), 165–72; John H. Crabtree, Jr., "The Comedy in Marlowe's *Dr. Faustus," Furman Studies,* IX.i (1961), 1–9; Charles N. Beall, "Definition of Theme by Unconsecutive Event: Structure as Induction in Marlowe's *Doctor Faustus," Ren.P 1962* (1963), 53–61; Clifford Leech, "Marlowe's Humor," in *Essays on Shakespeare and Elizabethan Drama in Honor of Hardin Craig,* ed. Richard Hosley (Columbia: University of Missouri Press, 1962), p. 70; Warren D. Smith, "The Nature of Evil in *Doctor Faustus," MLR,* LX (1965), 171–5; Sherman Hawkins, "The Education of Faustus," *SEL,* VI (1966), 193–209; Mutsumi Nozaki, "The Comic Sense in Marlowe Reconsidered," *Shakespeare Studies* (Japan), IX (1970–71), 1–27; and Linda Wyman, "How Plot and Subplot Unite in Marlowe's *Faustus," College English Association Critic,* XXXVII.i (1974), 14–16.

John Russell Brown
Doctor Faustus at Stratford-upon-Avon, 1968

Nine editions of Marlowe's *Faustus* before 1640, performances in Germany in the early seventeenth century, and in England until a year or two before the closure of the theaters for the Civil War in 1642—all attest the play's immediate popularity with audiences. And today it is one of the very few Elizabethan plays still to be seen on our stages: of plays written in England before 1600, its nearest rivals in popularity are the anonymous *Everyman,* first printed in the second decade of the sixteenth century, and Dekker's ebullient *Shoemakers' Holiday* written in the summer of 1599.

Productions today must lack much of the direct excitement of the earliest performances, for their audiences were accustomed to a belief in witchcraft and the sight of men and women convicted and burned for these practices. Several accounts of *Doctor Faustus* have survived, such as the Puritan William Prynne's report in 1633 of the

> visible apparition of the devil on the stage at the Belsavage Playhouse, in Queen Elizabeth's days (to the great amazement both of the actors and spectators)

whiles they were there prophanely playing the History of Faustus, the truth of which I have heard from
many now alive, who well remember it, there being
some distracted with that fearful sight.

Two versions of this story say that the actors themselves
fell to prayer and piety. This is not a twentieth-century
phenomenon, but nevertheless the devilry, which may
seem to be such a wasted asset or, even, liability in the
play today, is one of the two main reasons for present re-
vivals: it provides a large and fascinating opportunity for
the scene and costume designer, working with lights and
special-effects consultants. The enchantments, splendors
and tortures displayed in a sequence of eye-catching
coups de théâtre take possession of the audience's senses
and make it forget its disbelief in acceptance of a fantastic reality. The audience watches the play in something
of the same mind as we might explore a painting by Hi-
eronymus Bosch, his *Earthly Paradise* or *Seven Deadly
Sins*; costume designs for productions of *Faustus* are
often undisguised borrowings from these pictures. If a
modern audience cannot take the devils with intellectual assurance, it can respond eagerly to visual realiza-
tions of fantasies of desire and guilt.

The other major hold that the play has over modern
audiences is the star role: the opportunity for an actor
to dominate the production, speak magniloquent verse,
and attempt to create an outsized characterization that
can confront devils, sins, scholars, emperors, Helen of
Troy, and death.

At Stratford-upon-Avon in the summer of 1968, a
production designed by Abd'Elkader Farrah and directed, for the Royal Shakespeare Company, by Clifford Williams, blazed and threatened with sumptuous

theatricality. Many of the stage directions of the original quarto editions were cues for technological invention. Mephostophilis first appeared as a disembodied head with a shock of wild hair, vibrating in lurid light and with strange rhythmic sound in support; for perhaps as long as one minute its silent presence suggested a strange, unthinkable reality about to be released upon the stage. The Seven Deadly Sins had gross, distorted, distended, and discolored limbs, and were again supported with electronically doctored sound. The comic enchantments were staged rapidly and with seemingly endless resource: exploding grapes, a realistically articulated hand appearing from the center of a dish of food, wine that squirted up into the face of the Pope. Alexander and his paramour were lit in a circle of blue light and dressed in silver paint and silver spangles; they danced slowly to soft and lucid music. Maggie Wright, playing the mute Helen, was bronzed and gleaming; as she walked onstage naked, partly like a conventionally pretty nude and partly like a Cellini Venus, an unfamiliar quiet showed the audience to be held and perhaps disconcerted. At the end of the play there was a further moment of effective silence—when attention has been gained by visual means a director can readily take such liberties—which seemed to give Faustus a hope of survival after his last words, and then the squarish bulkheads at the back of the stage moved forward slowly, motivated by unseen power, and, still slowly, they then fell forward to reveal great gray spikes; through these came a crowd of silent devils. There was an enormous sound, with cries of pain and pleasure amplified stereophonically, as they encircled Faustus. When they moved away their satisfaction was only a murmur, and the stage was bare.

The text of the play was taken as an invitation to sensationalism. But it must be firmly controlled. Harold

Hobson, writing in *The Sunday Times* (June 30, 1968), found the Stratford production inconsistent and therefore unsatisfying:

> Let [Helen] be naked by all means, if that is how Mr. Williams wants her, but to normal eyes she should, if the production is consistent, be hideous, like the Seven Deadly Sins which Faustus finds so lovely and enticing.

The action of the play and Marlowe's keen verbal intelligence implicit in its words necessitate a careful significance for every detail, just proportion and a proper relation between each element.

For example, when Faustus has signed his pact with Lucifer in his blood, Mephostophilis on his own initiative decides to "fetch him somewhat to delight his mind" and a stage direction follows:

> *Enter Devils giving crowns and rich apparel to Faustus.*
> *They dance and then depart.*

It is this sight and the promise that he may raise such spirits when he pleases that persuade Faustus to hand the deed of gift of body and of soul into Mephostophilis' keeping. This is the first of a sequence of "shows"—pageant-like clarifications of the action—the most natural of them all and the one most directly "speaking" to Faustus. Its staging must mark all this; and the other "shows" must be graded in contrast both in splendor and realism. The she-devil who comes when Faustus asks for a wife may be both ridiculous and offensive as Faustus' response suggests, but the Seven Deadly Sins must be compelling as well so that they give "delight" to Faustus' soul as he instinctively exclaims.

The Stratford production failed noticeably in the papal scenes when compared to an earlier production by Michael Benthall for the Old Vic in 1961. Clifford Williams followed the demands for tricky practical jokes, but he disregarded the further insistence of both Quarto texts on the "pride" and high "solemnity" of the Vatican's ceremonies; his friars and prelates entered as if for farcical business. In contrast, the Old Vic production started here with "magnificence":

> The contrast between the fusty study and the riot of colour when [Faustus] lets loose as a magician is extremely effective. (*Punch,* August 30, 1961)

> When the papal court has been gradually assembled ... the scene is so impressive in its solemnity that almost any joke would seem tellingly out of place, and the final wrecking of all this grandeur by Faustus and Mephostophilis seems indeed a devilish outrage. (The London *Times,* August 23, 1961)

Marlowe uses spectacle, or "shows" as he would say, to very precise and, often, ironic effect. Contrasts and sequence are of crucial importance.

The Stratford production was perhaps too freely and consistently fantastic, without sufficient ordinary reality. Its careful staging of Faustus cutting his own arm for blood with which to sign, and the chafing of it in flame, showed how effective small-scale realism could be. But other opportunities were missed. It was incredible that the Emperor of Germany should wish to embrace the silvered phantoms of Alexander and his paramour, as he does in the Quarto of 1616; still less that he should wonder whether the lady had a wart or mole on her neck as he does in both Quartos. Yet the illusion of reality here is important as a preparation for Helen's entry, the awed silence with which she is greeted by Faustus on her first appearance and his unresisted kiss on her reappearance. Possibly the director wished the play to become progressively unreal, for the Old Man, who simply and bravely calls Faustus to repentance just before his last hour, entered in a red spotlight and had a woolly beard like another less resourceful stage-phantom: yet he should be clearly a man and not a spirit, one who can resist the torments of Mephostophilis. Even the Chorus, who speaks from outside the play's time and place, lacked a distinctive reality: the Stratford stage was theatrical space, without boundaries or permanent structure, and the Chorus was just one more illusory figure with no special point of vantage.

The director and designer must make their audience accept fantastic illusions, but they must also mark clearly the varying reality of each moment in the drama. Nor must they overwhelm the audience with large scale sensationalism. Some of the most significant moments are simply histrionic. When Faustus "pants and quivers" as he remembers his youth, when he finds "Heaven" in Helen's lips or boasts that he will sack Wittenberg for her sake, the physical transformations must be enacted and must dominate all other impressions. For the clarity of the play, and for its full excitement, Faustus must be seen to change from merriment to despair, to fear, to cruelty, and to sensual desire, all within a hundred or so lines at the beginning of the last scene. The spectacle must not overwhelm the acting, as it frequently does in twentieth-century theaters and as it did at Stratford.

For all its obvious attractions, the central role of *Faustus* poses serious problems for most twentieth-century actors. A common mistake is to choose a single definite "through-line" or an individual distinguishing mark for characterization; it will be too small a basis. For Irving Wardle, the drama critic of the London *Times,* Richard Burton's performance at the Oxford Playhouse and subsequently for a film version in 1967, was both plausible and "unsatisfactory" in "showing a bandy-legged little scholar seizing on magic to act out his frustrated sensual fantasies" (The London *Times,* June 28, 1968). Eric Porter at Stratford chose a dry, ascetic tone, dressed always in black and played with disdain rather than pride, quiet relish rather than delight or glutting pleasure as the text demands. In effect most actors lack weight: for the 1961 Old Vic production, "Paul Daneman . . . began in much too cavalier a manner; the entry into this dark world of ghostly temptation and deep doubt needs to be more subtle and awed. He dashed his books aside like a naughty schoolboy. The Latin he spouted seemed to mean nothing to him" (*The Guardian,* August 23, 1961). A seriousness is required, by both the theme and style of the play. So many large positive reactions are required—pleasure, fear, pride, humiliation, intellectual and imaginative energy—that the first and almost the last effort of the actor should be to find the reality, and a suitably clear, assured and true-to-life expression, for each element.

Edward Alleyn, who first created the role, was especially famed for his interpretation of Marlowe's earlier hero, Tamburlaine.[1] In a pamphlet of 1597, a man who "bent his brows and fetched stations up and down the room" was said to do so with "such furious gesture as if he had been playing Tamburlaine on a stage." Clearly Alleyn's acting was violent, stalking, astounding. When fashions changed and Alleyn's Tamburlaine was remem-

---

[1] Alleyn's style has been discussed by W. A. Armstrong and A. J. Gurr in *Shakespeare Survey,* VII (1954) and XVI (1963); both articles usefully quote contemporary assessments

bered as "flying from all humanity," it still was praised for the hold it kept over an audience: Joseph Hall's satire (1597) on "some upreared, high-aspiring swain" like "the turkish Tamburlaine" attests:

> He vaunts his voice upon an hired stage,
> With high-set steps, and princely carriage:
> Now swooping in side robes of royalty,
> That erst did scrub in lousy brokery.
> There if he can with terms italianate,
> Big-sounding sentences, and words of state,
> Fair patch me up his pure iambic verse,
> He ravishes the gazing scaffolders ...

Alleyn's acting was broad and violent, but while it could command popular attention it could also give special pleasure at Elizabeth's court where he was recalled from retirement to act before the Queen in 1600. Thomas Nashe, a dramatist and university-trained writer, said that his very name was "able to make an ill matter good" and that not even the famed Roman actor, Roscius, "could ever perform more in action than famous Ned Alleyn."

Alleyn did not act in Shakespeare's plays, and it is arguable that he could never have done so with much success. Marlowe's effects are not Shakespeare's, his "Big-sounding sentences and words of state" are quite unlike the developing and complex expressiveness of Shakespeare's mature verse. Quote any long speech from *Faustus* and Hamlet's advice will seem out of place: "Speak the speech ... as I pronounced it to you, trippingly on the tongue." But the opposite, a thundering Herod, is also wrong. Marlowe spoke of "working words," of "disputes," "concise syllogisms," words that "win," "incantations." Energy is the most important requirement, composed of force, clarity or control, and speed. When

the situation and reactions are complex, as they often
are, Marlowe does not write lines of allusive complexity
or multiple meaning; he divides to express the complexity, following one clear thought with another, perhaps its
opposite. Frequently two or three contrasted characters
speak successively about a single occurrence, as do the
scholars and the Good and Bad Angels who attend on
Faustus, or the speaker varies his reaction widely within
a single speech. Brecht's dramaturgy is more relevant
here than Shakespeare's: he asked for boldness, clarity, contradictions; he displayed complicated action and
reactions through "montage" rather than "growth"; the
event is "not to be read between the lines" but "directly
stated."

The physical demands of Faustus on the actor are at
one with the verbal; they need the same qualities. It is
instructive to observe how successive scenes start with
clearly contrasted moods, each requiring an entry in
strict contrast to previous ones, and an immediate effect.
For his second scene Faustus enters, as he says, "resolute" (1.3.14); his long study is already completed and
his prayers and sacrifice to devils: he is committed. For
his third scene (2.1) he is revealed "*in his study,*" not living in speculation of his art as he had left the stage, but
exclaiming that he must "needs be damned"; we are not
shown this change taking place, but its full effect; how
it is, not how it happens. Marlowe wishes us to observe,
wonder and question at the changes in Faustus not share
in the process of them. For his fourth scene, he is in debate with Mephostophilis, the first entry in duologue. In
the fifth scene, he starts by telling Mephostophilis of the
wonders of his travels, and the actor is set the task of
appearing as if he has just ridden across the firmament
on a dragon-drawn chariot. And so on through the play,
completing a series of appearances that give by montage

the complex impression of the mind and being of a man whose dominion "stretcheth as far as doth the mind of man."

The montage effect and the great economy in presentation of the central character may be illustrated by the soliloquy when Faustus is discovered in his study after the pact with Lucifer:

> Now, Faustus, must thou needs be
>   damned;
> Canst thou not be saved:—

The statement, sharpened by the emphasis on *Now* and *must,* is in two sections each representing a different involvement: *needs,* and then *canst.* The next line is a question, referring to thoughts immediately released:

> What boots it then to think of God or heaven?

There is nothing irresolute or nervous in the expression of any of these first lines; but an ejaculation follows defining the wildness and uncertainty that is another facet of Faustus' complicated state of mind and being:

> Away with such vain fancies, and despair.

Then at once there is a counterstatement, for two lines breaking the full run of the iambic pentameter with shorter thrusts and rhythms:

> Despair in God and trust in Belzebub!
> Now go not backward. Faustus, be
>   resolute!

And again a counterstatement: back to a question which expresses, not strength and purpose, but irresolution:

Why waver'st thou?

Then a description of a sudden sense of a different reality: Faustus' mind is impelled by a force he cannot control: this is experienced, described, rapidly questioned, and then almost as rapidly counterstated. Each of these short elements demands different vocal and physical representations for the varying emotional, intellectual, and physical realities implied:

Why waver'st thou? O something soundeth in mine
    ear,
"Abjure this magic, turn to God again."
Ay, and Faustus will turn to God again.
To God? He loves thee not. . . .

The speech does not build in effect: each element is self-contained and from this we gain an impression of a man of great energy and complexity. The soliloquy concludes with, first, a more sustained and temperate description of his new allegiance:

The God thou serv'st is thine own appetite
Wherein is fixed the love of Belzebub!

and then a new concern with *future* activity, in two stages, of which the second represents in one line a hitherto unknown element of cruelty and callowness:

To him I'll build an altar and a church,
And offer lukewarm blood of newborn babes!

The Good and Bad Angels enter on either side of the stage, to express visually and verbally the contrary possibilities that are available to Faustus; when they go, Faustus expresses yet further facets of his being. Here, rapidly, are love of wealth, sense of triumph, feelings of security, warmth and eagerness, and then committal and incantation:

> Wealth!
> Why, the signory of Emden shall be mine!
> When Mephostophilis shall stand by me
> What power can hurt me? Faustus, thou art safe.
> Cast no more doubts! Mephostophilis, come,
> And bring glad tidings from great Lucifer.
> Is't not midnight? Come Mephostophilis,
> *Veni, veni Mephostophile!*

The greatest challenge to the actor is the last soliloquy of the play. At Stratford, Eric Porter tried to sustain and unify it by a sense of terror and physical struggle. Most of it was spoken in white heat; Faustus writhed on the floor as if wrestling with a devil. In this way the astonishing variety of its demands was lessened and the play robbed of its climactic representation of Faustus' "dominion that ... Stretcheth as far as doth the mind of man," which realizes that dominion with economy, energy, and sensuous fullness. The actor should play the contradictions and the contrasts; he must not represent a general state of being which the audience may recognize and share, but open out the character's variety of impulse, sensation, and thought, anatomize him for the audience to see plainly and to wonder at, and not fully comprehend.

Clifford Williams' direction at Stratford had one expected success, and one unexpected. Most other productions have shown how effective is the contrast between Mephostophilis and Faustus, the spirit usually terse and often unvaried in his reactions, and independent even when obeying the magician's commands. For Harold

Hobson, "The controlled Mephostophilis of Terence Hardiman, occasionally allowing a flicker of torment to pass over his quiet face, is what does most to hold the production together" (The London *Sunday Times,* June 30, 1968). For Irving Wardle, "It is a pity that Terence Hardiman's Mephostophilis, as quiet and powerful as a coiled spring, did not meet a more challenging adversary" (The London *Times,* June 28, 1968).

The dramatic device of contrast is what justifies the comic subplots and the comic episodes of the main action: justifies them to the scholar and critic knowledgeable of the scriptural, medieval, and early Renaissance love of analogy, and able to mark the verbal connections between the comic and serious elements. But in performance the validity of the comedy, as practicable theater, has often been questionable. Mr. Williams, by encouraging robust and inventive performances by the minor characters, showed that these scenes are eminently playable; indeed that their verbal simplicity, in comparison with the obscurity of many of Shakespeare's low comedy episodes, makes them more immediately effective for twentieth-century audiences. For Irving Wardle, there was "good phallic fun between Robin (Bruce Myers) and Ralph." Ronald Bryden, writing in *The Observer* (June 30, 1968), noted with some surprise that "Richard Moore manages to make the servant Wagner's scenes of crude supernatural slapstick genuinely funny." These are not parts that play themselves: they require something of the independent and scene-stealing qualities of the Elizabethan personality comics. A renewal of interest in improvisational techniques and in popular, music-hall comedy is showing our actors the way toward, literally, reviving these parts.

But the problem that remains is how to relate Faustus' part in the comedy to his role as a whole. Why should he bother with the trivial concerns of the Duke and Duchess of Vanholt or the comic stubbornness of the Horse-courser? How can the audience accept from the same character metaphysical doubt and courtly subservience, sensitivity to beauty and childish exploitation of human absurdity? If the presentation of Faustus in his most obviously effective scenes is any clue, the answer must be to accept the contrasts and play them for all their local worth, to play each episode for itself (in the Brechtian manner) and leave the coherence to Marlowe, to the inward unity of the actor's performance (based as it must be in one individual man and his possibilities of suggestion), and to the audience's realization that however dignified or important a man may be there are usually absurdities and surprises deep within him. In full possession of magical powers, Faustus might well become irresponsible and childish; he might well play with the Emperor and the Duke of Vanholt in rather the same way as Mephostophilis has played with him. The practice of power may cause him to lose a sense of proportion. Familiarization with devilish practices and indulgence of his fancies may cause him to lose both his appearance of serious purpose and his sense of relevance.

Even in the height of the comedy in 4.5, Faustus returns for one speech to the earlier manner of obvious seriousness and high-pressured consciousness:

What art thou, Faustus, but a man condemned to die?
Thy fatal time draws to a final end;
Despair doth drive distrust into my thoughts.
Confound these passions with a quiet sleep.
Tush, Christ did call the thief upon the cross!
Then rest thee Faustus, quiet in conceit.

If the actor of Faustus creates this moment clearly and strongly, with its sharp transitions, with the firm, extended rhythm of the second line enforced with alliteration and monosyllabic stress, with the abrupt "Tush" followed by the simple New Testament reference, and with, lastly, the punning ambiguity of "rest," "quiet," and "conceit," the audience may sense the deep inward knowledge of judgment, confusion, and longing that in the comic scenes is banished from Faustus' consciousness by his petty activity.

The object of director and actors, and of scene designer and technicians, must be to reveal all with clarity, truth, and power, to give each element its own full effect and allow Marlowe's astonishingly varied and comprehensive drama to appear in meaningful sequence before the audience. To seek an easy unity, or to play one character, emotion, spectacle, or incident overwhelmingly, is to fight against the style in which the play was written. It is not an easy play for audience or performers: its subject, treated by an imaginative, speculative ironist, must warn us not to expect that; a study of its style must warn us that the audience should be continually alerted and that a sense of unity should be created by each member in his own imagination rather than made obvious and inescapable on the stage. Marlowe provides excitement, confrontation, and questions in plenty: he does not lead by the nose. *Doctor Faustus* is dialectic drama, in Brecht's sense; it is spectacular; and it lives in the imagination, freely and with complexity.

Kevin Dunn
Resolving Ambiguities in Marlowe's *Doctor Faustus*

In the first scene of *Doctor Faustus*, Marlowe's hero expresses the hope that spirits will "Resolve me of all ambiguities."[1] At the outset, then, he announces a leading motive for his pact with Mephostophilis: his desire to settle the questions plaguing his restless intellect, to solve the mysteries that had evaded philosophers, theologians and scientists through the centuries. This heroic desire to attain knowledge, however, stands cheek to jowl with another: the desire for "a world of profit and delight, / of power, of honor, and omnipotence" that can be earned by "the studious artisan" (1.1.51–3). The audience thus faces its own puzzle, since it is dared to decide whether it should see Faustus as a Promethean—or at least Quixotic—striver, a hypereducated and relentlessly curious hero who cannot tolerate "ambiguities," or as a bored pedant who trades his soul to realize a rather tawdry vision of power. This ambiguity is fueled by theatricality itself, the mode of literary representation that, rather than telling us directly (as a novel might) how to understand an ambiguous character like Faustus, places him in front of us on a blank stage and demands that we

---

[1] 1.1.77. All references are to the Signet Classics edition of the play and given by act, scene and line numbers. Subsequent references will be given parenthetically.

judge him based on the words and actions that unfold before us.

In fact, the great flowering of Elizabethan theater took place in a very broad context of cultural ambiguity, a context that engulfed and defined Marlowe as a poet and playwright. The latter half of the sixteenth century was a time of exciting but disconcerting mobility—social, economic, sexual and political—and Marlowe's plays concern themselves again and again with the vertigo-inducing potential of such mobility. Marlowe himself was the product of rapid advancement. Like Faustus, he was "born of parents of base stock" (Prologue 11) and achieved his considerable, if briefly enjoyed, fame largely as a result of his Cambridge education. That education in classical literature and rhetoric enabled him to move among the literary elite, including the so-called University Wits, the overeducated and underemployed group of writers (including men such as Thomas Nashe and Robert Greene) who, to put food (along with goodly amounts of beer and wine) on the table, produced the literary outpouring that became one foundation for the golden age of Elizabethan cultural production. Yet Marlowe and his associates did not, to say the least, resolve all ambiguities in their voluminous writings. If anything, the increasing sophistication bred by the competition of wit fueled even more uncertainty in an age already struggling to assimilate the gargantuan questions raised by the Protestant reformation and by Copernicus's challenge to the Ptolemaic, earth-centered model of the cosmos.

Marlowe sat, apparently, squarely in the middle of some of the more radical elements of this intellectual foment (see Introduction, pp. xv–xviii). When Mephostophilis himself openly tells Faustus that hell is real and horrible, Faustus exclaims, "I think hell's a fable"

(2.1.133). He thus identifies himself as the sort of radical skeptic that Marlowe's contemporaries felt the poet himself to be, a man anxious to reveal long-held beliefs as "fables." Much of the evidence for such involvement, unfortunately, comes either from rather suspect professional informants, or from letters written by a panicky Thomas Kyd, Marlowe's fellow playwright, who had been arrested after papers questioning the divinity of Jesus had been found in his chambers. Kyd, perhaps ignobly but not necessarily inaccurately, claimed under torture that the papers belonged to Marlowe, who had shared a writing space with him. Kyd's letters, written to the Lord Keeper, Sir John Puckering, shortly after Marlowe died either in a bar brawl or as a victim of political assassination—the records are scanty and suspicious—accuse Marlowe of all manner of deviance. Kyd wrote, "[I]t was his custom in table talk or otherwise to jest at the divine scriptures, gibe at prayers, and strive in argument to frustrate & confute what hath been spoke or write by prophets and such holy men."[2] Throw into this "atheistical" mix the charge that Marlowe was a fervid proponent of homosexuality and it is easy to see why he was a controversial figure, perhaps one who was in fact killed for espousing his beliefs so openly.[3] If any of these charges is true, it would suggest that Marlowe "resolved the ambiguities" by adopting the most extreme of stances available to him.

Perhaps, then, it is not surprising that Marlowe builds his dramas around what we have come to call anti-heroes, men who possess a kind of antithetical attraction, becoming more arresting to watch the further they depart from societal norms. These anti-heroes include

[2]Quoted in David Riggs, *The World of Christopher Marlowe* (New York: Henry Holt, 2004), p. 329.
[3]See Introduction xvi–xviii for more on Marlowe's beliefs and death.

Tamburlaine (*Tamburlaine the Great, Parts 1 and 2*), who mercilessly puts cities to the sword in his quest to rule the world; Barabas (*The Jew of Malta*), who tells his servant "see thou pitty none, / But to thy selfe smile when the Christians moane" (2.3.172–3);[4] Edward II and his lover Gaveston (*Edward II*), who place the enjoyment of their love over the administration of the state of England. Marlowe's predecessors and contemporaries certainly loved to hiss at overdrawn bad guys, but Marlowe neglects to provide what the other writers almost unfailingly do: a man in the white hat to cheer for. These characters take up all the space onstage, and we watch them with fascination, admiration, and even, as in the case of Edward II, sympathy.

These hero-villains are unimaginable without the institution of the public theater that Marlowe did so much to help shape. Commercial pressures rewarded more and more sensational roles, and dramatic form allowed Marlowe to present those characters with only a modicum of conventional moralizing. We can see the role of theatrical representation in creating the ambiguous figures who fascinate and repel if we look at the differing effects, both aesthetic and moral, of *Doctor Faustus* and of Marlowe's major source, the prose narrative *The Historie of the damnable life, and deserued death of Doctor Iohn Faustus*, often known simply as *The Faust Book*. As its title suggests, Marlowe's source, a translation of a German work published in 1587, provides little room for the reader to maneuver. Faustus's life was "damnable" and his death "deserved." At every turn, the narrator's voice herds the reader down a straight and narrow path. Even though the book undoubtedly works on our

---

[4] I am quoting from *The Complete Works of Christopher Marlowe*, volume IV (Oxford: Clarendon Press, 1995).

prurient interest in watching Faustus's transgressions, it never ceases to remind us that the narrative is *exemplary*, an attempt to show us the wages of sin. When he relates Faustus's conjuring up of Helen, the narrator tells us, "Wherefore a man may see that the devil blindeth and inflameth the heart with lust oftentimes, that men fall in love with harlots, nay even with furies, which afterward cannot lightly be removed."[5] Among the morals the narrator wants us to glean from Faustus's negative example is the danger of mobility itself: "Therefore I wish all Christians to take an example by this wicked Faustus and to be comforted in Christ, contenting themselves with that vocation whereunto it hath pleased God to call them . . ." (110). Since Marlowe was the son of a shoemaker who rose to practice a very different vocation and to travel in very different circles, he himself stands in the level of this moral.

Yet when Marlowe puts Faustus on the stage, the effect is quite different, by dint of, if nothing else, the stripping away of that narrative voice. It is of course possible for playwrights to create moralizing drama. Medieval morality plays such as *Everyman* staged allegorical virtues and vices to direct the audience's interpretation of what they saw. Much earlier, Greek and Roman tragedians used the chorus to provide moral and philosophical context for the actions of the characters and even to advise the characters directly. Marlowe, in fact, adopts both of these techniques, borrowing his good and bad angels from morality plays and beginning and ending *Doctor Faustus* with a chorus.[6] For good measure he throws

---

[5] I quote from the excerpts reprinted in the back of this volume, p. 142.
[6] For Marlowe's debt to morality plays, see David Bevington's study, *From Mankind to Marlowe: Growth of Structure in the Popular Drama of Tudor England* (Cambridge: Harvard University Press, 1962). Bevington's final chapter is devoted to *Doctor Faustus*.

in the concerned Scholars of 1.2, 5.2 and 5.3, and from *The Faust Book* he borrows the Old Man who exhorts Faustus to repent. All these moralizing voices, however, create not so much an overwhelming condemnation of Faustus as a bewildering, cacophonous over-kill. They begin to feel like high-toned bric-a-brac, a necessary sop to conventional morals that may be pared away, leaving Marlowe's hero naked on the stage for us to puzzle out and judge according to his own actions and words. Theatrical representation, after all, while putatively more realistic than narrative poetry or prose, in that it puts sentiments and ideas into the mouths of living actors standing on the stage, in fact openly begs the questions of literary fiction: how seriously are we to take this story? do we need to condemn someone who is, after all, only an actor? is an entertainment sometimes just an entertainment? A generation before Marlowe wrote *Doctor Faustus*, Sir Philip Sidney argued that poets frankly show us a make-believe world and that hence "of all writers under the sun the poet is the least liar" because "he nothing affirms and therefore never lieth."[7] Marlowe seems to take Sidney's claim further, daring us to consider that not only does the playwright not "affirm" objective truth, he also does not force any moral interpretation on the viewer.

The potential for radical skepticism presented by theatrical representation echoes Faustus's own belief in a world of intellectual endeavor cut free not just from conventional morality but even from the evidence of the senses. When Faustus contracts the original "Faustian bargain," he has, or should have, the already secured knowledge that a deal with the devil cannot, in the end,

[7]Sidney, *The Defense of Poesy*, in Katherine Duncan-Jones, ed., *Sir Philip Sidney: A Critical Edition of the Major Works* (Oxford: Oxford University Press, 1989), p. 235.

go well, but he swaps that rather commonplace, widely possessed knowledge for an initiation into the powers of black magic. The deal involves, as his own words make clear, a willful looking away from what is right before his eyes:

> This word "damnation" terrifies not me
> For I confound hell in Elysium:
> My ghost be with the old philosophers!
> But leaving these vain trifles of men's souls,
> Tell me, what is that Lucifer thy lord? (1.3.57–61)

Faustus here takes a cogent philosophical position known as "nominalism," which holds that we should not confuse a word like "damnation" for an abstract reality standing behind that word,[8] and perverts it into the arrogant assertion that if he can't see it, then it's just a name and doesn't really exist. Somewhat contradictorily, he asserts his ability to "confound" hell with Elysium, that is, to assert that two things he cannot see (heaven and hell) are in fact the same place. In similar fashion, he then seems to believe in a non-hellish afterlife in a place where virtuous pagan philosophers would reside (usually called Limbo, a place that is neither heaven nor hell).

There is, then, a kind of heroic stupidity to Faust in the play.[9] Skeptical speculation about hell is all well and good, after all, unless one is speaking to the emissary of Satan; in that case, it begins to look like wishful thinking.

---

[8]The opposing philosophical stance, called "realism," holds that words can name a generalizable abstraction behind them; "round," therefore, would refer not just to a spherical ball, but to a very real idea of roundness that informs all round things. A nominalist believes only in roundness as found in particular balls, peas, plates, etc.

[9]Patrick Cheney connects sublimity and skepticism in *Marlowe's Republican Authorship: Lucan, Liberty, and the Sublime* (Basingstoke: Palgrave Macmillan, 2009), Chapter 5.

Faustus's limitations show themselves in the relatively trivial ways that he employs his power, in what amounts to little more than a series of spectacles and practical jokes. He speaks of riches and sexual exploits, but we see little of the former and he turns to Helen of Troy as an afterthought, to distract him as his end draws near, to "extinguish clear / Those thoughts that do dissuade me from my vow, / And keep mine oath I made to Lucifer" (5.1.91–93). The famous speech that follows—"Was this the face that launched a thousand ships?"—for all its rhetorical power can only highlight the sharp distinction between the epic sweep of the *Iliad, Odyssey* and *Aeneid*, and the story of a man who victimizes an ignorant horse courser with a fake leg, a story derived not from classical literature but from *The Faust Book*, which is little more than a pamphlet.

Faustus's extreme nominalism recapitulates the claims of theater itself. What you get may be what you see, but what you see is *not* what you get; there is a boy under Helen of Troy's dress, a struggling theatrical "artisan" beneath the robes of the German Emperor. A play folds the audience into its own skeptical structure, and a central part of that skepticism is directed toward playing itself. *Doctor Faustus*, as much as any play by Marlowe, refuses to present us with an unambiguous triumph over the bonds of religion, society and nation. In fact, it can almost seem as if Marlowe is scoffing at skepticism itself, trying to expose the bonds that tie even the most rebellious imagination.

Marlowe, the great poet of power, reveals here the limits to the imagination, imposed by the desire for that power. It is one thing, Marlowe would seem to say, to throw off the bonds of convention; it is another to know what to do next. Stephen Greenblatt goes so far as to argue that "Marlovian rebels and skeptics remain embedded within this orthodoxy: they simply reverse the paradigms and embrace what the society brands as evil."[10] Faustus, for instance, despite the seemingly unlimited scope of his magic, never attempts to rule the world or even become Emperor, unlike Tamburlaine, who though born a shepherd aspires from the first moments he appears onstage to be "Monarch of the East."[11] Faustus is satisfied to "Both love and serve the German Emperor" (4.2.16), to make himself indispensable to the great by providing them entertainment and by annoying their enemies. He becomes a kind of master of the revels, an MC, perhaps akin to what Marlowe's contemporaries might have called a "juggler," both a jester and a magician, a sleight-of-hand artist. Since the play gives itself over to so many cheap thrills and crude jokes, one can wonder if Marlowe isn't having some fun with his own role in the "culture industry," with his place as someone who provides entertainments, however searching and sophisticated. Or is he staking out a clear difference and distance between Faustus's literal-minded and even childish notions of power with his own powers of creation?

Marlowe sees to it that these questions have no answers, or at least no easy ones. The final lines of the play are remarkably ambiguous; the Chorus commands us to

> . . .regard his hellish fall,
> Whose fiendful fortune may exhort the wise
> Only to wonder at unlawful things,
> Whose deepness doth entice such forward wits
> To practice more than heavenly power permits.

[10]Greenblatt, *Renaissance Self-Fashioning from More to Shakespeare* (Chicago: University of Chicago Press, 1980), p. 209.
[11]*Tamburlaine the Great, Part 1*, 1.2.185. I am quoting from volume V of *The Complete Works of Christopher Marlowe* (Oxford: Clarendon Press, 1998).

We are in effect asked to look without being enticed, a request quite contrary to the basic business of the stage. More importantly, the phrase "only to wonder," while it certainly must mean primarily "to wonder but not practice," strikes the ear first and foremost as an exhortation for us to be enticed by "unlawful things" alone. When the Prologue asks the audience to accept that author and actor are compelled to "perform / The form of Faustus' fortunes, good or bad" (7–8), it is introducing the playgoer into the principle of anti-heroism itself. Faustus, unmoored from the shackles of convention, has the power, Marlowe knows, to rivet those who witness him. Anticipating Coleridge's dictum that the reader of poetry must practice "the willing suspension of disbelief,"[12] the Chorus points us to the performance rather than the moral. Rather than asking us to choose the good, Marlowe asks us not to resolve ambiguities, not to reconcile our repulsion at Faustus's choice with our fascination with his conjuring or even with the high-jinks of Wagner, Robin and Faustus himself, but rather simply to marvel at the performance itself, the matter we see staged before us, "good or bad."

[12]Coleridge, *Biographia Literaria*, Chapter 14.

Sylvan Barnet
Marlowe's *Doctor Faustus* on the Stage

The date of the composition of *Doctor Faustus* is uncertain, but it probably was first performed during the winter of 1592–93, and it was certainly performed in September 1594, with Edward Alleyn—the leading tragic actor of the period—in the title role. We know that it was popular for the next few years, and we know that in 1602 Philip Henslowe, a theater owner and manager, paid William Birde and Samuel Rowley for "additions" to the play. Subsequent performances, therefore—including those of today—surely include some material that Marlowe did not write. Unfortunately, it is not certain which scenes or lines are the "additions."

The play was popular until the theaters were closed in 1642, at the outbreak of the English Civil War. We can get some idea of what these early performances were like from Sir John Melton, who in a work published in 1620 says that at a production of *Doctor Faustus*

> a man may behold shagge-hayr'd Deuills runne roaring ouer the Stage with Squibs [i.e., firecrackers] in their mouthes, while Drummers make thunder in the Tyring-house [i.e., the area at the back of the project-

A slightly revised version of Sylvan Barnet, "The Play in Performance," in *Types of Drama*, 7th ed. (Longman, 1997), pp. 219–21.

ing stage], and the twelue-penny Hirelings [i.e., stage-hands] make artificial Lightning in their heauens.

The text of the play supports Melton's comment. For instance, 1.3 begins with "thunder"; in 2.1 when Faustus calls for a wife, Mephostophilis provides a female devil with fireworks; 3.2 tells us that Faustus and Mephostophilis "fling fireworks" at the friars. We know for certain that the stage effects were not only frightening but also were comic, since (for instance) when Faustus gives up his desire for a wife, he jokes that the fireworks-throwing female devil is "a hot whore indeed." (With the word "hot," he is punning on her lasciviousness and also suggesting that she is burning with venereal disease.) It may be hard for some of us to take seriously the spectacular events and the talk of the supernatural, but apparently the Elizabethans were impressed. For instance, stories circulated that during a performance the actors suddenly found one devil more on the stage than there should have been. According to one report, when the actors perceived that the devil himself was among them, they were so unnerved that they terminated the performance. Edward Alleyn's retirement was traditionally attributed to the appearance of a devil during the play.

Beyond the fact that drums provided the thunder, and firecrackers and lightning were used, what do we know about the earliest productions of the play? Not a great deal for sure, but we probably can make some safe guesses. The Chorus, who opens the play, probably wore a black cloak—traditional for such a role—and possibly he wore a crown of bays, emblematic of the poet. When he ends his first speech with "And this the man that in his study sits," he probably pulls back a curtain at the rear of the stage, revealing Faustus in his study.

From here, however, we enter upon less firm ground.

Probably the study was equipped with some books and with some magic symbols, for instance a magic circle on the floor, as is seen on the title page of an edition of the play. (This picture [see p. ii] shows a dragon emerging from the floor; possibly in the play a devil appeared in the form of a dragon.) Faustus probably wore a scholar's robe—maybe the fur-trimmed gown of a Doctor of Divinity—and he may have held a magician's wand, again as in the woodcut facing the title page. Probably when Faustus dismissed each field of learning in his first speech (philosophy, medicine, law, theology) he read from a different book, and then cast it aside. With the entrance of Wagner in the first scene, Faustus probably came forth from the alcove at the rear and moved forward, onto the platform stage, in a sense bringing his locale with him. The audience would then understand that (so long as Faustus was on the stage) the scene was still within his study, even though whatever scenery there was—for instance an astrological chart—probably was confined to the alcove at the rear of the platform.

The Good Angel and the Bad Angel entered and exited through different doors (the text says they enter "at several doors"); possibly some or all devils showed their underworld nature by entering onto the stage through a trapdoor. Perhaps during his last speech, when he says he will burn his books, Faustus rushed into his study, an alcove at the rear of the stage, and perhaps devils then pulled him down into an opened trap. In keeping with the other medieval aspects of the play, this trap may have been covered by a conventional medieval hellmouth, a gaping mouth of a monster or a devil, from which infernal smoke issued. The curtain could then have been pulled closed, the hellmouth removed, and when the curtain was drawn back the limbs of Faustus would be discovered.

We know, of course, that the Elizabethan stage not only made use of traps, but it also made use of playing spaces *above* the stage. When Lucifer begins 5.2 by saying, "Thus from infernal Dis [the underworld] do we ascend," he and his cohorts may have climbed out of a trapdoor and then continued climbing onto an elevated position above the stage, where for a while they looked down on their victim. An area above the platform stage is also indicated by a stage direction in 5.2, which tells us that "the throne descends," that is, a symbol from heaven manifests itself on the stage.

From 1642 to 1660, during the Civil War between the Parliamentarians and the Royalists (1642–52) and during the Commonwealth Period (1649–60) when Oliver Cromwell and his son were dictators, the theaters were closed, but in 1662, during the Restoration, *Doctor Faustus* was revived. The play was performed again in 1675, and then it disappeared from the stage for more than two hundred years, until July 1896, when William Poel, founder of the Elizabethan Stage Society, revived it on a stage that approximated an Elizabethan stage.

Perhaps a director's first act of interpretation is the decision about which text to use—the 1604 text, or the longer (chiefly because of comic scenes) 1616 text. The choice makes a big difference not only in the playing time but also in the interpretation of the central figure, because the abundant comic scenes of 1616 tend to trivialize Faustus. Directors who wish to suggest that Faustus is a grand Renaissance hero whose fault—let's say an overly aspiring mind—is tragic, usually choose the shorter text.

For the 1896 production (and again for a revival in 1906), William Poel relied chiefly on the shorter text, partly because he believed that the longer text included additions not by Marlowe, and partly because he saw Faustus as a heroic figure, driven by a quest for knowledge. In keeping with the ideals of the Elizabethan Stage Society—the idea was to produce the plays as they might have been done in the sixteenth century, with relatively little scenery and therefore with no intervals between changes of scene—Poel dispensed with the usual Victorian scenery that clearly established the particular setting as a room or a forest or whatever. The players merely entered the stage through curtains, in effect establishing the particular locale by their dialogue and their costumes (for instance, the costumes of cardinals or of a pope indicated that the scene was Rome). A reviewer of Poel's production tells us that for some scenes, however, a curtain at the rear was drawn back to reveal "a great dragon's mouth wide open, representing the mouth of hell. Out of this mouth came Mephostophilis, and under his escort the Seven Deadly Sins, Alexander and his paramour, and Helen."

Three other points about Poel's production should be mentioned. (1) The Chorus was a woman (odd, since the Elizabethan Stage Society sought to imitate Elizabethan practice, and the Elizabethan stage did not use actresses). (2) Faustus's encounter with Helen was very chaste (Helen kissed his forehead, and he kissed her hand), though in the 1906 revival, Poel—or Faustus— was a little bolder, since Faustus brushed Helen's cheek with his lips. (3) The devil-wife of 2:1, seen from the front, seemed a beautiful woman, but when she turned around the audience perceived a skeleton—an interesting idea that to the best of our knowledge has not been used in later productions.

We cannot discuss all of the subsequent productions, but a few deserve special mention. In 1937 Orson Welles—not yet twenty-two and therefore still regarded as a boy genius—produced the play under the auspices of the Federal Theatre Project (part of Franklin Delano Roosevelt's Works Project Administration, a plan to find work for the unemployed during the Depression). John Houseman (later known to a vast public as the law professor in the television series *Paper Chase*) was the director of the unit in which Welles worked, and the two staged an impressive version. In fact, Welles was a devoted amateur magician, and—given his high estimate of himself and his fondness for breaking rules—he must have identified strongly with the role of Faustus. He cut much of the comedy and stressed the heroic aspects of Faustus, but he did retain some of the comedy where he could indulge in conjuring. Thus, the cardinals' hats flew through the air, the pope's miter arose, splendidly dressed papal servants carrying dishes of food were astonished to find the food—a side of beef, a pudding, roasted chickens—fly through the air and disappear. Welles' set appeared to be not much more than a background of black velvet, but this set was the key to the magic. Houseman, in *Run-Through,* an autobiography, explains a system that professional magicians call "black magic."

> Used for vanishing acts and miraculous appearances, it exploits the absorbent properties of black velvet so that, under certain lighting conditions, not only do black surfaces become totally invisible against each other, but all normal sense of space, depth and perspective becomes lost and confused in the eye of the spectator. . . . By using almost no front light and crisscrossing the stage with parallel light curtains and clusters of units carefully focused from the sides and overhead, [Welles] was able to achieve mystifications that would have impressed the great Thurston. . . .
>
> This mystification was accomplished with the aid of eight dancers, dressed from head to foot in black

velvet, moving alongside the procession [of servants carrying food], just far enough upstage to be out of the blaze of the light curtain and thus completely invisible to the audience against the darkness of black velvet. In their black-gloved hands, they held ... thin, black, flexible steel rods whose ends were affixed to the meats, the pudding and the episcopal headgear that were marked for flight. On cue the boys in black swung those loaded rods up over their heads and brought them down behind them where their own black costumes formed a screen for them till they were able to leave the stage unobserved in the confusion of the dissolving parade.

(233–34)

Although most of the comedy was cut, those clown scenes that were staged were played strictly for comedy—Faustus was just fooling around—and they did not seem to interfere with Welles' heroic interpretation of the role. The Seven Deadly Sins were puppets that appeared onstage by wriggling up through openings in the floor; as we will see in a moment, later productions follow Welles in tending to use puppets rather than human actors for the Seven Deadly Sins.

One other point should be made about this production. Welles used an African-American actor, Jack Carter, in the role of Mephostophilis. The employment of a single black actor in the role of a devil today scarcely seems to be daring, but it was an innovation in the 1930s, when casts were almost never integrated.

In 1968 Clifford Williams directed the Royal Shakespeare Company's production of *Doctor Faustus,* with Eric Porter in the title role. Because this production is discussed in John Russell Brown's essay included in this volume, we need not comment at length here, but we do want briefly to describe the staging of Faustus' last exit.

Faustus groveled in terror as he made his final speech,
but when the clock finished striking twelve and nothing
happened, he raised his head, looked at the emptiness
around, and then laughed. At this point, sections of the
back wall fell away, revealing a red glow, through which
were seen steel spikes, the teeth of a hellmouth. Devils
slowly came forward, surrounded Faustus, and then carried him screaming back into the hellmouth, which then
closed.

The 1974 production by John Barton, first in Edinburgh and then in London, starred Ian McKellen as
Faustus. Barton cut almost all of the comedy, replacing
some of it with passages from the source of the play, a
prose account of Faustus. All of the action took place
within Faustus' study, and Barton gave the final lines of
the play, in the original spoken by the Chorus, to a devil.
Despite the deletion of the comic material, which might
indicate that the director was aiming at an heroic Faustus,
Barton's Faustus was not a grand figure but rather struck
most viewers as a neurotic pedant. He peered through
spectacles, twitched, grimaced, and hugged himself with
glee. All of the magical figures—the Seven Deadly Sins,
Helen, and so forth—were puppets or dummies of one
sort or another. The Good Angel and Bad Angel, for instance, were hand puppets manipulated by Faustus, who
spoke their lines. Helen of Troy was merely a blond wig,
a mask, and a bit of cloth, which Faustus caressed and
took to bed. The effect was to diminish Faustus. After
all, what sort of a man would be delighted with these
toys? Reviews tended to be unfavorable, with much se-
vere talk about the director who dared to cut the text
and to impose his views on what was left of it, but, as we
have seen, no one really knows what Marlowe's original
text was like.

Although this brief discussion of the stage history of

Marlowe's *Doctor Faustus* is necessarily highly selective, it should mention two curious productions that take off from Marlowe's play. The first of these is Jerzy Grotowski's *Dr. Faustus: Textual Montage,* a production staged at Grotowski's Laboratory Theater in Opole, Poland, about sixty miles from Auschwitz. In a room that seated only fifty or sixty spectators, Grotowski staged a "montage" of Marlowe's texts, shifting the sequence of some scenes and omitting others. The whole was conceived as a flashback, remembered during Faustus' last hour on earth. For Faustus and Grotowski, God is a tyrant, Faustus a martyr. In a note on the production Grotowski said,

> Faustus is a saint and his saintliness shows itself as an absolute desire for pure truth. If the saint is to become one with his sainthood, he must rebel against God, Creator of the world, because the laws of the world are traps contradicting morality and truth. . . . Whatever we do—good or bad—we are damned. The saint is not able to accept as his model this God who ambushes man. God's laws are lies, He spies on the dishonor in our souls the better to damn us. Therefore, if one wants sainthood, one must be against God.

For this passage, and a fairly full description of the production, see Jerzy Grotowski, *Dr. Faustus,* translated by Richard Schechner, in *TDR* 8 (1964):120–33, reprinted in Grotowski's *Towards a Poor Theatre* (1975).

Schechner himself apparently went several steps further in 1993, when he staged *Faust/Gastronome* at La Mama in New York. The text consisted of material from Marlowe's source, from Goethe's *Faust,* and from speeches of Hitler; Schechner's Faust is a cook, not an alchemist, who at the end of the production ends up in his own vast cauldron. A publicity release (February 1993) announced that "Schechner envisions the play—

complete with dances and a magic show—as more a Breughel painting for the twentieth century than a formalist, postmodern exercise in visual theater."

The twenty-first century has already seen some interesting productions of *Doctor Faustus,* beginning with a version (2002) for the Young Vic, directed by David Lan, in which Jude Law, twenty-nine years old and a teenage heartthrob, played the role of the elderly magician. The A-text, some six hundred lines shorter than the B-text, was used (much of the missing material is comic), with a few additions from the B-text, including B's lines, at the end, where Mephostophilis confesses that he trapped Faustus (5.2.99–105). The omitted comic material was not lamented, but reviewers did like the comic material that was staged, praising Law especially in these scenes. Also praised was Richard McCabe, who played a cynical but dignified Mephostophilis, unleashing his hatred only at the end of the play, when Faustus lay sobbing on the ground. But what especially evoked comment was the presentation of the scene in which Faustus conjures up a spirit who represents Helen, evoking the play's most famous passage.

> Was this the face that launched a thousand ships,
> And burnt the topless towers of Ilium?
> Sweet Helen, make me immortal with a kiss.
>
> (5.1.96–98)

In Lan's production, no spirit represented Helen. Rather, when Faustus spoke the lines about Helen he embraced a mirror provided by Mephostophilis and then kissed it. There is much to be said for this interpretation: Although the lines about Helen are often interpreted as typifying the Renaissance celebration of the classical world, this celebration is undercut by

an image of destruction ("burnt the topless towers")
brought by unbridled self-assertion. This emphasis on
Faustus's narcissism was evident in another unusual detail: In the scene showing the Seven Deadly Sins, Jude
Law himself played Pride. (The cast consisted of only
seven performers, so inevitably there was a good deal
of doubling, but this particular bit of doubling was of
special, i.e. symbolic, significance.)

The setting of this production was also symbolic: A
narrow, elevated wooden ramp bisected the auditorium,
suggesting that life requires a delicate balancing act.
Coal fires burned beneath the ramp, heightening the
sense of danger. The play ended with Faustus departing through a red-lit doorway, escorted by Lucifer, and
watched by Mephostophilis. But sometimes conventional symbolism was subverted: The Good Angel wore
a black body suit, the Bad Angel a white body suit. And
sometimes there seemed to be no symbolism at all, just
a bit of eccentricity: The Pope was played by a female.
Still, the production apparently was highly interesting,
and it was well received.

A second English production of 2002, this one at the
Royal and Derngate Theatres (in Northampton), should
be briefly mentioned. The comic scenes were replaced
with a new play-within-the-play, with the result that
Marlowe's play in effect became merely a part of a new
play.

In 2004 Paul Garnault in Cardiff directed the Wales
Actors Company in a ninety-minute production of an
abridged A-text of *Doctor Faustus*. Gone were the king,
the popes and cardinals and the archbishop. Four actors
played the remaining roles: One played Faustus, and the
other three played the Good and Bad Angels and the
other surviving roles. The Good Angel (in a white suit)
and the Bad Angel (in a dark suit, with a red shirt) when

not performing remained onstage throughout. The setting was sparse—some furniture that was not shifted—with the implication that what was significant was Faustus's mind, not particular places. At the beginning of each of the two parts of the play, images of orbiting planets, a DNA double-helix, and pterodactyls in flight were projected, suggesting current and future scientific threats to orthodox religion. And during the performance, images of the performance itself were projected, some from behind, thus showing the actors' backs. When the bond was signed in blood, a close-up of Faustus's arm was shown. In short, although the setting was simple, there was plenty of visual activity. The play ended in a most unusual way: Faustus shot and killed Mephostophilis with a pistol, then put the pistol into Mephostophilis's hand in order to make it look as though the devil had committed suicide. A calm Faust then walked off, not sent to Hell—unless viewers chose to assume that damnation is a matter of one's state of mind.

In the summer of 2005 the Utah Shakespeare Festival performed a straightforward version that was well received, indicating—perhaps to the surprise of the audience and to the great relief of the company—that an old-fashioned play can resonate with today's public.

Much more elaborate (though done in modern dress) was the production staged by the drama department of the University of North Carolina at Charlotte, directed by Andrew Hartley. In addition to using thirty-two actors, this production made use of dancers, puppeteers, and stilt-walkers. When Alexander and Thaïs entered the stage, at the court of Charles V, they were accompanied by photographers. Faustus removed his eyeglasses in order to better contemplate her. Several male roles were performed by women, the most significant of which was Mephostophilis, who was first dressed as a male, later dressed as a nun, and still later as a woman in an evening gown.

Probably the most important production of the century thus far was the one done in 2008 at Notre Dame, directed by Anton Juan, who used the A-text when it suited him, and the B-text when it suited him. At the center of the stage was a globe which divided to form a Hell Mouth, out of which Lucifer and Belzebub came. Belzebub was dressed like a circus trainer, Lucifer was in golden body tights with wings fanned out behind him. When Belzebub announced the show of the Seven Deadly Sins, he cracked a whip, again like a circus trainer, and out of the Hell Mouth came a giant tent, which proved to be the skirt of Pride. Out of a slit in her skirt came the other sins. Greed was a slot machine; Gluttony ate a plate of rats, vomited them, and ate them again. After each sin did its bit, the whip was cracked and the sin took the posture of a contestant in a beauty pageant.

Helen (or, rather, the demon impersonating Helen), like a white marble statue, entered, carried by a devil. After uttering "Sweet Helen, make me immortal with a kiss," Faustus closed his eyes, Helen turned around, lifted her skirt, and Faustus kissed her anus. The audience was both greatly shocked and greatly amused. Helen moved away from the globe, Faustus (eyes opened) following, still enamored. The statue/Helen then put her hand to her face, gathered a lump of plaster, and gave it to Faustus when he said (5.1.115),

And none but thou shalt be my paramour.

Faustus looked at his hand, and let the plaster fall where Helen a moment ago had stood.

The clerics—popes, and all—were depicted as grotesque puppets, though in fact they were actors, not puppets, some with giant papal crowns, all of which was very well received at this Roman Catholic institution of higher learning.

For further discussions of productions, see Michael Hattaway, *Elizabethan Popular Theatre* (1982, chiefly on the earliest production); William Tydeman, *Doctor Faustus:Text and Performance* (1984, on productions in the later twentieth century); Christopher Marlowe, *Doctor Faustus: A- and B-texts (1604, 1616),* ed. David Bevington and Eric Rasmussen (1993). *Theatre Record* and *Shakespeare Bulletin* are useful sources. I also wish to thank Alan Dessen, Peter Holland, Anton Juan, and Paul Whitfield White for valuable assistance.

SUGGESTED REFERENCES

Among modern editions of the play, three are especially valuable: *Marlowe's Doctor Faustus: 1604–1616: Parallel Texts*, ed. W. W. Greg (Oxford: Clarendon Press, 1950), gives the A- and B-texts on facing pages and contains a long discussion of the textual problems. Greg favors the B-text, but his arguments have been challenged in four important editions: *Doctor Faustus: A- and B-texts (1604, 1616)*, ed. David Bevington and Eric Rasmussen (Manchester, England: Manchester University Press, 1993); *Doctor Faustus: The A-Text*, ed. David Ormerod and Christopher Wortham (Nedlands, Australia: University of Western Australia Press, 1985); *Doctor Faustus* (the A-text, with B-text scenes in an appendix), ed. Roma Gill, revised third edition by Ros King (London: Methuen, 2008), and *Doctor Faustus with the English Faust Book,* ed. David Wooton (Indianapolis: Hacklett, 2005). The Bevington-Rasmussen edition includes excellent critical apparatus.

Several collections of essays on Marlowe include material on *Doctor Faustus.* See the volumes, listed below, by Emily Bartels (1997), Harold Bloom (1988), Willard Farnham (1969), and Richard Wilson (1999).

Among critical studies, the following may provide a useful beginning:

Bartels, Emily C., ed. *Critical Essays on Christopher Marlowe.* New York: G. K. Hall, 1997.

Bartels, Emily C. *Spectacles of Strangeness: Imperialism, Alienation, and Marlowe.* Philadelphia: University of Pennsylvania Press, 1993.

Bloom, Harold, ed. *Christopher Marlowe's Doctor Faustus.* New York: Chelsea, 1988.

Cheney, Patrick, ed. *Cambridge Companion to Marlowe.* New York: Cambridge University Press, 2004.

Craik, T. W. "Faustus's Damnation Reconsidered," *Renaissance Drama,* new series, 2 (1969): 189–96.

Deats, Sarah Munson, and Robert A. Logan. *Placing the Plays of Christopher Marlowe: Fresh Cultural Contexts.* Aldershot: Ashgate, 2008.

Dollimore, Jonathan. *Radical Tragedy: Religion, Ideology and Power in the Drama of Shakespeare and His Contemporaries.* Brighton: Harvester, 1984.

Farnham, Willard, ed. *Twentieth-Century Interpretations of Doctor Faustus.* Englewood Cliffs: Prentice, 1969.

Grantley, Darryll, and Peter Roberts, eds. *Christopher Marlowe and English Renaissance Culture.* Aldershot: Scolar Press, 1996.

Greenblatt, Stephen. *Renaissance Self-Fashioning: From More to Shakespeare.* Chicago: University of Chicago Press, 1980.

Hattaway, Michael. *Elizabethan Popular Theatre: Plays in Performance.* Boston: Routledge, 1982.

Hopkins, Lisa. *Christopher Marlowe: A Literary Life.* Basingstoke: Palgrave, 2000.

Kuriyama, Constance Brown. *Christopher Marlowe: A Renaissance Life.* Ithaca: Cornell University Press, 2002.

Levin, Harry. *The Overreacher: A Study of Christopher Marlowe.* Cambridge: Harvard University Press, 1964.

Maclure, Millar, ed. *Marlowe: The Critical Heritage.* Boston: Routledge, 1979.

McAlindon, T. *Doctor Faustus: Divine in Show.* New York: Twayne, 1994.

Rasmussen, Eric. *A Textual Companion to Doctor Faustus.* Manchester: Manchester University Press, 1993.

Ricks, Christopher. "Doctor Faustus and Hell on Earth." *Essays in Criticism* 35 (1985): 101–20.

Riggs, David. *The World of Christopher Marlowe.* London: Faber, 2004.

Sale, Roger. *Christopher Marlowe.* New York: St. Martin's, 1991.

Sewall, Richard B. *The Vision of Tragedy.* New Haven: Yale University Press, 1959.

Simkin, Stevie. *Marlowe: The Plays.* Basingstoke: Palgrave, 2001.

Shepherd, Simon. *Marlowe and the Politics of Elizabethan Theater.* Brighton: Harvester, 1986.

Steane, J. B. *Marlowe: A Critical Study.* Cambridge: Cambridge University Press, 1964.

Sullivan, Garrett A., Jr. *Memory and Forgetting in English Renaissance Drama: Shakespeare, Marlowe, Webster.* New York: Cambridge University Press, 2006.

Thomas, Vivien, and William Tydeman, eds. *Christopher Marlowe: The Plays and Their Sources.* New York: Routledge, 1994.

Tromly, Fred B. *Playing with Desire: Christopher Marlowe and the Art of Tantalization.* Toronto: University of Toronto Press, 1998.

Tydeman, William. *Doctor Faustus: Text and Performance.* Basingstoke: Macmillan, 1984.

Westlund, Joseph. "The Orthodox Christian Framework

of Marlowe's Faustus." *Studies in English Literature* 3 (1963): 191–205.

White, Paul Whitfield., ed. *Marlowe, History, and Sensuality; New Critical Essays on Christopher Marlowe.* New York: AMS, 1998.

Wilson, Richard, ed. *Christopher Marlowe.* New York: Longman, 1999.

The Signet Classics Shakespeare Series:

The Tragedies

extensively revised and updated expert commentary
provides more enjoyment through a greater
understanding of the texts

ANTONY AND CLEOPATRA, Barbara Everett, ed.

CORIOLANUS, Ruben Brower, ed.

HAMLET, Sylvan Barnet, ed.

JULIUS CAESAR, William and Barbara Rosen, ed.

KING LEAR, Russell Faser, ed.

MACBETH, Sylvan Barnet, ed.

OTHELLO, Alvin Kernan, ed.

ROMEO AND JULIET, J.A. Bryant, Jr., ed.

TROILUS AND CRESSIDA. Daniel Seltzer, ed.

Available wherever books are sold or at
signetclassics.com

READ THE TOP 20
SIGNET CLASSICS

Texas hurricane or tornado. Papa said they were real bad storms.

Papa looked down at Hope and winked. She winked back, grinned, and crinkled her nose. She did love her papa.